THE
NEW CASE
AGAINST IMMIGRATION

THE
NEW CASE
AGAINST IMMIGRATION

Both Legal and Illegal

MARK KRIKORIAN

SENTINEL

SENTINEL
Published by the Penguin Group
Penguin Group (USA) Inc., 375 Hudson Street,
New York, New York 10014, U.S.A.
Penguin Group (Canada), 90 Eglinton Avenue East, Suite 700,
Toronto, Ontario, Canada M4P 2Y3
(a division of Pearson Penguin Canada Inc.)
Penguin Books Ltd, 80 Strand, London WC2R 0RL, England
Penguin Ireland, 25 St. Stephen's Green, Dublin 2, Ireland (a division of Penguin Books Ltd)
Penguin Books Australia Ltd, 250 Camberwell Road, Camberwell, Victoria 3124, Australia
(a division of Pearson Australia Group Pty Ltd)
Penguin Books India Pvt Ltd, 11 Community Centre, Panchsheel Park,
New Delhi – 110 017, India
Penguin Group (NZ), 67 Apollo Drive, Rosedale, North Shore 0632,
New Zealand (a division of Pearson New Zealand Ltd)
Penguin Books (South Africa) (Pty) Ltd, 24 Sturdee Avenue,
Rosebank, Johannesburg 2196, South Africa

Penguin Books Ltd, Registered Offices:
80 Strand, London WC2R 0RL, England

First published in 2008 by Sentinel,
a member of Penguin Group (USA) Inc.

3   5   7   9   10   8   6   4   2

LIBRARY OF CONGRESS CATALOGING IN PUBLICATION DATA
Krikorian, Mark.
    The new case against immigration : both legal and illegal / Mark Krikorian.
        p.   cm.
    Includes bibliographial references and index.
    ISBN 978-1-59523-035-5
    1. United States—Emigration and immigration.   2. Americanization.   3. Assimilation
(Sociology)—United States.   I. Title.
    JV6465.K75 2007
    325.73—dc22   2007043555

Printed in the United States of America
Set in Bembo
Designed by Spring Hoteling

For Alex, Ben, and Theo

Contents

THE
NEW CASE
AGAINST IMMIGRATION

INTRODUCTION

I t's not the immigrants—it's us.

What's different about immigration today as opposed to a century ago is not the characteristics of the newcomers but the characteristics of our society. Immigrants are what they've always been: not the poorest of the poor but one step up from the bottom, strivers looking for better lives for their children, coming from rural or small-town backgrounds in traditional—what we would call third-world—societies. But the changes that define modern America—in our society, economy, government, and technology, for example—are so fundamental that our past success in dealing with immigration is simply no longer relevant.

This is a new argument. It's not that previous critiques of immigration have been wrong—indeed, much of what follows in this book is based on the outstanding work of others over the years. Instead, the source of the problems created by immigration has usually been located in differences between *immigrants* past and present rather than in differences between *America* past and present. Immigrants in the past, it is said, were white, but now they're not; they used to want to assimilate, but now they don't; or they used to be self-sufficient, but now they seek out government assistance. We've all heard the laments: "My grandpa from Sicily learned English, and my grandma from Minsk got by without welfare—what's the problem with immigrants today?"

The problem is that the America your grandparents immigrated to a century ago no longer exists. This is neither a good nor bad thing—it just *is*. Of course, some of the changes brought by modernity are generally positive, others negative. We all welcome, for instance, the spread of easy and cheap communications and transportation but mourn the weakening of our communities. Other changes will be embraced by some but not by others; the growth in government, for instance, is seen by the Left as a recognition of our social responsibility to the poor and marginalized but feared by the Right as likely to erode liberty and personal responsibility.

But whatever steps we take to accentuate what we consider positive about modern life and ameliorate what we see as negative, the basic features of modern society are not subject to debate. The social and other changes briefly outlined below are inherent characteristics of a mature society; we cannot say that "immigration would be fine if only we got rid of (fill in the blank)" when what we fill in the blank with is an inextricable part of how we live today. Instead, immigration undermines many of the objectives that our modern, middle-class society sets for itself and exacerbates many of the problems brought on by modernization.

In short, mass immigration is incompatible with a modern society. As Hudson Institute scholar John Fonte has written, "It's not 1900 any more."[1]

The subsequent chapters will spell out exactly how the changes that distinguish a modern, mature society are incompatible with continued immigration, but for now it will suffice to say that they paint a picture of a country fundamentally different from the past. Some examples:[2]

ECONOMY. A century ago, what economists call the primary sector of the economy (farming, fishing, hunting, and herding) still employed more Americans than any other, as it had since the dawn of humankind. Today only 2 percent of our workforce occupies itself in this way. Meanwhile, the tertiary sector (service industries) now employs 80 percent of working Americans, and the percentage is climbing.

EDUCATION. Along with the change in the economy, education has become more widespread. Nearly a quarter of American adults had less than five years of schooling in 1910; as of 2000, that figure is less than 2 percent. Likewise, the percentage who had completed high school increased sixfold, from about 13 percent of the total to 84 percent. And the percentage of college graduates increased tenfold, from 2.7 to 27 percent. Another way to look at it is that in 1900, only a little more than 10 percent of high-school-age children were actually enrolled in school; in 2001, nearly 95 percent were.

TECHNOLOGY. In 1915, a three-minute call from New York to San Francisco cost about $20.70 (about $343 in 2000 dollars); the same call in 2000 cost 36 cents. In 1908, a Model T cost more than two years' worth of the typical worker's wages; a Ford Taurus in 1997 (a much better car) cost eight months' work. A thousand-mile airline trip in 1920 would have cost the average American 220 work hours; by 2000, it cost perhaps 11 work hours.

DEMOGRAPHY. The birthrate fell by half during the past century, while infant mortality fell by 93 percent. In 1915, sixty-one out of ten thousand mothers died during childbirth; in 2001, only one out of one hundred thousand did. Life expectancy went from forty-seven years in 1900 to seventy-seven a century later, while people sixty-five and older have tripled as a share of the nation's total population, from about 4 percent to more than 12 percent.

GOVERNMENT. In 1900, total government spending at all levels equaled about 5.5 percent of the economy; by 2003, it was more than 36 percent. Total government employment (federal, state, and local) went from a little more than 1 million in 1900 (about 4 percent of the workforce) to more than 22 million in 2000 (more than 16 percent of the workforce).

LIFESTYLE. America's population was still 60 percent rural in 1900; in 2000, only 21 percent of Americans lived in rural areas (and only a tiny fraction were involved in farming). The average household went from more than 4.5 people to a little more than 2.5, while the number of people per room in the average house fell from 1.1 in 1910 to 0.4 in 1997.

Other changes are harder to quantify but are just as real in marking modern society as a break with the past: a weakening sense of community and civic engagement, increased religious skepticism, a greater sense of responsibility for the less fortunate, rejection of racial and religious discrimination, and concern for our stewardship of the natural world.

These changes have brought both benefits and woe, but whatever we might do to deal with harmful side effects, modernization itself is irreversible, because people don't want it to be reversed; anyone who has spent time in a premodern village understands that Marx's observation about "the idiocy of rural life" has more than a little truth to it. Or in the words of the popular World War I song, "How Ya Gonna Keep 'Em Down on the Farm (After They've Seen Paree)?"

These social changes marking national adulthood don't mean that mass immigration was out of place during our country's adolescence. America ended up a stronger nation because of the mass-immigration phase of our development, a phase that extended for seventy-odd years, from the late 1840s until the early 1920s. Had we not experienced that period of mass immigration, our population, derived mainly from descendants of a relatively small number of preindependence settlers, would still have grown rapidly, but it would have been smaller; in 1990, about half of America's population was attributable to post-1790 immigrants and their descendants.[3] The first part of the immigration phase, dominated by northern Europeans, helped settle much of the land; this happened both because some immigrants went directly to the Midwest and West to establish farms and ranches and because others moved to eastern cities, filling in behind old-stock Americans who had moved west. The latter part of our nation's adolescent immigration phase was dominated by immigrants from eastern and southern Europe who settled mainly in the cities and contributed mightily to industrialization.

Samuel Huntington pointed out in his book *Who Are We?* that describing America as a nation of immigrants is only a partial truth; we are a nation of both settlers and immigrants, two very different ways of moving to the New World. Settlers arrived as a group to create a new community where there is none; immigrants came from one preexisting society to another one. As Huntington puts it, "Before immigrants could come to America, settlers had to found America."

But as different as they are, these two methods of peopling America share one thing—they were phases in our national development that we have outgrown. In 1890, the superintendent of the census declared that the frontier could no longer be said to exist, ending nearly three centuries of westward settlement. As the historian Frederick Jackson Turner wrote in *The Frontier in American History,* "the frontier has gone, and with its going has closed the first period of American history."

A generation later, Congress declared that the period of mass immigration was also closed by passing the immigration laws of 1921 and 1924. In the latter year, the number of immigrants was about 700,000, already down from 1.2 million in 1914, right before the outbreak of World War I; in 1925 it fell to less than 300,000. It was sixty-five years before immigration again reached the level of 1924. As one supporter wrote at the time, "The passage of the Immigration Act of 1924 marks the close of an epoch in the history of the United States."[4]

President Franklin Roosevelt made the same point in his speech on the occasion of the fiftieth anniversary of the Statute of Liberty: "Within this generation that stream from abroad has largely stopped. We have within our shores today the materials out of which we shall continue to build an even better home for liberty."

When the sweeping overhaul of the immigration law was debated in the 1960s, culminating in the 1965 Hart-Celler Immigration Act, supporters readily asserted that the changes, important as they were, would be mainly cosmetic. Though important for moral and foreign-policy reasons, the new law was not intended to return America to a bygone phase in its national life. Representative Sidney Yates (D-IL), for instance, supported the bill but said, "It is obvious in any event that the great days of immigration have long since run their course. World population trends have changed, and changing economic and social conditions at home and abroad dictate a changing migratory pattern."[5]

Likewise, immigration subcommittee member Representative Peter Rodino (D–NJ), another supporter of the changes, testified that "We will not be admitting substantially more immigrants, times and possibilities have changed, we can no longer admit everyone who wishes to come here and it is with sadness that we modify Miss Liberty's invitation."[6] And President Johnson put it most succinctly in his remarks upon signing the new immigration law: "The days of unlimited immigration are past."[7]

The closing of the frontier was irreversible—once it was gone, there was no way to get it back. But prospective immigrants continued to be available in abundance. And so, starting with the 1965 immigration law, America resumed its adolescent policy of immigration, leading to the largest wave of newcomers in its history. The total foreign-born population has ballooned, from fewer than 10 million in 1970 (less than 5 percent of the nation's population) to nearly 38 million in 2007 (12.6 percent of the population). Annual legal immigration—the number of people awarded permanent residency, potentially leading to citizenship—has gone from fewer than 400,000 in 1970 to nearly 1.3 million in 2006. And illegal immigration has become a major phenomenon, with today's illegal population totaling perhaps 12 million and growing by around half a million each year.

One last figure will suggest the magnitude of what was ignited in 1965: Fully one third of all the people ever to move to the United States, starting from the first Siberian to cross the Bering land bridge in search of game, have arrived since 1965.[8]

The objective of this book is to demonstrate how this new immigration wave clashes with modern America, how a policy that served us well in our adolescence is harmful in our maturity. This is not a strictly conservative argument, though I am a conservative. While there may be anti-Americans on the hard Left or post-Americans on the libertarian Right, whose ideologies lead them to welcome the effects of mass immigration, this book is intended for Americans in the patriotic mainstream, liberal and conservative, who can agree on the broad contours of a desirable society, though obviously not on all the details nor on how best to achieve it. Nothing is this book assumes a particular set of views on other issues, like abortion or the minimum wage, but it does assume certain broadly shared goals for modern America:

- A strong sense of shared national identity
- Opportunities for upward mobility, especially for the poor, the less educated, and generally those at the margins of the society
- The availability of high-wage jobs in knowledge-intensive, capital-intensive industries
- A large middle class, with the gap between rich and poor not growing inordinately
- A functional, responsible, and affordable system of social provision for the poor
- Middle-class norms of behavior, such as orderliness and cleanliness of public places, residential occupancy limits and zoning rules, and obeying traffic laws
- Government spending on certain kinds of infrastructure, such as schools, roads, and public amenities like national parks
- Environmental stewardship, to provide clean air and water to our descendants, and historical stewardship, to preserve the treasures handed down to us by our ancestors

There are other characteristics common to all modern societies which, when combined with mass immigration, undermine these goals, such as:

- Easier and cheaper means of long-distance communication and transportation
- The trend toward smaller families

- The spread of cosmopolitanism or post-Americanism among our elites
- Social atomization, disengagement, and anonymity

In effect, this book offers a "unified field theory" of immigration restriction, explaining why the different impacts of immigration (on the economy, assimilation, security, and so on) are really all part of the same phenomenon. There is some legitimacy to the complaints of immigration boosters that immigration critics seem to have been offering a Chinese menu of objections: If you're a conservative, pick a problem from column A (tax burden or national security); if you're a liberal, choose from column B (effects on the poor or on sprawl).

It's not that these objections are baseless—in fact, they're spot-on. The problem is that they have never been integrated into a coherent whole. Immigration critics across the political spectrum have been like the proverbial blind men feeling different parts of an elephant and imagining they're touching different things, not realizing that it's all the same animal. Likewise, immigration critics concerned about security, for instance, may dismiss concerns about the harm done to low-skilled workers, while those worried about artificial population growth may frown on concerns related to assimilation. In fact, they're all identifying different facets of the same problem.

It's important to note that this critique is not focused on any particular kind of immigration or any particular means of immigration. Specifically, the problem we face is not confined to the arrival of illegal aliens. The stubborn refusal of America's political class to enforce the immigration law is an enormous problem, and thus it is only appropriate that most political activity related to immigration has been directed toward controlling illegal immigration. After all, until we develop the will and the means to enforce current immigration law, changing that law will have little effect.

But as the rest of this book will argue, the central problem is the large-scale settlement of people from abroad, whoever they are and however they get here: legal or illegal, skilled or unskilled, immigrants or guest workers, European or Latin or Asian or African. Obviously, different kinds of immigrants will have different impacts; an illegal alien, for instance, undermines the rule of law but places less of a burden on government services than an otherwise similar legal immigrant. Likewise, a skilled immigrant does not have trouble learning and speaking English, but he may be more susceptible than his low-skilled counterpart to a politics of ethnic grievance and be more able to pursue dual citizenship and a transnational lifestyle. Despite the different effects that different kinds of immigrants may have, the common thread remains— modern America has outgrown mass immigration.

This is not a pessimistic or declinist argument. The problem is not that America has become decadent and weak and is thus unable to take full advantage of the blessings of mass immigration as it once did. Rather, a policy that served America's interests during our national adolescence no longer serves those interests now, during our national maturity. President Reagan was right when he said America's best days lie ahead. But only if we heed the words of his greatest predecessor, Abraham Lincoln: "As our case is new, so we must think anew and act anew. We must disenthrall ourselves, and then we shall save our country."

CHAPTER 1

Assimilation: The Cracked Melting Pot

The most important long-term measure of success in immigration is assimilation. The American model of immigration has been based on turning immigrants and their descendants fully into Americans. Theodore Roosevelt summed up this Americanization tradition when he wrote that "if the immigrant who comes here does in good faith become an American and assimilates himself to us, he shall be treated on an exact equality with every one else, for it is an outrage to discriminate against any such man because of creed or birthplace or origin."[1]

This is unlike the practice of other countries, such as Germany or the Persian Gulf sheikhdoms, and even our own historical lapses (African slavery, the Know-Nothing movement, and the Bracero program for Mexican guest workers), which all have one thing in common—the willingness to employ the labor of foreign workers without admitting them to membership in the society.

This process of Americanizing immigrants was tumultuous and wrenching for everyone involved but eventually very successful. The descendants of those who came in generations past—from Ireland or Poland, Mexico or Sweden, China or Germany, Britain or Armenia—have indeed become one people. This has been possible, of course, because American nationality is not based on blood relations, like a biological family, but is more like a family growing partly through adoption, where new immigrants attach themselves to their new country and embrace the cultural and civic values of their native-born brethren as their own.

Lincoln described the adoption of immigrants this way:

> If they look back through this history to trace their connection with those days [the founding era] by blood, they find they have none, they cannot carry themselves back into that glorious epoch and make themselves feel that they are part of us, but when they look through that old Declaration of Independence they find that those old men say that "We hold these truths to be self-evident, that all men are created equal," and then they feel that that moral sentiment taught in that day evidences their relation to those men, that it is the father of all moral principle in them, and that they have a right to claim it as though they were blood of the blood, and flesh of the flesh of the men who wrote that Declaration, and so they are.[2]

Likewise, political scientist Lawrence Fuchs describes Japanese American children in Honolulu's McKinley High School in the 1920s referring to "our Pilgrim forefathers" and reciting the Gettysburg Address from memory.[3]

But this offer of complete adoption into the American nation was always based on the requirement that the immigrant "assimilates himself to us." Such assimilation is more than the surface changes that are easily observed; future Supreme Court Justice Louis Brandeis put it well in a 1915 speech:

> But the adoption of our language, manners and customs is only a small part of the process. To become

Americanized, the change wrought must be fundamental. However great his outward conformity, the
immigrant is not Americanized unless his interests and
affections have become deeply rooted here. And we
properly demand of the immigrant even more than
this. He must be brought into complete harmony with
our ideals and aspirations and cooperate with us for
their attainment. Only when this has been done, will
he possess the national consciousness of an American.[4]

This adoption of "the national consciousness of an American" is what
Hudson Institute scholar John Fonte calls patriotic assimilation[5]—an
identification with Americans as the immigrant's new countrymen,
converting, in a secular sense, from membership in one national community to membership in another. Political psychologist Stanley Renshon describes the issue as one of cultivating an emotional attachment
to the United States, which is essential because "strong emotional attachments are not only critical to the American civic process but also
help provide the glue that keeps the country together and serve as the
basis for united action in tough times."[6]

The model for this—again, in a secular sense—is in the Bible,
where the foreigner Ruth says to Naomi, her Israelite mother-in-law,
"Whither thou goest, I will go; and where thou lodgest, I will lodge:
thy people shall be my people, and thy God my God: Where thou diest,
will I die, and there will I be buried."[7]

Unfortunately, the conditions of modern society make such assimilation increasingly difficult. It is characteristic of modern societies that
they have great difficulty in assimilating large numbers of newcomers
into the model of a territorial nation-state, with a common language
and civic culture helping to cultivate the patriotic solidarity necessary
for both mutual sacrifice and respect for individual rights.

This is not because of any intrinsic differences between immigrants
past and present; the simple fact that most immigrants now come from

Latin America and Asia, rather than from Europe, is of less importance with regard to assimilation than some observers seem to think. Instead, it is *we* who have changed.

Our modern society is different in two major ways that relate to assimilation, one practical, the other political. The first, practical, difference is that modern technology now enables newcomers to retain ties to their homelands, even to the extent of living in both countries simultaneously; thus, becoming "deeply rooted here," in Brandeis's words, is simply less likely to happen. This leads to what scholars call transnationalism—living in such a way as not to be rooted in one nation, but rather living across two or more nations. As one student of the subject has put it, "Transnational communities are groups whose identity is not primarily based on attachment to a specific territory. They therefore present a powerful challenge to traditional ideas of nation-state belonging."[8]

Second, and perhaps more important, is the political change. Elites in all modern societies, including ours, come to devalue their own nation and culture and thus recoil from the idea that newcomers should even be required to adopt "our language, manners and customs," let alone "be brought into complete harmony with our ideals and aspirations"— assuming we can even agree, in this contentious age, on what those ideals and aspirations are. This loss of confidence expresses itself in an ideology of multiculturalism, which rejects the idea of bonds tying together all members of a society.

The combination of these two modern traits—transnationalism and multiculturalism—means that mass immigration today is much less likely to result in the kind of deep assimilation of the vast majority of immigrants and their children that is necessary for immigration to be successful. This is true regardless of the characteristics of the immigrants—their legal status, country of origin, or even level of education—because the problem is inherent to modern society and the way that modernity limits our ability to replicate the successes of the past.

CHANGING ORIGINS

Some observers misinterpret the assimilation problem as resulting from the ethnic makeup of the immigrant flow itself rather than changes in our own society. It is true, of course, that the source countries of immigrants have changed over the generations. In the 1890s, for instance, Europeans accounted for 97 percent of immigration, while in the 1990s, Europeans accounted for only 14 percent, almost all the rest coming from the third world.[9] The shift away from Europe is continuing; a snapshot of the total immigrant population in 2005 showed that Europe was the birthplace of 24 percent of those immigrants who had arrived before 1980 but only 8.5 percent of those who arrived 2000–2005.[10] This is why Pat Buchanan's book on immigration is titled *State of Emergency: The Third World Invasion and Conquest of America*.

But rather than a break with the past, today's Latin and Asian immigration actually represents a continuation of the expansion of "Us"—the majority population, the group into which assimilation is supposed to take place—a process that's been ongoing since colonial times.[11] In mid-seventeenth-century Massachusetts, for instance, even Quakers—fellow English Protestants, but of the "wrong" kind—were banished by the Puritans as unfit for membership in the community, and several of them who kept returning were actually hanged.

Soon, British Protestants in general came to be considered part of the Us, but other northern European Protestants were still excluded. In 1751, for example, Benjamin Franklin complained of Protestant German immigrants as unassimilable: "Why should the Palatine Boors be suffered to swarm into our Settlements, and by herding together establish their Language and Manners to the Exclusion of ours? Why should Pennsylvania, founded by the English, become a Colony of Aliens, who will shortly be so numerous as to Germanize us instead of our Anglifying them, and will never adopt our Language or Customs, any more than they can acquire our Complexion."[12]

In time, successful assimilation caused the circle of the American Us to expand to include all northern European Protestants—not just

Germans but also Swiss (like Albert Gallatin, fourth secretary of the treasury), French Huguenots (like Paul Revere's father), and Dutch (like Revolutionary War general Philip Schuyler's forebears). But Roman Catholics, even those from northern Europe, were not included, an issue that flared when hundreds of thousands of Irish and German Catholics began immigrating in the late 1840s, kicking off America's first wave of mass immigration. The Know-Nothing movement sprang up at that time, not to limit immigration but specifically to prevent the incorporation of Catholic immigrants into the American nation.[13]

As the source countries of immigration changed yet again (and as the Irish became fierce American patriots), northern Europeans in general, both Protestant and Catholic, came to be seen as legitimate material for Americanization. But the new immigration wave from southern and eastern Europe, starting around 1880, brought in Italians, Poles, Jews, and others whose fitness for membership in the American nation was suspect. A vigorous government and private-sector program of patriotic assimilation, along with a long pause in immigration and the shared experience of depression and war, turned the descendants of this immigration wave, as well, into patriotic Americans.

So the pool of those considered suitable raw material for new Americans consisted of, first, certain varieties of English Protestants, then British Protestants in general, then northern European Protestants, then northern Europeans in general, and finally, by midcentury, those of any sort of European ancestry. This last stage is what prompted Peter Brimelow, author of *Alien Nation,* to describe the current wave as "so huge and so systematically different from anything that had gone before as to transform . . . the American nation, as it had evolved by the middle of the twentieth century."[14]

The current wave is certainly huge, and it is indeed transforming the nation in myriad detrimental ways. But today's raw material for assimilation—the immigrants from Asia and Latin America—is not "systematically different from anything that had gone before" but instead a continuation of the expansion of "Us." Asian and Latin immigrants (and especially their children) who have undergone the initial steps of assimilation—i.e., those who speak English, are educated, have a steady job, and pay their taxes—are, for all intents and purposes, "white," and are accepted as members of the majority community (at least socially, if not legally) for whom ethnic identity is optional. As improbable as this expansion of the concept of whiteness may seem today, it's only slightly more improbable than the inclusion of Sicilians, Portuguese, Armenians, and others not originally considered white. We already see this acceptance in intermarriage rates, for instance; among native-born women with immigrant parents, one third of Asians and one fourth of Hispanics are married to men of a different group, mostly whites.[15]

In fact, today's "systematically different" immigrants are simply continuing the traditional pattern (common among the Irish and Italians and others in the past) of trying to climb over the backs of black Americans to achieve assimilation. To begin with, nearly half (48 percent) of Hispanics selected "white" as their racial category in the 2000 census, even when presented with a variety of other choices.[16] Furthermore, research on the views of Hispanic immigrants has shown that, far from identifying with black Americans as nonwhites, they identify themselves with whites and harbor much more negative views of blacks than do non-Hispanic white Americans.[17] It was telling when a Hispanic activist in North Carolina complained that immigration enforcement was interfering with efforts toward acceptance: "It used to be everybody here loved the Latinos. They would say, 'We like you more than the blacks.' Now we're like the Big Bad Wolf."[18]

In a sense, third-world immigration has been happening from very early on, if we interpret "third world" broadly to mean "the kind of unsavory places that people want to leave." What was Franklin's complaint about the Germans, after all, or later complaints about the Irish or Italians, if not laments about third-world immigration? At the risk of being crude, the British wisecrack that "the wogs start at Calais" (i.e., the uncivilized world begins just across the English Channel) describes the approach most human communities take toward outsiders, but the location of "Calais" for America, at least with regard to potential new Americans, has been consistently moving outward.

The white/nonwhite divide in American culture and history is, for the purposes of immigration at least, not very relevant. Despite a lot of hokum about how nonwhite immigration is blurring the white/nonwhite divide, what's proven much more important historically is the divide between blacks and nonblacks, and Hispanics and Asians are simply the latest immigrant groups trying to use their location on the nonblack side of the divide as an assimilation tool. Bridging this basic divide in American society between black and nonblack—bringing our black countrymen into full membership in the American nation in every respect—is our most urgent long-term domestic concern, one in which we have made some hard-won progress over the past fifty years. But the relation of today's immigration to that divide is the same as in previous waves.

WHAT DIVERSITY?

This is the place to discuss the one major difference that does exist in today's immigration flow (if not in the immigrants themselves) compared to the past: its remarkable lack of diversity. "Diverse," of course, has come to mean "nonwhite" in the stilted language of business, government, and journalism, which is why today's immigration is endlessly applauded as increasing "diversity." But if we use the word's actual meaning—"made up of distinct characteristics, qualities, or elements"—there's no denying that immigration today is radically *less* diverse than in the past.

It's true, of course, that today's immigrants come from a greater number of countries than ever before. Indeed, there is no corner of the world, no matter how small or remote, that does not send immigrants here; in 2006, permanent residence was granted to seventy-eight immigrants from Bhutan, thirty from Papua New Guinea, twenty-five from Brunei, fifteen from the Seychelles, thirteen from Equatorial Guinea, and eleven from Swaziland.

But today's extraordinarily wide variety of sending countries masks a growing domination of the immigrant flow by one ethnic group.

Mexicans now account for some 31 percent of the total immigrant population—legal and illegal, naturalized and noncitizen—and accounted for fully 43 percent of the growth in the total immigrant population in the 1990s.[19] The 12 million Mexican immigrants are more than the number of people from the next 10 countries of origin *combined.*[20]

And today's immigration flow is even less diverse than these figures suggest. A meaningful comparison to the past would require looking at immigration from Spanish-speaking Latin America as a whole. Naturally, there are significant regional differences among Hispanic sending countries, just as there were regional differences between German speakers from Prussia, Switzerland, Austria, and Russia, or between Chinese from the People's Republic, Taiwan, and Malaysia, or Italians from Naples, Sicily, and Milan, or Yiddish-speaking Ashkenazi Jews from Lithuania, Romania, and the Ukraine. But the shared sense of ethnic and linguistic and cultural identity—both in the homelands and in the United States—requires examining Hispanic immigrants together, just as we examine these other groups together. What's more, the United States' own complex system of race laws (and the racial-identity organizations that have sprung up in response to these race laws) treats Hispanics as a single group, notwithstanding internal variations.

When viewed this way, the lack of diversity in current immigration is even more profound. During the 1990s, Hispanics went from 37 percent to 46 percent of the total immigrant population.[21] This is because people from Spanish-speaking countries accounted for more than 60 percent of the growth in the foreign born during that decade and became the largest immigrant group in 32 states (plus the District of Columbia), including all the main immigration states.

Noted demographer Michael Teitelbaum wrote presciently (in 1980!) that "Such linguistic concentration is quite unprecedented in the long history of U.S. immigration. While there were substantial concentrations of a particular language group in past decades . . . previous immigration flows generally were characterized by a broad diversity of linguistic groups ranging from the Chinese to Polish to Spanish to Swedish. Furthermore, those concentrations that did occur proved to be short-lived."[22]

A look at the 1910 census illustrates this. At that time, the peak of the prior wave of immigration, the picture was much more diverse, despite the fact that virtually all immigrants were what we would now consider white. About one quarter of the immigrant population was English- or Irish-speaking (from Ireland, Britain, and Canada), and the other three quarters spoke a wide variety of languages: About 21 percent of all immigrants spoke German, 10 percent Italian (in a variety of very different dialects), 10 percent Scandinavian languages (again, different from one another), about 7 percent each Yiddish and Polish, and so on.[23]

Today's profound and growing lack of diversity has major implications for assimilation. Simply as a practical matter, the diversity of ethnicities and languages in the past made it impossible to interact with the larger world of school and work without learning English and venturing out of the economic and cultural niches that immigrants naturally create for themselves. But today's unprecedented volume of immigration dominated by a single ethnic group lays the groundwork for the development of a parallel, foreign-language, mainstream culture, a locally grown Hispanic identity shaped by but different from the various regional characteristics immigrants bring with them. The possibility, then, is that immigrants will assimilate into this new people, forming, in the extreme case, not an ethnic subculture like so many others (which will fade in importance over time) but instead a separate national community, a Hispanic *Volk*, demanding recognition on par with Anglos. This is what Samuel Huntington was getting at in pointing to Miami as a possible model for much of the country if immigration (and other policies) remained unchanged.[24]

Even short of such an extreme development, today's lack of immigrant diversity slows the kinds of initial, surface assimilation that are precursors to patriotic or emotional assimilation. With regard to language, for instance, the dominant position of Spanish allows the development of ever-larger enclaves, eliminating for an increasing number of people the need for any daily interaction in English, thus reducing the incentive to learn. Huntington quoted a writer who observed that "an entrepreneur who spoke no English could still, in Miami, buy, sell, negotiate, leverage assets, float bonds, and, if he were so inclined, attend galas twice a week in black tie."[25] The effect this has on mastery of English is exactly what you'd expect; research into immigrant language use has found that "the greater the extent to which an individual can avoid communicating in the destination language, the slower is likely to be the rate of acquisition of dominant language skills."[26]

In addition to simple proximity of an immigrant to a larger number of Spanish-speakers, the lack of diversity in today's immigration creates a critical mass for, among other things, Spanish-language mass media, further reducing exposure to, and thus acquisition of, English. There are now two nationwide Spanish-language television networks, Univision and Telemundo, serving scores of stations and producing an increasingly large share of their programming domestically rather than importing it from abroad. Almost 80 percent of Hispanics (immigrant and native born) watch Spanish-language television, half of them as their primary source of TV.[27] The spread of such outlets is the reason that ratings research has found that Spanish speakers are watching less and less English-language programming.[28]

Academic advocates for mass immigration have claimed that the undiverse concentration of Spanish speakers is completely benign and will not have any different results from past immigration. A 2006 study of language retention among immigrant groups in Southern California, which was prepared specifically to make this case (the authors described the article as a test of Huntington's hypothesis that mass immigration will ensure the permanence of Spanish), actually suggests quite the opposite of what the authors intended.[29] They claim their finding that "only" 17 percent of the American-born grandchildren of Mexican immigrants (one out of six) speak *fluent* Spanish proves that foreign languages will die out in the United States. While they acknowledge that the same percentage for the grandchildren of European immigrants is close to zero, they do not note that these Spanish-retaining people are the grandchildren of people who immigrated—and thus began the process of assimilation—fifty to seventy-five years ago, at a time of radically lower levels of immigration, before the embrace of post-Americanism and multiculturalism by the elite, and before the term "bilingual education" even came into existence. That one out of six of the grandchildren of *those* immigrants still speaks Spanish fluently is actually disturbing evidence of the persistence of foreign attachments and suggests that the grandchildren of *today's* immigrants will retain the ancestral foreign language at even higher rates.

TRANSNATIONALISM

The lack of ethnic diversity in today's mass immigration is a problem that could theoretically be fixed; in fact there are two provisions of the immigration law intended to increase the diversity of the immigration flow.[30] But assuming such measures were successful (they have not been and, as a practical matter, cannot be[31]), would that take care of the problem? In other words, if immigration were kept at its current high levels but somehow magically made more diverse (i.e., less Hispanic), wouldn't that address our assimilation concerns?

No, because, as mentioned earlier, there is a systemic incompatibility between mass immigration—regardless of its origin—and assimilation in a modern society. The first reason for this incompatibility is modern technology: easy and cheap communications and transportation over very long distances make it easier for immigrants to maintain ties with the old country, making it less likely that such ties will atrophy over time and thus focus the attention and affections of the newcomer (and his children) on his new country.

The desire to retain ties with family and friends back home is perfectly natural—in fact, there's probably something wrong with an immigrant who doesn't occasionally feel some kind of longing for home, however unpleasant the circumstances of his departure. A *New Yorker* cartoon of an elderly immigrant talking to his grandchildren captures this sentiment: "The country grandpa came from was a stinking hellhole of unspeakable poverty where everyone was always happy."

But a century ago, this normal human sentiment ran up against practical realities: Travel, though cheaper and easier than it had been, was still expensive, time-consuming, and unpleasant. Many immigrants a century ago did go home (perhaps as many as a third of those who passed through Ellis Island), but their residence was sequential—first they lived in Italy, say, then they came to work in New York, and after several years, they took the long trip back.

Likewise, communication with home was difficult in the past, limited to hand-written letters, which took weeks or months to cross the ocean, if they arrived at all. The title of the final volume of a tale of nineteenth-century Swedish immigrants in the Midwest captures the tenuous nature of their ties with the old country: *The Last Letter Home*.[32]

Princeton University sociologist Alejandro Portes summed up the situation: "Earlier in the twentieth century, the expense and difficulty of long-distance communication and travel simply made it impossible to lead a dual existence in two countries. Polish peasants couldn't just hop a plane—or make a phone call, for that matter—to check out how things were going at home over the weekend."[33]

But now they can. As one article puts it: "Armed with cut-rate phone cards and frequent-flier miles, with modems, fax machines and videocameras, immigrants can participate in the lives of their families back home—be they in Barbados or Tibet—with an immediacy unknown to any previous generation."[34]

These modern technologies foster the creation of transnational immigrant communities that cross boundaries and undermine the rootedness needed to foster emotional assimilation and national cohesion. Wellesley College sociologist Peggy Levitt calls communities like this transnational villages.[35] As an example of this spreading phenomenon, she describes a community split between the original village in the

Dominican Republic and its other half in Boston: People watch the same soap operas, telephone contacts become ever more frequent as rates fall, gossip travels instantly between the two halves of the village, parents in one half try to raise children in the other, the same political parties operate in both places, and air travel allows people to go home for long weekends or split their time between the two communities. In short, modern technology "keeps people connected to one another in unprecedented ways and reinforces their ties to one another."[36]

Transnationalism allows ties to be maintained even beyond death: According to Deborah Sontag and Celia Dugger, "In 1996, more than half the Dominicans and Mexicans who died in New York City were sent home for burial, as were a third of the Ecuadoreans, a fifth of the Jamaicans and 16 percent of the Greeks."[37] So much for "Where thou diest, will I die, and there will I be buried."

As one Mexican immigrant, whose community similarly straddles two countries, put it, "We really don't have to choose between here and there."[38] The result, in one scholar's words, is that "they're redefining what it means to be American."[39]

This redefinition of Americanness caused by transnationalism isn't just informal—it's being institutionalized by the rapid spread of dual citizenship.

Whenever people have moved from one country to another, the issue of dual and competing citizenships has arisen; one of the causes of the War of 1812, after all, was the British crown's policy of "once an Englishman, always an Englishman"—that is, Britain's refusal to recognize American naturalization and its seizure of British-born American citizens on American ships.

But mass immigration combined with modern technology is making the exercise of dual citizenship a pervasive phenomenon, no longer limited to the handful of globe-trotting rich. More than 80 percent of today's immigrants come from countries that provide for some form of dual citizenship, and of the major countries immigrants leave for the United States, only three—China, Cuba, and South Korea—do not have some form of dual citizenship.[40] Since dual citizenship in almost all cases passes to the American-born children as well (and in some cases to grandchildren), the number of potential dual citizens is quite large; Renshon estimates a total of more than 40 million people,[41] and the total number grows by something like 1.5 million each year.[42]

Of course, potential dual citizenship is one thing, the reality is another. There were large numbers of potential dual citizens created by past immigration waves, but because of technological limitations, immigrants had little practical alternative to complying with their American citizenship oath: ". . . I absolutely and entirely renounce and abjure all allegiance and fidelity to any foreign prince, potentate, state or sovereignty, of whom or which I have heretofore been a subject or citizen . . ."

But the same modern technological advances that permit informal, social forms of transnationalism are also making possible the spread of political transnationalism—i.e., dual citizenship. One harbinger of things to come is Jesus Galvis, a Colombian immigrant who became an American citizen and eventually got elected to the Hackensack, New Jersey, City Council. Then, in 1998, he ran for the Senate—the Colombian Senate. Had he won, he would have held elective office in two nations simultaneously, a first in American history.

In 2000, for the first time, several Mexican immigrants who had become American citizens ran for local political offices in Mexico, something made possible by Mexico's 1997 law permitting dual nationality. In 2004, one Manuel de la Cruz, a naturalized American citizen from Los Angeles, was elected to the legislature of the Mexican state of Zacatecas.[43] And in 2006, Andrés Bermúdez, one of the naturalized U.S. citizens elected to a local office in 2000, moved up to the national Chamber of Deputies, the lower house of Mexico's national legislature, where he swore an oath to uphold that nation's constitution.

Of course, relatively few immigrants will run for office in their home countries. But many more might be willing to vote in foreign elections, and modern technology could make that possible in ways unimaginable a century ago. A 2005 survey by the Pew Hispanic Center found that nearly 90 percent of the Mexican immigrants polled (including illegal aliens, legal immigrants, and naturalized American dual citizens) said they would vote in Mexico's 2006 elections if they could.[44] In the event, fewer than half the Mexicans in the United States were deemed eligible to vote in Mexico, and then only for Mexico's president (and not in the congressional races), and the rules for doing so were made quite onerous. Nevertheless, nearly thirty thousand did vote from the United States, following in the footsteps of dual citizens from Poland, Iraq, Colombia, Italy, and elsewhere who have voted in elections held in countries to which they supposedly renounced allegiance.

POST-AMERICANISM

But the transnational possibilities created by modern technology wouldn't matter so much in inhibiting assimilation if it weren't for the second, political, factor: All modern societies, or at least their elites, lose the cultural self-confidence needed to induce patriotic assimilation.

Past waves of immigration encountered strongly assimilationist attitudes among America's elites. The Founding Fathers insisted that patriotic assimilation was key; Alexander Hamilton, for instance, said that the success of the American republic depended upon "the preservation of a national spirit and national character" among native born and immigrant alike.[45]

Later, John Quincy Adams told a German aristocrat contemplating immigration that immigrants "must cast off the European skin, never to resume it. They must look forward to their posterity rather than backward to their ancestors."[46]

Theodore Roosevelt was quoted earlier on the necessity of assimilation, but he was seconded, if only on this matter, by his bitter political rival, Woodrow Wilson, who admonished new citizens, "You cannot dedicate yourself to America unless you become in every respect and with every purpose of your will thoroughly Americans."[47]

Nor was the robust promotion of Americanization confined to the federal government; state and local governments and the private sector were also actively involved. The first sentence that Henry Ford's immigrant workers learned in their company-supported English classes was "I am a good American."[48] *National Review* reporter John Miller, in his valuable look at Americanization, *The Unmaking of Americans,* tells of the Americanization program launched by the town fathers of Lawrence, Massachusetts, after a bitter 1912 strike involving immigrants. One local group published a pamphlet, "Lawrence—Here She Stands: For God and Country!" while the public schools developed an "American Plan for Education in Citizenship," which included lessons in history to teach "love and loyalty for America" and promoted things "which the American spirit holds dear."[49]

Miller also describes the North American Civic League for Immigrants, founded in 1907, as "a group of philanthropists, social workers, writers, and industrialists" who promoted Americanization by, among other means, a series of public lectures and pamphlets on such topics as "The Story of the American People," "Abraham Lincoln," and "George Washington."[50]

One need only imagine what "a group of philanthropists, social workers, writers, and industrialists" today would teach immigrants about America to see how much we've changed. The reason is that elites in modern societies change from being nationalist to being cosmopolitan, so that, as Huntington writes, they "abandon commitment to their nation and their fellow citizens and argue the moral superiority of identifying with humanity at large."[51] Another way of saying this is that our elites—in government, business, education, religion, philanthropy, journalism, and other fields—have become "post-American."[52] Post-Americans are not necessarily anti-American; it's just that their chief political allegiance is no longer with the United States. They don't feel the visceral emotional attachment to the American national community that is the mark of patriotism, instead seeing themselves chiefly as "citizens of the world" or perhaps as part of a multinational corporation or of an ethnic or other group that is the chief object of their affections and attachment.

Consumer activist Ralph Nader pulled a stunt a few years ago that highlighted the post-Americanism of the nation's business leaders. On the occasion of Flag Day in 1996, Nader sent letters to the CEOs of the one hundred largest Fortune 500 corporations, asking that they open their next shareholders' meeting by reciting the Pledge of Allegiance on behalf of their corporation, which is chartered, subsidized, and protected by the people of the United States.[53] All but one of the companies that responded rejected the idea out of hand: One called it "a grim reminder of the loyalty oaths of the 1950s," while another denounced it as "someone else's imposed litmus test regarding our corporation's allegiance to the United States of America." And especially ironic, in light of Henry Ford's Americanizing efforts, was the response of the Ford Motor Company: "We do not believe that the concept of 'corporate allegiance' is possible."

Along these same lines are the perennial calls by the *Wall Street Journal* editors for an amendment to the Constitution saying, "There shall be open borders," reiterated in one form or another at least seven times.[54] The fact that all of these calls for the abolition of America's borders have been tied to Independence Day highlights the rejection by this element of the elite of the very legitimacy of the United States as a distinct nation-state.

This same outlook was revealed by a sociological study of executives of nominally American multinational corporations: "Again and again, we heard them say that they thought of themselves more as 'citizens of the world' who happen to carry an American passport than as U.S. citizens who happen to work in a global organization."[55]

But this post-Americanism is not limited to America's economic elites, as shown by survey research from the Chicago Council on Foreign Relations.[56] This 2002 survey on a broad range of foreign policy-related issues compared the views of the public and of "opinion leaders," including not just executives of Fortune 1000 corporations but also presidents of the largest labor unions, television and radio news directors, network newscasters, newspaper editors and columnists, religious leaders, presidents of large special interest groups and think tanks with an emphasis on foreign policy matters, presidents and faculty of universities, members of Congress, and senior staff in the administration.

Among the topics discussed, immigration policy was clearly the one that best highlighted issues of national identity and national attachment. Not coincidentally, immigration was also the source of the widest differences between the public and the opinion-leading elite. For instance, 60 percent of the public agreed that the present level of immigration was a "critical threat to the vital interests of the United States," compared to only 14 percent of the elite. Likewise, 70 percent of the public viewed controlling and reducing illegal immigration as a "very important" foreign policy goal, compared to only 22 percent of the elite. And 55 percent of the public wanted legal immigration to be reduced, compared to only 18 percent of the elite.

The broad sampling of the elite for this survey, beyond merely business leaders, suggests these huge differences in views on immigration were driven by the elite's post-Americanism rather than simply by narrow economic concerns, such as access to cheap labor.

MULTICULTURALISM

Post-Americanism's downgrading of allegiance to the national community leads to a broad policy of multiculturalism, "understood not just as tolerance of cultural diversity in de facto multicultural societies but as the demand for legal recognition of the rights of ethnic, racial, religious, or cultural groups, [which] has now become established in virtually all modern liberal democracies."[57] The genesis of multiculturalism had nothing to do with immigrants, of course; the groups demanding legal recognition initially included black Americans and women, then homosexuals, the deaf, the obese, and others.

The idea of multiculturalism for immigrants isn't entirely new; philosopher Horace Kallen wrote way back in 1915 that, thanks to immigration, "the United States are in the process of becoming a federal state not merely as a union of geographical and administrative unities, but also as a cooperation of cultural diversities, as a federation or commonwealth of national cultures."[58]

But given the elite's assimilationist, nationalist self-confidence at that time, this protomulticulturalism could not gain any traction. Instead, immigrants learned what Victor Davis Hanson calls a tough Americanism based on "simplistic but unmistakable assumptions about the immigrant: he was here to stay and become an American, not to go back and forth between the old and the new country. He was to become one of us, not we one of him. He was here because he chose to be here, and so was required to learn about us, not we about him."[59] In the same vein, Hanson observed that in the past, American teachers "seemed to know that the Mexican immigrant could and should retain a pride in his ethnic heritage—to be expressed in music, dance, art, literature, religion and cuisine *only*—while being mature enough to see that the core political, economic and social values of his abandoned country were to be properly and rapidly forgotten."[60]

Under multiculturalism, today's circumstances are very different: "The goal of assimilation that was once the standard, if unspoken, orthodoxy in our schools and government is now ridiculed as racist and untrue,"[61] largely because "the self-confidence that taught values to the immigrant has nearly vanished from our schools."[62] After all, as one political scientist asks, "If we cannot be confident of our values and the society that supports them, how can we expect others to view them as objects of emulation?"[63]

The corrosive effect of this modern loss of self-confidence on patriotic assimilation shows itself in a variety of ways:

ENGLISH. Perhaps the most obvious is language policy. Although learning English is certainly not sufficient for genuine assimilation, it is obviously the first step, and the unwillingness by government to insist on the primacy of English in the public sphere sends a clear signal to newcomers that, while English may be useful in getting a job, there is no moral obligation to master it as part of acquiring a new national identity.

The elite viewed immigrant acquisition of English very differently in the past. Theodore Roosevelt again: "We have room for but one language here, and that is the English language, for we intend to see

that the crucible turns our people out as Americans, and American nationality, not as dwellers in a polyglot boarding house."[64]

Today, on the other hand, something as innocuous as declaring English the official language of a jurisdiction (even with all the usual cave-
ats about emergency services and the like) is fiercely opposed by elites.
The first such measure to arise during this new wave of immigration
was a ballot measure in 1980 declaring English the official language of
Dade County, Florida, home of the city of Miami. The chief newspaper
denounced it as "civic and social madness," and the Greater Miami
Chamber of Commerce called it "destructive and disunifying."[65] It
passed, and has been followed by similar measures in states and localities
across the country, always with much more public than elite support.

The elite's anti-Americanization message regarding language goes
beyond resisting largely symbolic measures, like official-English desig-
nations, to actively *preventing* acquisition of English. For instance, federal, state, and local governments spend hundreds of millions a year on
bilingual education programs, which no longer even pretend to ease the
transition to English but are now specifically intended to maintain foreign languages and cultures.[66] Furthermore, despite the requirement
that immigrants demonstrate a knowledge of English to receive citizenship, the Voting Rights Act was amended in 1975 to require ballots
in foreign languages, and that "temporary" measure was renewed in
2006.[67] President Clinton signed, and President Bush has reaffirmed,
Executive Order 13166, which requires all federal agencies and all recipients of federal funds to provide all services in whatever foreign language anyone demands.[68]

The ambivalence of the elite on these sorts of language issues shows
up in opinion surveys as well. A 2006 poll asked a variety of language-
related questions and correlated them with various characteristics of the
respondents; one of the characteristics asked about in the poll that can
serve as a rough yardstick to gauge elite verses nonelite opinion is how
often the respondent shopped at Wal-Mart.[69] Those who never shopped
at Wal-Mart were significantly less likely to support proassimilation
language policies than those who shopped there weekly. For instance,

compared to Wal-Mart no-shows, frequent Wal-Mart shoppers were about 15 percent more likely to support declaring English our official language, 25 percent more likely to support printing ballots only in English, and 33 percent more likely to require that immigrants pass a driver's license exam in English.

SCHOOLS. Our public school system was created in the nineteenth century in large part to Americanize immigrant children, and it performed remarkably well. Economist and political philosopher Friedrich Hayek observed, in *The Constitution of Liberty,* "That the United States would not have become such an effective 'melting pot' and would probably have faced extremely difficult problems if it had not been for a deliberate policy of 'Americanization' through the public school system seems fairly certain."[70]

Because of multiculturalism, however, schools today are failing utterly to pass on the history and heroes and legends of our past. In fact, schools are more likely to engage in a deliberate policy of *de-*Americanization, having become a battleground in a "conflict between those who want to *transmit* the American regime and those who want to *transform* it."[71] Social studies curricula, for instance, routinely promote the notion of the American "peoples," rejecting the very idea of a unifying American identity into which newcomers might assimilate.[72] History textbooks present the United States as "exploitative, unequal, and almost unredeemable in its general nastiness," according to a review by two prominent scholars.[73]

A 2006 study by the Intercollegiate Studies Institute found that American students arrive at college knowing very little about American history and government, and learn virtually nothing about them during their four years of higher education.[74] Such stories have become almost comically routine, but they are alarming nonetheless: Given multiple-choice tests, the majority of college seniors surveyed did not know in which *century* the Jamestown colony was established, what battle ended the American Revolution, that the Bill of Rights prohibits an established church, or that the Declaration of Independence was the source of the phrase "We hold these truths to be self-evident, that all men are created equal." It was telling that the more elite the college, the lower the level of civic learning.

Research has actually documented our schools' de-Americanizing effect on children from immigrant families. Sociologists Alejandro Portes and Ruben Rumbaut studied thousands of children of immigrants in San Diego and South Florida over a period of several years.[75] Most interesting for our purposes was their analysis of how these young people identified themselves in terms of ethnic or national identity, something the students were asked when starting high school and again when they were finishing.

When first surveyed, the majority of the students identified themselves as American in some form, either as simply "American" or as a "hyphenated" American (Cuban American, for instance, or Filipino American). After several years of American high school, barely one third still identified themselves as Americans, the majority choosing an identification with no American component at all, opting for either a foreign national-origin identity (Cuban, Filipino) or a panracial identity (Hispanic, Asian). The antiassimilationist slant of modern American education is perhaps most visible from this fact: Of the one eighth of immigrant children in the study who identified themselves as simply "American" at the beginning of high school, only 15 percent still thought of themselves that way at the end of high school. The most dramatic abandonment of "American" identity was seen among Cubans in private schools; in the first survey, fully one third identified themselves as simply American. By the end of high school, only 2 percent still did.

As the authors sum up: "The shift, therefore, has not been toward mainstream identities but toward a more militant reaffirmation of the immigrant identity for some groups (notably Mexicans and Filipinos in California and Haitians and Nicaraguans in Florida) and toward panethnic minority-group identities for others."[76]

DUAL CITIZENSHIP. Dual citizenship has not spread merely because of the technological reasons discussed earlier but also—perhaps mainly—because of our modern elite's post-Americanism, leading the government to shrug its figurative shoulders at the idea of multiple national attachments. The clear message being sent to immigrants is that American citizenship is a mere formality, a passport of convenience, rather than the formal, legal recognition of an emotional change in nationality.

Theodore Roosevelt, always reliable in these matters, called dual citizenship "a self-evident absurdity." Franklin Roosevelt appointed a cabinet committee that concluded "it is not believed that an American national should be permitted to participate in the political affairs of a foreign state and at the same time retain his American nationality. The two facts would seem to be inconsistent with each other."[77]

Stanley Renshon connects dual citizenship with multiculturalism:

> No country, and certainly no democracy, can afford to have large numbers of citizens with shallow national and civic attachments. No country facing divisive domestic issues arising out of its increasing diversity, as America does, benefits from large-scale immigration of those with multiple loyalties and attachments. And no country striving to reconnect its citizens to a coherent civic identity and culture can afford to encourage its citizens to look elsewhere for their most basic national attachments.[78]

While the requirement of renouncing other allegiances (and prohibiting the exercise of dual citizenship) remains in U.S. law,[79] our modern elite's diffidence about patriotism and national commitment has rendered it a dead letter. In 1967, the Supreme Court in a 5–4 decision overturned the long-standing practice of stripping a person of his American citizenship if he committed an "expatriating act," like swearing allegiance to a foreign power or serving in a foreign military engaged in hostilities against the United States. That decision, *Afroyim v. Rusk,* held that "Congress has no power under the Constitution to divest a person of his United States citizenship absent his voluntary renunciation thereof."[80]

Whatever the merits of the Warren Court's constitutional reasoning in this case (it overturned a precedent reaffirmed by the Court just nine years earlier in a decision authored by Justice Felix Frankfurter), Congress had options for accommodating this novel interpretation while still upholding the principle of exclusive American citizenship. Namely, it could have taken its cue from Justice Earl Warren's dissent in that case of nine years earlier (*Perez v. Brownell,* 356 U.S. 44), where Warren wrote that while he thought that stripping someone of his citizenship should not be permitted, "If the Government determines that certain conduct by United States citizens should be prohibited because of anticipated injurious consequences to the conduct of foreign affairs or to some other legitimate governmental interest, it may within the limits of the Constitution proscribe such activity and assess appropriate punishment." In other words, Congress could simply change the law in question so that instead of losing his citizenship, an American who committed an expatriating act could instead be punished with a fine or prison.

In 1967, this may never have occurred to anyone, because mass immigration was seen as a relic of a bygone era and there just weren't many people such a legal provision would apply to. But by the time mass immigration (and changes in the laws of sending countries) made dual citizenship an unavoidable issue, post-Americanism had become widespread enough among the elite to dissuade Congress from acting. Instead, in 1986, Congress passed, and President Reagan signed, a measure that amended the Immigration and Nationality Act to conform with the Supreme Court decision, without adding any other punishments for the prohibited acts.

And far from being an accident, dual citizenship is seen as desirable by backers of mass immigration precisely because of its corrosive effect on national cohesion. Portes, the Princeton sociologist, has written approvingly that "transnationality and its political counterpart, dual citizenship, may not be a sign of imminent civic breakdown but the vanguard of the direction that new notions of community and society will be taking in the next century."[81]

AFFIRMATIVE ACTION FOR IMMIGRANTS. Another way that the modern phenomenon of multiculturalism impedes assimilation is through affirmative action, the government-mandated system (now also broadly adopted by the private sector) that gives preferences in hiring, promotion, government contracts, and university admissions to members of certain ethnic and racial groups. Whatever the merits of affirmative action, it would not be an assimilation issue if most new immigrants were what bureaucrats now call "non-Hispanic whites," and thus ineligible for affirmative-action benefits. But the overwhelming majority of immigrants are immediately eligible as members of "protected classes." Immigrants from Latin America, sub-Saharan Africa, and East and South Asia—i.e., "minorities"—accounted for 87 percent of new immigration during the first half of this decade. The percentage of immigrants eligible for affirmative-action preferences may actually be higher, both because of nonwhite immigration from Canada and Europe and because some jurisdictions consider even immigrants from Spain and Portugal as members of minorities in need of special preferences.

By institutionalizing the "otherness" of immigrants, the racial framework of affirmative action transforms what was originally billed as a temporary policy of compensation for the descendants of slaves into a permanent means of managing "diversity." In this sense it is like bilingual education, which has likewise changed from a transitional tool to a permanent feature of American education.

This is especially problematic at a time when the expansion of "whiteness" means that Hispanic and Asian ethnicity is increasingly voluntary, like Italian or Irish or Jewish ethnicity. Inclusion of almost all immigrants in the system of minority preferences serves as a formal message from the government of their new country that immigrants should not—cannot—ever be truly assimilated. By seeking to harden these increasingly optional identities into legally solidified ones, affirmative action impedes deep assimilation. Portes and Rumbaut, in their study of immigrant children referenced earlier, found exactly this effect: "Second-generation youths seemed to become increasingly aware of

and adopt the ethnoracial markers in which they are persistently classi-
fied by the schools and other U.S. institutions."[82]

It wasn't supposed to be that way. At the start, what we now call
affirmative action was conceived as specific to black Americans. In his
1965 commencement speech at Howard University, the nation's premier black college, President Lyndon Johnson said, "You do not take a
person who, for years, has been hobbled by chains and liberate him,
bring him up to the starting line of a race and then say, 'You're free to
compete with all the others,' and justly believe that you have been completely fair."

From the very beginnings of the modern system of racial categori-
zation in the 1950s (when Washington sought to ensure that federal
contractors were complying with nondiscrimination rules), nonblack
groups were simply tacked on as an afterthought. The congressional
hearings and public debates shaping civil rights policy included much
discussion of the legacy of slavery but, in the words of Hugh Davis Graham, author of *Collision Course: The Strange Convergence of Affirmative
Action and Immigration Policy in America,* "The record showed almost no
discussion of why other minority groups in America were included (for
example, Chinese, Argentinians, Pakistanis, Cubans, Spaniards, Portuguese) or excluded (Jews, Italians, Jehovah's Witnesses, Mormons,
Palestinians, Iranians)."[83]

Instead, bureaucrats simply made up categories of people presumably suffering from discrimination, in closed deliberations, with no
explanations or rationale provided, and under pressure from ethnic lobbyists who wanted equal billing with blacks. Dubious as such policy
making might be, it happened mainly during a period of low immigration, long after the era of mass immigration was thought to have ended,
and thus was seen as having little practical effect. But by the end of the
1990s, as Graham writes, "Mass immigration from Latin America and
Asia had undermined affirmative action's original, black-centered rationale. It did this by bringing to America more than 25 million immigrants whose national origins automatically qualified them as official
minorities eligible for affirmative action benefits."[84]

Though immigrants were included in affirmative action programs almost by accident, there were some illuminating incidents in which a public decision had to be made. Graham recounts an Indonesian immigrant who sought inclusion in the Small Business Administration's minority set-aside program in 1988.[85] Her original request to the SBA outlined her immigrant success story, complete with long hours of hard work, struggles to master English, and finally starting a business and becoming a naturalized American. But she was turned down, because Indonesians were not on the SBA's list of oppressed groups.

She took the hint and quickly ditched the language of Americanization and embraced instead the modern language of grievance and deassimilation. Graham quotes from her revised, and successful, petition:

> My color is yellow like other Indonesians I know. Asian Pacific Americans have suffered the chronic effects of discriminatory practices for a very long time, over which they have no control, and, Indonesian Americans most definitely included, have suffered economic deprivation. This has impacted all the Indonesian Americans I know in a most negative way. Good jobs are scarce regardless of talent. Language and color are a barrier to both employment and a good education. Indonesian Americans have no business history.

This immigrant's adoption of modern America's ambivalence about itself highlights a second antiassimilationist aspect of affirmative action. It's not just that this policy officially demarcates and almost sacralizes group divisions for immigrants that would otherwise be fluid and optional; in addition, the need to justify continued inclusion of immigrants forces supporters to adopt the narrative of black American history, arguing that America is irredeemably racist and thus the government needs to keep its thumb on the scales for "minorities" for the indefinite future. But if America is so rotten at its core that the government must permanently protect Hispanics and Asians, as though they were in the same tenuous position as, say, Christians in the Middle East or Chinese in Indonesia, then why would immigrants want to identify with this America and embrace its history and heroes as their own?

JUST END MULTICULTURALISM?

Some who recognize the antiassimilationist effects of multiculturalism nevertheless argue that the solution is simply to end multiculturalism while continuing the federal immigration program at record levels. But even if multiculturalism were the only concern regarding Americaniza-tion (which the earlier discussion of advances in technology shows it's not) and even if assimilation were the only concern regarding modern immigration (as the rest of this book argues it's not), the fact would re-main that multiculturalism is not something that can be eliminated by a single piece of legislation or administrative decision, like lowering the voting age or raising the tax rate.

Instead, multiculturalism is an ideology that is virtually universal among elites in modern societies, including ours, and its assumptions are now deeply rooted in every American institution—every univer-sity, obviously, but also every public and private elementary and high school, every day-care center, every library, every corporate human-resources department, every newspaper, every church and synagogue, every police station, every town council, every courtroom, every civic club—everywhere.

This is not to say that those concerned about the antiassimilationist effects of multiculturalism should merely accept it as a given in modern society and do nothing to try to limit its scope and move toward resto-ration of a common civic culture. After all, whatever immigration policies we adopt in the future, there are millions of legal immigrants, and their American-born young children, already here. Furthermore, even under an immigration system more in tune with the needs and characteristics of modern America, there will still be some nontrivial amount of ongoing immigration (see the final chapter for an outline of such a system), and those future immigrants will also need to be assimilated.

This means that efforts to refocus public debate on the ideal of an inclusive, nonracial American patriotism are vital and need to continue. Ballot measures like California's Proposition 209 (prohibiting the state government from considering race or ethnicity in contracting, hiring, or schooling) and Proposition 227 (limiting bilingual education in public schools) were important examples of a patriotic public pushing back against a post-American elite. More recent measures of this kind were successful 2006 ballot initiatives in Arizona (declaring English the state's official language) and Michigan (like California's Proposition 209, barring race-based government policies).

But even the most optimistic supporter of such efforts would have to acknowledge that progress will be very slow and incomplete. In the meantime, millions of newcomers keep arriving from abroad and are introduced to America by the multiculturalists. As Miller writes in *The Unmaking of Americans,* "If the schools miss their chance [to inculcate American language and values], un-Americanized children grow up to become un-Americanized adults—at which point their Americanization becomes much more difficult and unlikely."[86]

LIFESTYLE CHANGES

In addition to transnationalism and multiculturalism, there is a final cluster of concerns regarding the difficulties of assimilation in modern society, which can be grouped, for want of a better word, under the rubric of lifestyle changes in our society.

These concerns are not really related to the goal of Americanizing immigrants by shifting their political allegiance from their old countries to the United States. Instead, these are features that distinguish modern society and complicate the incorporation of immigrants into the daily life and social norms of contemporary America.

First, there is a larger gap between the lifestyles and assumptions of today's new arrivals and today's American norms than was the case in the past. At the risk of sounding glib, immigrants in the nineteenth century came from towns and villages with horse manure in the streets and found the same situation in New York and Boston. In other words, immigrants came from what we would now describe as third-world environments to an America that was, in many respects, also a third-world country.

Today's immigrants, on the other hand, come from places very much like the homelands of their nineteenth-century predecessors, but are coming to a twenty-first-century society with modern, middle-class, developed-nation social norms. There were criticisms of the conflict between immigrant and American mores in the past as well, of course. But despite the difficulty in measuring such a thing, it seems pretty clear that the mainstream social norms of modern America are much further removed from the assumptions that immigrants bring with them than was the case in the past. Political scientist Peter Skerry describes the conflict between immigrant and native norms as a matter of "social disorder," examples of which "are highly visible in immigrant neighborhoods and have surfaced as the focus of disputes and controversies between immigrants and nonimmigrants [i.e., native-born Americans] across the United States."[87] He cites things like immigrants' crowing roosters waking up neighbors, overcrowded housing in immigrant neighborhoods (in violation of modern housing codes), trash and health concerns involving immigrant food vendors, high rates of pedestrian accidents in immigrant neighborhoods, and more. These are what Skerry and a coauthor have described as "the social strains and disorder that inevitably accompany any movement of large numbers of unskilled immigrants into advanced democratic societies."[88]

Such a critique is not meant to stigmatize immigrants as somehow inherently backward; after all, the reason immigrants' backwardness was less of a problem in the past is that we were, in many ways, similarly backward. Nor are immigrants incapable of adopting modern American social norms; Skerry notes the example of a long-term working-class Mexican immigrant who moved her family out of the old neighborhood to a gated community north of Las Vegas because

"People from Mexico—we call them paesanos—were burning tires. They played radios real loud. I was afraid of Cecelia [their daughter] playing outside, that someone would run her over. Here it's quiet and safe for her."[89] Note that this is not a concern about violent crime nor even strictly about economics, but rather the conflict between old-country and American assumptions and behaviors, and the immigrant in question had come to adopt some significant portion of mainstream American social views.

This larger gap between immigrant and American social norms makes it that much more difficult to successfully press huge numbers of newcomers to abandon their premodern habits and assumptions for more modern behavior. Even in the previous wave of immigration, the closing of that period's smaller social gap between newcomers and Americans was significantly aided by the cutoff of immigration in the 1920s. How much more important it is to reduce numbers today in order to enable immigrants to cross the much larger social gap that lies between them and America's mainstream.

BOWLING *SOLAMENTE*

This first lifestyle concern is the result of a generally positive aspect of modernity—higher standards of decorum and conduct that people in modern societies internalize and come to expect. But one of the negative social consequences of modernity also makes mass immigration problematic: social atomization and loss of what Robert Putnam, author of *Bowling Alone,* calls social capital and civic engagement. Putnam describes social capital as "connections among individuals—social networks and the norms of reciprocity and trustworthiness that arise from them."[90] Putnam traces the decline in such connections in a wide variety of areas: less citizen participation in politics, declining membership in civic groups across the board, from the PTA and the Elks to Hadassah and the Boy Scouts, as well as declining church attendance, membership in unions and professional associations, even informal activities like having friends over for dinner.

Putnam identifies the reasons for this pervasive decline in a variety of factors that distinguish modern society: two-career families and other modern pressures related to work; suburbanization, commuting, and sprawl; the effect of television privatizing our leisure time; and generation change—that is, the passing of a generation raised in more traditional times and its replacement by a generation raised in modernity.[91]

The problem here for mass immigration is twofold: First, immigrants are harder to absorb socially in a bowling-alone society, because the institutions that did the assimilating in the past have declined significantly; and second, mass immigration exacerbates the bowling-alone tendencies in the broader society.

As to the first, unions and urban political machines were among the most important institutions involved in immigrant assimilation; the decline of the first and the disappearance of the second are well documented. Specifically with regard to machines, Skerry writes, "Our political institutions have been transformed. They have in many respects become more modern. As a result, they offer little help in negotiating the gulf between the traditional values that newcomers bring with them and those of contemporary American society."[92] Even the Roman Catholic Church, the nominal religious home of the majority of new immigrants, has seen a large, steady decline in attendance at Mass, donations from members, and new priests.

Nor are today's immigrants creating their own large membership-based organizations as they did in the past. The groups started by immigrants in previous eras—the Knights of Columbus, the Steuben Society, the various Slavic Sokol groups, AHEPA (the American Hellenic Educational Progressive Association, for Greeks), and many others—served both to provide mutual support (financial and emotional) and to be vehicles for integration into the rest of society. "Such institutions," Skerry writes, "performed this task [changing old-world immigrant values] by providing opportunities for newcomers to learn to behave like Americans, but without cutting them off from their native languages or heritages."[93]

But today's immigrants live in today's America, and in that bowling-alone environment of social atomization, new grassroots immigrant organizations seldom rise above the level of small, tenuous hometown associations comprised of people who hail from the same part of the old country.[94] The high-profile groups claiming to speak for today's immigrants do not, in fact, have much real membership at all, consisting instead of professional staff paid from grants by foundations, corporations, and government. Skerry describes the Mexican American Legal Defense and Educational Fund (MALDEF), "the most visible Mexican-American presence in the national arena," as a group that "has no mass membership base among Mexican Americans" and that during the 1980s received from one third to nearly one half of its funding from the Ford Foundation alone.[95]

As Gregory Rodriguez has written, "In Los Angeles, home to more Mexicans than any other city in the U.S., there is not one ethnic Mexican hospital, college, cemetery, or broad-based charity."[96] It could well be that there are cultural or other reasons that Mexican immigrants are especially deficient in institution building, but they nonetheless reflect a broader trend in modern society.

What's more, mass immigration seems to exacerbate the bowling-alone tendencies of modern society, actually contributing to the decline in social capital by overloading the society with more diversity than it can handle. Putnam has said that "the effect of diversity is worse than had been imagined. And it's not just that we don't trust people who are not like us. In diverse communities, we don't trust people who *do* look like us."[97] Specifically, Putnam describes the effects of immigration-driven diversity:

> Diversity does not produce "bad race relations" or ethnically-defined group hostility, our findings suggest. Rather, inhabitants of diverse communities tend to withdraw from collective life, to distrust their neighbours, regardless of the colour of their skin, to withdraw even from close friends, to expect the worst from

their community and its leaders, to volunteer less, give less to charity and work on community projects less often, to register to vote less, to agitate for social reform *more,* but have less faith that they can actually make a difference, and to huddle unhappily in front of the television. Note that this pattern encompasses attitudes and behavior, bridging and bonding social capital, public and private connections.[98]

He uses an evocative image: "In colloquial language, people living in ethnically diverse settings appear to 'hunker down'—that is, to pull in like a turtle."[99] Los Angeles, which immigration has made what Putnam calls "the most diverse human habitation in human history," not coincidentally has the lowest level of trust of the communities he and his team studied.

Nor are these findings entirely unexpected. Two economists from MIT and the Fletcher School of Law and Diplomacy reviewed empirical studies of the issue several years ago and found that "all of these studies have the same punch line: heterogeneity reduces civic engagement. In more diverse communities, people participate less as measured by how they allocate their time, their money, their voting, and their willingness to take risks to help others."[100] A later study by two economists in Germany found a significant "anti-social effect" on society at large due to low-skilled immigration.[101]

Either to maintain his own cognitive balance or preserve his professional viability in academia, Putnam tries to explain away the socially corrosive effects of mass immigration by arguing that in the long run "successful immigrant societies have overcome such fragmentation by creating new, cross-cutting forms of social solidarity and more encompassing identities."[102] That is indeed what successful immigrant societies like ours have done—*in the past.* But these "cross-cutting forms of social solidarity and more encompassing identities"—in other words, an overarching American identity held by people of different ethnic groups and classes and regions and religions—are precisely what modern societies have greater trouble developing, for the reasons, both technological and ideological, that this chapter has explored.

In short, Americanization is much more difficult under modern conditions than in the past. Rather than turning out new Americans who are "blood of the blood, and flesh of the flesh of the men who wrote that Declaration," mass immigration today is helping transform the United States into what one anthropologist approvingly calls "one node in a post-national network of diasporas."[103] Ending mass immigration does not guarantee the restoration of a common civic culture, but continuing it does guarantee that any attempt at such restoration will fail.

CHAPTER 2

Mass Immigration Versus American Sovereignty

The same aspects of modern society that make patriotic assimilation more difficult than in the past also serve to make mass immigration a serious challenge to America's sovereignty.

"Sovereignty" here means the ability of the American people, through their government, to exercise exclusive authority within the territory of the United States. In the modern environment of cheap and easy transportation and communications combined with the loss of self-confidence experienced by the elites in a modern society, mass immigration presents an opportunity for other nations to expand their sovereignty at the expense of ours.

Although any nation that sends large numbers of immigrants can take advantage of such an opportunity, as a practical matter, it is our neighbors who would obviously be in the best position to expand the scope of their sovereignty at our expense. Canada, though, sends us relatively few immigrants, and its elites are even more debilitated by the modern loss of cultural self-confidence than ours.

Mexico, on the other hand, has sent fifteen times as many immigrants here as Canada—more than 10 percent of its entire adult population—and has proven eager to exploit that fact to expand its authority within the United States. This expansion of Mexico's sovereignty northward is most obvious in a network of consulates unlike any other in the world, with officials of Mexico's foreign ministry directly involved in American politics, advocacy groups, courts, police, and schools.

The role of this consular network in American domestic affairs is so taken for granted by Mexico that failed presidential candidate Andrés Manuel López Obrador said during the 2006 campaign that he would formalize it by opening branches of the Mexican Attorney General's office in all of Mexico's consulates to defend Mexicans against "discrimination" (that is, to defend them against the workings of American law).[1]

Does this mean that today's massive Mexican immigration into the Southwest will enable Mexico to take back territories it briefly held in the nineteenth century? Did the huge illegal-alien marches in the spring of 2006 mark the beginning of a reconquest—*reconquista*—of Aztlán, the name some Mexican chauvinists use for the American Southwest? Will California and Texas be lost to the Union?

The answer is no. But what is happening is arguably worse, and it's unavoidable so long as mass immigration continues. And the cause is not ultimately something in the immigrants themselves but rather in the conditions of a modern society.

The boasts by Mexican nationalists about *reconquista* used to sound comical to most American ears, little more than banana-republic bravado. Americans who took this *reconquista* rhetoric seriously were breezily dismissed as cranks or alarmists, "black helicopter" people imagining world events controlled by the Trilateral Commission or, worse, by the Elders of Zion.

But as Mexican immigration—most of it illegal—has continued at levels unprecedented in history, and as illegal aliens have massed in the streets issuing demands to the American people, concern over *reconquista* has entered the mainstream.[2] Ron Maxwell, for instance, acclaimed film director of *Gettysburg* and *Gods and Generals,* wrote in an open letter to President Bush in the *Washington Times* in 2006, "It may already be too late to avoid a future annexation of the Southwest by Mexico or the evolution of a Mexican-dominated satellite state."[3] Syndicated columnist Michelle Malkin wrote a piece in May 2006 entitled "Reconquista Is Real."[4]

This concern is justified, as this chapter will outline. But the specific outcome that these writers point to is not going to happen. There will be no secession of the Southwest from the Union. Even if federal immigration policy remains unchanged and artificially creates a Hispanic majority in the Southwest (something that the 2007 Bush-Kennedy amnesty bill would have accelerated), there are still too many non-Hispanics, and too much diversity of opinion among Hispanics themselves, for a successful irredentist movement—one in which an ethnic group breaks away and joins its coethnics in a neighboring state.

But that doesn't mean there isn't a problem. Mass immigration under modern conditions *is* bringing about a kind of *reconquista*—it's just not the old-fashioned version in which territory is lost, but rather a new, twenty-first-century variety. What we are seeing right now is the gradual development of a new constitutional order of shared sovereignty in which the nominal borders stay the same but, through an accumulation of seemingly small American capitulations, the Mexican government gradually acquires more and more authority over the decision making of federal, state, and local governments all over the United States—i.e., it expands its sovereignty beyond its nominal borders. Under the pretext of protecting its compatriots (a group of people that Mexico defines very broadly, as we'll see later), Mexico City is moving toward becoming, in effect, a second federal government that American mayors and governors must answer to.

This is different from the concerns expressed by many about possible movement toward a North American Union, along the lines of the European Union. Such a development would go beyond measures like NAFTA that facilitate trade and would actually create new governmental institutions that could overrule the decisions of Congress or the president.

This is not a baseless fear. The Council on Foreign Relations has published a blueprint for "Creating a North American Community," and many critics have pointed to the trilateral (United States, Mexico, and Canada) governmental initiative called the Security and Prosperity Partnership as the germ of such a new political union.[5]

But the erosion of sovereignty promoted by mass immigration does not lead in the direction of a North American Union. Instead, what continued mass immigration will lead to, in practical terms, is a situation in which, for example, it becomes a binding custom that the governor of California would have to receive permission from the Mexican consul general in Sacramento before signing legislation that affects Hispanics in the state, such as any measures related to education, health care, welfare, occupational safety, unions, and the like. The Mexican embassy staff in Washington would work on an increasingly regular basis with the staff of congressional committees in framing legislation and conducting hearings on such matters, as well as on matters specific to the federal government, such as immigration, affirmative action, voting rights, and military personnel issues. Hispanic defendants would receive favorable treatment at police stations and county courthouses around the country out of concern for objections from the Mexican consulate with oversight of their area—and maybe even from a consular representative in the police station or courthouse itself.

This looks a lot like extraterritoriality, a concept in international law by which foreigners are exempt from local laws. The best known example of such extraterritoriality was the status of Westerners in China during much of the nineteenth century, starting with the British after the Treaty of Nanking in 1842. This meant that when a legal issue arose with regard to Westerners in China, their local consuls resolved the matter according to their own country's laws rather than China's.

But what's happening now between the United States and Mexico goes beyond extraterritoriality. It's more like the role France and Russia asserted as protectors of the oppressed Christian minorities in the Ottoman Empire. Starting in the 1600s, as part of a series of commercial agreements the Ottoman Turks came to call the Capitulations, France asserted itself as protector of Catholic sites and clergy in the Holy Land, and this role expanded gradually until, in the mid-1700s, France was regarded as protector of all the various Ottoman Christian communities affiliated with Rome. Russia later claimed a similar role with regard to Orthodox Christians, starting with a 1774 treaty that made the tsar the guarantor of commitments by the Turkish sultan to protect Ottoman Christians.

Actually, though, mass Mexican immigration is creating in the United States a situation that goes beyond even the European role in the internal affairs of the declining Ottoman Empire. The role that the Mexican government is acquiring in America's internal affairs is not merely defensive, as was the Ottoman case, in which European powers were, among other things, trying to limit rapacious Muslim assaults on persecuted Christians. Rather, Mexico is in the unprecedented position of proactively working with governments at all levels in the United States to shape new policies, in general becoming a permanent participant in the day-to-day business of governance.

This is what in international law is called "condominium"—not an apartment complex but literally "joint dominion," an arrangement whereby two powers jointly exercise their sovereignty in the same territory without dividing it up. It's a relatively unusual situation; recent examples include the British-French condominium in the Pacific island chain of the New Hebrides (now the independent country of Vanuatu) and Anglo-Egyptian rule over the Sudan until its independence. But in both these cases, two outside powers agreed to jointly administer a third country as a colony. Our situation with regard to Mexico does not seem to have any precedent in world history—a stronger country allowing itself to, in effect, be colonized by ceding sovereignty to a weaker power.

A NEW CONSTITUTIONAL ORDER

In other words, mass immigration isn't laying the groundwork for a dramatic switch in sovereignty and loss of territory at some point in the *future*—it's restricting America's sovereignty *right now*, a little bit at a time, all over the country (not just in the Southwest), as Mexico's government increasingly insinuates itself into American politics and governance. This is not the kind of expansionism we've seen in history—the Spanish expulsion of the Arab invaders from the Iberian Peninsula, for instance (the original *Reconquista*), or the medieval German expansion into the Sudetenland and elsewhere—but it might be seen as the twenty-first-century version of *reconquista,* one that leaves in place the lines on the map but changes the realities of power.

And this is actually a greater threat than conventional *reconquista,* because even the most supine, multiculturalist, post-American administration in Washington would be forced to respond to an ethnically driven secessionist movement in the Southwest. But the current reality—the slow but steady development of a new, nationwide constitutional order within our existing borders—can always be ignored or explained away because of its gradualism, like the proverbial frog in the pot on the stove, who doesn't notice the increasing water temperature until it's too late to escape. And the implausibility of old-fashioned irredentism and secession make it harder to get the American public and political class to focus on the very real threat to America's sovereignty that is growing right under our noses as a result of mass immigration under modern conditions.

This progressive retreat of American sovereignty is an inevitable consequence of mass immigration into our modern society for two reasons. First, modern communications and transportation technologies enable the governments of immigrant-sending countries to maintain ties with immigrants in a way never before possible, allowing those governments to act immediately and decisively as intermediaries between the immigrants and our government.

But technology would be irrelevant without the second factor: Elites in modern nations like ours have lost the self-confidence in the value of their own society and culture that is needed to assert sovereign rights in the face of immigration-driven challenges from foreign nations. In the domestic context, this loss of elite self-confidence translates into multiculturalism and identity-group politics, the result being a refusal to impose the new country's standards upon immigrants and, in fact, a sense that their norms are superior to our own. The effect on our sovereignty is even greater because, since most immigrants are members of federally designated minority groups—called protected classes in recent law and jurisprudence—mass immigration becomes a kind of affirmative-action program, with the sending-country governments becoming important players in America's domestic identity-group politics under the guise of protecting the "protected classes" that they claim responsibility for.

Whatever the pluses or minuses of identity politics, none of the other groups engaging in it represents a threat to American sovereignty. No African nation, for instance, presumes to speak for black Americans, nor is there a sovereignty issue regarding the claims of the various nonethnically based identity groups—feminists, homosexuals, the deaf, smokers, the obese, and others.

It is, of course, theoretically possible to address this part of the immigration challenge by restoring the elite's self-confidence in the desirability of American norms and sovereignty. As libertarians are wont to say, there's nothing wrong with mass immigration that ending multiculturalism won't fix.

But our modern elite's cosmopolitanism, as Samuel Huntington called it in his book *Who Are We?* (or what I have called "post-Americanism"[6]) is a systemic problem, deeply rooted in every institution of our society—every corporation, every school, every church, every day-care center, every police department, every university, every government agency. Trying to make a zealous defense of the nation's sovereignty the default position of America's elite again is a worthwhile, even urgent, goal but success is a long, long way off. Curtailing immigration, on the other hand, is simple in comparison, and since the combination of elite cosmopolitanism and mass immigration is toxic, the preservation of our sovereignty requires that we end one of them as soon as possible.

It's important to note that the challenge to modern America's sovereignty posed by mass immigration isn't limited to Mexico. The combination of modern technology and elite post-Americanism enables other immigrant-sending countries to impose themselves between their former citizens and the government of the United States. But Mexico, already the eight-hundred-pound gorilla of immigration policy, is the eight-thousand-pound gorilla with regard to sovereignty, due to its domination of the immigration flow, its proximity, and the historical resentments that many of its people harbor toward our country.

DRIVE TO THE NORTH

Although the Southwest isn't going to become our Sudetenland, you can see why people would fear *reconquista* of the traditional kind. Under modern conditions, the results will be different, but the Mexican surge to the north is very real, a *"Drang nach Norden,"* comparable to the *"Drang nach Osten"* (Drive toward the East), the term used for the German demographic expansion into the Baltic and Slavic areas of central and eastern Europe during the Middle Ages.

Start with the numbers. There are some 12 million Mexican-born people in the United States (legal and illegal, citizens and noncitizens), accounting for about one third of all immigrants. The large majority have arrived since 1990, with the total growing by more than 25 percent just from 2000 to 2005.[7] This is a huge change from the relatively recent past; in 1970, there were fewer than 800,000 Mexicans in the entire country, and they represented less than 8 percent of all immigrants.[8]

And there are no immediate prospects of this surge in immigration from Mexico tapering off on its own, despite claims to the contrary by supporters of open borders. Then-president Vicente Fox, for instance, said in early 2006 that in ten years the United States would be begging for Mexican workers because immigration would have ended.[9] But his own census bureau, Mexico's National Population Council, refutes this; it has projected that under any combination of assumptions about job growth and the like, Mexico will continue to send to the United States between 3.5 million and 5 million immigrants every decade until at least 2030 (barring a change in American immigration policy, of course).[10]

One of the reasons open-borders supporters claim that immigration from Mexico will taper off soon is that the country's Total Fertility Rate (or TFR, essentially the number of children born to the average woman during her lifetime) has been falling dramatically, from 6.5 children in 1970 to about 2.2 today, and is expected to keep dropping.[11] There are two problems with this claim. First, a drop in a nation's fertility rate doesn't necessarily translate into falling emigration. Simple math would suggest that if the birthrate were low enough for long enough, there'd be no one left in a country to emigrate. But the real world doesn't work that way. Immigration is a function of family connections and other networks, and it often takes on a momentum of its own and continues long after the circumstances that caused it have disappeared. Emigration from Ireland, for instance, continued for generations after the Potato Famine ended, and it was only recently, 150 years after that catastrophe, that the tide reversed and Ireland began to see a net inflow of people from abroad.

Looking specifically at falling fertility, South Korea, a prosperous country with one of the lowest fertility rates in the world at 1.21, continues to send immigrants to the United States in large numbers. From 1996 through 2005, more than 175,000 Koreans received green cards, and the flow during the first decade of this century looks as though it will exceed that of the 1990s.

And Russia, which also has a very low fertility rate of 1.34 and has actually started declining in population, nonetheless sent almost 168,000 legal immigrants to the United States from 1996 through 2005.

What's more, since this chapter deals with the sovereignty challenge, and Mexico claims authority over not only immigrants but their American-born children as well, it's important to note that the fertility of Mexican women actually goes *up* after they move to the United States.[12] Comparing the UN's data for Mexico (for the 2000–2005 period) with 2002 data on Mexican immigrants from our Census Bureau, it turns out that the average woman in Mexico then had a TFR of 2.4, but the average Mexican immigrant in the United States had a TFR of 3.5. Well, you might say, the women leaving Mexico probably have less education than the average person there and so would have had more children anyway. No—women in Mexico with the same education as Mexican immigrant women in the United States had a TFR of only 2.3, which means the actual increase in births is even greater than the average fertility rate for Mexico would suggest.

This very large and continuing flow of immigration from Mexico is, as you would expect from Mexico's geographic proximity, highly concentrated in a handful of states. Although they have begun to spread out in recent years, some 70 percent of Mexican immigrants are still in the four border states of California, Arizona, New Mexico, and Texas.

The combination of huge inflows and concentration means that the Hispanic share (immigrant and native born) of the population in the Southwest is rising rapidly. The California Department of Finance projects that the state's population, 33 percent Hispanic in 2000, will become majority Hispanic by 2040.[13] In Texas, 32 percent Hispanic in 2000, the Office of the State Demographer projects a Hispanic majority by 2035.[14]

And this huge, concentrated population is marginalized from the American mainstream. Mexicans have the lowest citizenship rate of any major immigrant group, with less than 19 percent of Mexican immigrants having become citizens, as opposed to 42 percent of Canadians, 21 percent of Salvadorans, 54 percent of Chinese, and 61 percent of Filipinos, to name just a few other large groups. This is partly because so many Mexicans are illegal aliens but also because even Mexican legal immigrants are less likely than those from most other countries to seek U.S. citizenship.

Mexican immigrants are also isolated from mainstream America by their poverty. They are the least-educated major immigrant group, with 62 percent of all Mexican immigrants lacking a high school diploma; even among the children and grandchildren of Mexican immigrants, the dropout rate is stuck at 25 percent, nearly triple the rate for other native-born Americans.

Consequently, Mexicans have the highest poverty rate of any major immigrant group, with 26 percent falling below the poverty line and fully 63 percent in or near poverty (in other words, earning less than 200 percent of the poverty threshold). More than half (54 percent) lack health insurance, the second-highest rate after the much smaller number of Guatemalans, while 43 percent of households headed by Mexican immigrants use at least one major welfare program, and 50 percent are eligible for the Earned Income Tax Credit. Even among the third generation—the native-born grandchildren of long-ago Mexican immigrants—welfare use is triple the rate for other natives, and nearly half live in or near poverty.

Finally, Mexicans have one of the lowest rates of entrepreneurship, with only 7 percent of them self-employed, well below the average for all immigrants of 11 percent and the average for the native born of 13 percent.

ETHNIC CHAUVINISM

Now, when you combine these phenomena—a large, rapidly growing, geographically concentrated, poor population from a neighboring country—with Mexican ethnic chauvinism and resentment toward the United States, both on the fringe and in the mainstream, both in Mexico and in the United States, then *reconquista* doesn't look so crazy after all.

A revanchist (from the French for "revenge") attitude toward the United States is part of the background music of Mexican discourse about the United States. An early example tying mass immigration to reconquest is from a 1982 column in the Mexican newspaper *Excelsior,* entitled "The Great Invasion: Mexico Recovers Its Own."[15] The writer says the American Southwest is "slowly returning to the jurisdiction of Mexico without the firing of a single shot, nor requiring the least diplomatic action, by means of a steady, spontaneous, and uninterrupted occupation." This was not written by a gadfly journalist, but by Carlos Loret de Mola, former governor of the Mexican state of Yucatán and a prominent member of the then-ruling Partido Revolucionario Institucional (Institutional Revolutionary Party, or PRI).

Mexican writer Elena Poniatowska continued this theme more recently; in 2001 she wrote, "Mexico is recovering the territories ceded to the United States with migratory tactics."[16] She is also not a marginal figure; a well-known essayist, she helped found one of Mexico City's major daily papers, the country's first feminist magazine, a prestigious publishing house, and the nation's film archive.

In the same year, another Mexican writer, Carlos Fuentes, one of Latin America's most prominent men of letters, cheered the "silent reconquest of the United States" through Mexican immigration.[17]

Several years later, when hundreds of thousands of Hispanic illegal aliens and others marched in Los Angeles in March 2006, Mexican television reporter Alberto Tinoco was described as "almost giddy" when he told the viewers of the Televisa network's nightly newscast, "With all due respect to Uncle Sam, this shows that Los Angeles has never stopped being ours."[18]

Even Mexico's consul in Los Angeles, José Ángel Pescador Osuna, felt secure enough about this to say during a 1998 symposium on the 150th anniversary of the Treaty of Guadalupe Hidalgo: "Even though I'm saying this part serious, part joking, I think we are practicing La Reconquista in California."[19]

The *reconquista* perspective is not confined to Mexico's elite. A 2002 Zogby poll found that 58 percent of Mexicans believed that "the territory of the United States' Southwest rightfully belongs to Mexico," while 57 percent agreed with the statement that "Mexicans should have the right to enter the U.S. without U.S. permission."[20]

Nor is this talk of *reconquista* and the rejection of American sovereignty limited to chauvinists living in Mexico itself. People in the United States of Mexican origin—both immigrant and native born—and not just those on the fringe make similar claims.

Of course, Hispanic racist organizations, the equivalents of the Nation of Islam or the Ku Klux Klan, talk of *reconquista* with great relish. Especially colorful was Augustin Cebeda of the Brown Berets, a group modeled on the Black Panthers, who said at a Fourth of July rally in Los Angeles in 1996, "Go back to Boston! Go back to the Plymouth Rock,

Pilgrims! Get out! We are the future. You're old and tired. Go on. We have beaten you; leave like beaten rats. You old white people, it is your duty to die."[21]

The Brown Berets are a paramilitary offshoot of MEChA, the Movimiento Estudiantil Chicano de Aztlán, a racial-identity group with hundreds of chapters in colleges and high schools around the country. ("Chicano" is an ethnic nationalist term for Mexican American.) Its founding document is El Plan Espiritual de Aztlán (The Spiritual Plan of Aztlán), which decries the "brutal gringo invasion" and includes the exhortation "Por La Raza todo. Fuera de La Raza nada." (For the [Hispanic] Race, everything. For those outside the Race, nothing.) Its logo is an eagle superimposed on a large red star, the eagle holding an Indian tomahawk-like weapon in one talon and a lit stick of dynamite in the other.

So much for kooks and college students. But chauvinist vitriol is also spewed by more mainstream figures. Particularly egregious are professors of Chicano studies. For instance, Charles Truxillo, a Chicano studies professor at the University of New Mexico, described in great detail his plans for an ethnic-separatist "República del Norte" carved out of the Southwest.[22] As he told a gathering at a ceremony at the university library, "We will one day be a majority and reclaim our birthright by any means necessary."

Another such example is José Ángel Gutiérrez, a political science professor at the University of Texas, Arlington, and founder of its Center for Mexican American Studies.[23] He also helped found two racial-identity groups, the La Raza Unida Party and the Mexican American Youth Organization; the latter was denounced by Representative Henry Gonzalez in 1969 as drawing its inspiration "from the deepest wellsprings of hate."[24] Gutiérrez at the time had said it was necessary to "resist and eliminate the gringo."

His racial chauvinism and rejection of American sovereignty have not dissipated with age. In 1995 he said, "We cannot—we will not—and we must not be made illegal in our own homeland. We are not immigrants that came from another country to another country. We are migrants, free to travel the length and breadth of the Americas because we belong here." And as recently as 2004, Gutiérrez said at a rally in Kansas City, "We are the future of America. Unlike any prior generation, we now have a critical mass. We're going to Latinize this country."[25]

And then there's Rodolfo Acuña, professor of Chicana/o studies at the California State University, Northridge, and author of *Occupied America: A History of Chicanos*. At a MEChA-sponsored conference in 1996, he warned of "being taken to the intellectual ovens" and denounced "the Nazi United States of America."[26] Or Armando Navarro, professor of ethnic studies at the University of California, Riverside, who recently published the book *The Mexicano Political Experience in Occupied Aztlán: Struggles and Change*.

POLITICIANS, TOO?

Well, maybe you can't expect any better from professors, given the entrenched America-hatred in academia, though the views of any group's intellectual elite matter more than the elite's small numbers would suggest. But what about government officials and other mainstream political figures?

Let's start with Mario Obledo, former California state secretary of health and welfare, former president of the League of United Latin American Citizens (LULAC), and cofounder of the Mexican American Legal Defense and Educational Fund (MALDEF). In 1998, the same year he was awarded the Presidential Medal of Freedom by Bill Clinton, he said, "Eventually, we're going to take over all the political institutions of California."[27] It wasn't a slip of the tongue; on another occasion the same year he said, "California is going to become a Hispanic state, and if anyone doesn't like it they should leave . . . they ought to go back to Europe."

Or Art Torres, former California state senator and current (as of 2007) chairman of the California Democratic Party, who said in 1995 that Proposition 187 (a ballot initiative to limit state-funded services for illegal aliens) "is the last gasp of white America in California."

And Richard Alatorre, former Los Angeles city councilman and "godfather" of a Hispanic political machine (a title he lived up to later when he plead guilty of felony tax evasion for bribes he'd received), who said in 1996: "They're afraid we're going to take over the government institutions . . . they're right, we will take them over."

Just to show this isn't confined to Democrats, Xavier Hermosillo, a businessman and radio host who was California chairman of the Republican National Hispanic Assembly, said in 1993: "We are taking Los Angeles back, house by house and block by block."[28]

And here's a list of prominent officials who have not made comments as incendiary as these but who are former members of MEChA and haven't gone out of their way to renounce their past affiliation in the radical student group: U.S. representative Raul Grijalva (D-AZ), U.S. representative Joe Baca (D-CA), California lieutenant governor Cruz Bustamante, and California state senator Gil Cedillo, plus Los Angeles mayor Antonio Villaraigosa, who did not publicly renounce MEChA's racist principles until the week before his 2005 election. It's not that these politicians are violent radicals but rather that they consider the anti-American chauvinism and resentment articulated by MEChA an acceptable part of public discourse, even though the politicians themselves have likely outgrown it.

Something similar is true for ordinary Mexican immigrants and Mexican Americans. *Reconquista* radicalism is largely absent, but a stubborn resentment against the United States is nonetheless widespread. This is different from the class-based animosity or political rivalry that earlier immigrants felt toward some native-born Americans; with Mexican immigrants, America itself is the issue. For instance, the Grammy-winning musical group, Los Tigres del Norte, are very popular among their fellow immigrants, singing often of the Mexican immigrant experience. Notable among their many love songs and ballads about drug smugglers is "Somos Más Americanos"—"We Are More American."[29] It contains lyrics such as "Let me remind the Gringo / That I didn't cross the border, the border crossed me" and "We are more American / Than any son of the Anglo-Saxon." The fact that this resonates deeply with ordinary Mexican immigrants doesn't mean they will demand an Anschluss between California and Mexico, but rather that ambivalence runs very deep—and not ambivalence normal to any stranger in a strange land, but ambivalence about America as such.

Political scientist Peter Skerry mentions the same phenomenon in his book *Mexican Americans: The Ambivalent Minority:* "Similarly vivid in my mind are the countless conversations about U.S. immigration policy that I have had with Mexican Americans of varied backgrounds and political orientations. Seldom in the course of such exchanges have my interlocutors failed to remind me that 'We were here first,' or 'This was our land and you stole it from us.' "[30]

All this so far—the huge numbers of poor, geographically concentrated immigrants, the historic resentments shared by the Mexican-origin elite and the public—would certainly be enough on its own to raise concerns about assimilation and the possible development of our own version of Quebec. But this wouldn't be relevant to America's sovereignty without the last element: an expansionist stance by the government of Mexico. "Expansionist," of course, does not mean territorial expansion; no Mexican political figure seriously foresees a change in the borders. But what Mexico has done is aggressively pursue expansion of its sovereignty into the United States by claiming the role of spokesman and intercessor for Mexican immigrants, for naturalized Mexican Americans, for native-born Americans of Mexican origin, and increasingly for Hispanics in general.

A government is supposed to speak up for citizens abroad, of course—we would expect nothing less of our own government if we got into trouble in a foreign country. To get an idea of what normal services a government provides its citizens abroad, see this from our State Department's Web site:

> U.S. consular officers assist Americans who encounter
> serious legal, medical, or financial difficulties. Although
> consular officers cannot act as your legal counsel or

representative, they can provide the names of local attorneys and doctors, provide loans to destitute Americans, and provide information about dangerous conditions affecting your overseas travel or residence. Consular officers also perform non-emergency services, helping Americans with absentee voting, selective service registration, receiving federal benefits, and filing U.S. tax forms.[31]

But when the number of one country's citizens concentrated in another country becomes large enough, there can be a qualitative change in the role of the sending country's government, a difference in kind, not just in degree. The government of the sending country (in this case Mexico) at that point is no longer just looking out for the well-being of individual compatriots but is rather speaking for a portion of the nation itself. In other words, what was once simply a service function becomes a political one.

Precisely when Mexico reached that stage is hard to say, but it clearly did so at some point during the rapid increase in the Mexican immigrant population over the past generation. Prior to that, Mexico's relationship with its former residents was cool, at best; nationalists either dismissed emigrants as traitors or conducted outreach mainly to persuade people to come home. As George Sanchez wrote in *Becoming Mexican American,* during the 1920s, "a central goal of all programs initiated by the Mexican consulate was the preservation of the cultural integrity of Mexican emigrants through the establishment of institutions to foster Mexican patriotism, with the long-term goal of encouraging return migration."[32]

But at least by 1990, things had begun to change fundamentally. That was the year President Carlos Salinas created the Program for Mexican Communities Abroad, the first permanent government agency in charge of outreach to those in the United States, implicitly accepting both the permanence and the legitimacy of those communities.[33]

GREATER MEXICO

But it was Salinas's successor, Ernesto Zedillo, who formally moved Mexico from a modern nation-state, responsible for governing only the inhabitants of its territory, to what might be called Greater Mexico. This embrace of an older, racialist conception of membership is a process sociologist Robert Smith has described as the "redefinition of the Mexican nation."[34] In 1997, Zedillo told the National Council of La Raza in Chicago, "I have proudly affirmed that the Mexican nation extends beyond the territory enclosed by its borders and that Mexican migrants are an important, a very important part of it."[35] Zedillo's 1995 development plan suggested the sweeping nature of this conceptual change; under the heading Sovereignty, the plan lists among its objectives the defense not merely of the rights of Mexicans abroad, but also of their quality of life, something usually considered a domestic-policy concern and not the bailiwick of consular officials assisting their sojourning compatriots.[36]

A major step toward Greater Mexico came in 1997 with a change in the Mexican constitution permitting dual nationality. John Fonte, a scholar at the Hudson Institute, quotes a Mexican congressman on the significance of the change:

> Fellow senators: the reports [on dual nationality] that we present today have historical importance, because they complete a qualitative change in the judicial conception that until now, we have had of Mexican heritage. It signifies the recognition that nations are more than concrete, specific territorial resources. . . . The reports recognize that Mexicans abroad are equal to those of us who inhabit Mexican national territory. Belonging to Mexico is fixed in bonds of a cultural and spiritual order, in customs, aspirations and convictions that today are the essence of a universally recognized civilization.[37]

An important point about the dual-nationality law is that it not only permits Mexican immigrants to naturalize in the United States without losing citizenship rights in Mexico, but it also permits native-born Americans of Mexican origin to acquire Mexican nationality without having to go through the immigration process that other foreigners would.

Zedillo's successor eagerly built on this ideology of Greater Mexico. Vicente Fox pledged when he was elected "to govern for 118 million Mexicans," a number that included 18 million in the United States—many of them native-born Americans. Fox merged Zedillo's outreach program into a new Presidential Office of Mexicans Abroad, headed by U.S.-born Chicano studies professor Juan Hernández.

The office has since evolved into a different form, but this is how its Web site described its functions several years ago (as translated by writer Allan Wall): "To attend to the millions of Mexicans and Mexican-Americans who live in the United States as citizens, residents, temporary workers and undocumented. . . ."[38]

Nor is this supposed to be a temporary phenomenon, as Hernández made clear on ABC's *Nightline* in 2001, when he said, "I want the third generation, the seventh generation, I want them all to think 'Mexico first.'"[39]

The nature of Hernández's activities, again from his office's Web site, was also telling:

> Dr. Hernández spends at least three days of each week in the U.S., holding meetings with governors, state and federal officials, and most importantly, with members and leaders of the Mexican communities abroad, from Alaska to Florida, from the Bronx to the east [sic] of the United States. He serves as a channel of communication between President Fox and Mexicans living abroad—hearing their complaints, resolving their needs and problems, and receiving innumerable petitions from millions of Mexicans living in different states in the United States.

He has also been commissioned to bring a strong and clear message from the President to the Mexicans abroad—Mexico is one nation of 123 million citizens—100 million who live in Mexico and 23 million who live in the United States—and most importantly to say that although far, they are not alone.

The administration of Felipe Calderón, who succeeded Fox as president in 2006, has undertaken something of a tactical, or at least rhetorical, shift. His ambassador to Washington has said of Mexico's involvement in American politics, "I think the previous Mexican government did itself and those that believe in comprehensive immigration reform a lot of damage by the way it tried to position itself publicly in an internal debate in the United States."[40] Nonetheless, the basic perspective has not changed; as President Calderón said in his September 2007 state-of-the-nation address, "Mexico does not end at its borders. . . . Where there is a Mexican, there is Mexico."[41]

This redefinition of the Mexican nation was formalized when Mexicans abroad (including native-born Americans) were permitted to vote in the 2006 presidential election. Only about 28,000 ballots were mailed in from the United States due to the extraordinarily complex and expensive process required but, as the Mexican government's coordinator for the expatriate vote said, "This was a first step of a historic vote. It planted the seeds for years to come."[42]

In addition to voting, American citizens now hold elective office in Mexico as well. Naturalized American citizen Manuel de la Cruz, for instance, was elected to the Zacatecas state legislature in 2004, while Andrés Bermúdez, another naturalized American, was elected to the lower house of Mexico's national Congress in 2006.[43] There are also a number of naturalized American citizens elected as mayors in Mexico, and in 2007 Michoacán became the first state to allow expatriate voting in state elections.[44]

Mexico's transition to a racial conception of nationhood is all the more obvious when you contrast the recent addition to the legislature of a naturalized American of Mexican origin with the provision in Mexico's constitution that bars naturalized Mexican citizens (i.e., immigrants from abroad who have moved to Mexico and received Mexican citizenship) from serving in the same legislature.[45]

PAN-HISPANISM

As if aspiring to become a parallel government for Mexican immigrants (and Mexican Americans) weren't enough, the Mexican government is claiming additional authority by seeking to become the paramount spokesman for Hispanics in general in the United States. Today's system of identity politics actually fosters this. Mexicans are part of a broader identity-group category under current American race laws; our system of racial classification, which developed haphazardly in the 1960s and 1970s, has no category for Mexicans, only for Hispanics. The majority of Hispanics are indeed of Mexican origin, but not all. The 12 million Mexican-born people in the United States today are joined by perhaps 17 million native-born Americans of Mexican origin, plus another perhaps 16 million people, immigrant and native born, whose ancestors are from Cuba, Puerto Rico, the Dominican Republic, El Salvador, and elsewhere in Central and South America.

Thus both the logic of our race laws and the self-interest of the Mexican government in magnifying its power within the United States argue for Mexico's expanding its claims beyond Mexican immigrants and beyond Americans of Mexican ancestry to encompass all people of Latin origin in the United States. You get a lot more attention claiming to be the spokesman and intercessor for 45 million Hispanics than for 12 million Mexican immigrants.

Whether Americans of Mexican and other Hispanic origin actually *want* the Mexican government to be their intermediary with the American government in Washington (and state and local governments) is irrelevant. The genuine American patriotism of millions of Hispanic citizens doesn't change the fact that Mexico is already actively involved in American domestic politics ostensibly on their behalf. After all, the two largest Hispanic "civil rights" organizations—the Mexican American Legal Defense and Educational Fund (MALDEF) and the National Council of La Raza—are not membership organizations funded mainly by citizens, and yet they claim to be speaking on behalf of millions of people. Why should the Mexican government, aspiring to the role of spokesman for Hispanics in America, be any different?

The Mexican government's activities in the United States bear this out. Look at its frequent appearances before the big three Hispanic organizations, none of which is specifically Mexican. The National Council of La Raza, the League of United Latin American Citizens (LULAC), and even MALDEF all claim to speak not for Mexican immigrants and Mexican Americans but rather for the entire Hispanic *Volk* ("Raza" in Spanish).

For instance, Mexican ambassador Jesús Silva Herzog complained about American domestic policies regarding immigration before LULAC's annual convention in 1997, saying, "Make no mistake about it, this is racism and xenophobia, and it has a negative impact on *every person of Hispanic origin* living in this country, regardless of their migratory status [emphasis added]."[46]

In 2002, during a dispute with the Mexican Congress over a planned visit to the United States, Vicente Fox sought to justify the trip by saying he'd be visiting "crucial states for the Hispanic vote."[47] Not the "Mexican vote," the "Hispanic vote."

Foreign Minister Luis Ernesto Derbez in 2003 spoke to a summit of Latin American countries in Peru, presenting his country's efforts to help Mexican illegal aliens as trailblazing for other Hispanic immigrants. According to Allan Wall, "He [Derbez] pointed out that these actions could benefit migrants from other countries, 'because the law (U.S. law) will not be able to discriminate between migrants,' and the U.S. government will not say: this is a law only for Mexican migrants.'"[48] Continuing that role as standard-bearer for all Hispanics, Mexico brought together officials from other Latin American countries in January 2006 to demand amnesty for all their illegal aliens, increased legal immigration, reduced enforcement, and other changes in U.S. domestic policy.[49]

And symbolically important is the Ohtli Award, which is presented by the Institute for Mexicans Abroad (the current iteration of the government office responsible for outreach in the United States) but which is broadening into a means for recognition of Hispanics in general. For instance, Representative Robert Menendez (who is of Cuban heritage) was given the award in 2004 "in recognition for his commitment in improving the well-being of Hispanics in the United States." Not Mexicans, but Hispanics. The same reason was given for the 2005 Ohtli award to Rubin Barrales, the Bush White House's director of intergovernmental affairs.

"BEACHHEADS OF LOBBYING"

Empowered by mass immigration, Mexico is carrying out this role of "protector" of Hispanics in America in a wide variety of ways, mainly centered on its network of consulates, the institutional structure for this neo-*reconquista*.

Of course, consulates are a normal part of every nation's diplomatic presence abroad, but Mexico's network of consulates in the United States is without parallel in the world: fifty-six consulates and consular agencies (or honorary consuls, who perform consular services on a part-time basis) in twenty-six states plus the District of Columbia and Puerto Rico, the largest such network anywhere. The United States, on the other hand, has only nine consulates, plus thirteen consular agencies, in Mexico.[50]

Mexico makes no effort to hide the activist nature of this network in America's domestic politics. A visiting Mexican official in Texas told the Spanish-language press that one of the goals of Mexican consulates is to "form a common front that represents . . . the interests of the Hispanic community."[51]

The complete silence or even acquiescence of the U.S. government to Mexico's recent consular interference is a departure from the past. For instance, in 1924, when Japan's ambassador prepared a memorandum claiming that the immigration law then being considered by Congress would have "grave consequences," Congress "expressed annoyance at Japan's intrusion into a domestic matter."[52]

Likewise, in a 1926 letter, Mussolini's ambassador in Washington, "keenly aware of American hostility toward consular interference in local ethnic associations in the 1920s, warned that consular influence must be exerted 'under conditions of utmost prudence and without assuming an attitude that contrasts with the American program. . . . To organize the Italian communities through consular authority would be the most serious error.' "[53]

With regard to Mexico specifically, the U.S. government in the past responded appropriately to incidents of consular interference. In 1936, for example, Army intelligence warned that the Mexican consul in Laredo, Texas, was working to unionize Mexican workers and organize a strike. After objections from Congress and the State Department, the consul was recalled and "a contrite Mexican ambassador, F. Castillo Najera, assured the U.S. State Department that the Mexican government was already taking the 'appropriate measures to prevent the repetition of acts capable of giving rise to difficulties.' Further, 'all members of the Mexican consular service [were instructed] to abstain from . . . meetings of any kind alien to the consular functions.' "[54]

The unprecedented nature of Mexico's current interference in U.S. internal affairs is recognized even by its supporters. Armand Peschard-Sverdrup, director of the Mexico Project at the Center for Strategic and International Studies, a Washington-based think tank, has said, "What we're now seeing is a consular system being evolved into an advocacy/educational role. It's never been done before."[55]

The reason it's never been done before is that it's an unambiguous violation of the Vienna Convention on Consular Relations, the international treaty that governs such matters. Article 55 of the convention says, "Without prejudice to their privileges and immunities, it is the duty of all persons enjoying such privileges and immunities [i.e., consular personnel] to respect the laws and regulations of the receiving State. They also have a duty not to interfere in the internal affairs of the State."[56]

But interfere they do—and massively.

Mexico's lobbying on big-picture immigration policy really is re-markably shameless.[57] Its rejection of America's sovereignty over its own borders is sweeping; in response to a 1996 U.S. law intended to limit illegal immigration, President Zedillo actually said that "We will not tolerate foreign forces dictating and enacting laws on Mexicans."[58] For-eign Minister Jorge Castañeda explained to the Mexican press in 2002 how Mexico's strategy had as its starting point an effort to get the Amer-ican government to agree to subject its domestic immigration policy to international debate: "First, making [migration] a central part of our agenda with the United States and opening it to a bilateral negotiation, something we had never managed to do before."[59]

Another part of the strategy was to "build the social and political coalition [in the United States]—legislators of both parties, unions, em-ployees, state and local authorities, civic leaders, non-governmental organizations and means—that we'll need to support negotiations." Castañeda was more blunt when discussing this strategy with other Mexican officials; to Mexico's Congressional Foreign Affairs Commis-sion he said, "We are already giving instructions to our consulates that they begin propagating militant activities—if you will—in their com-munities."[60]

The ambassador of the current administration made essentially the same point in 2006: "Certainly the only way in which Mexico can ad-vance a comprehensive agenda [i.e., amnesty for illegal aliens] with the United States is if we use the [Mexican] embassy and the network of consulates as 'beachheads' of lobbying for the image, the interests and the agenda of Mexico in all of U.S. territory and with all sectors of American society."[61]

It is in the area of working outside Washington—in the field, with illegal aliens and local advocacy groups, as well as lobbying local and state governments—that Mexico's consular network is most active and the expansion of Mexico's sovereignty is most noticeable. For starters, con-sulates actively subvert American law by advising ordinary illegal aliens on how to evade deportation. They have distributed the "Guide for the

Mexican Migrant," a comic book–style pamphlet presented as a safety measure (it provides advice on how to safely sneak across the Rio Grande and the Arizona desert), but it also advises readers how to avoid deportation by not calling attention to themselves, by not drinking and driving, and by avoiding loud parties where the police might be called.[62]

The San Francisco consulate has published "10 Golden Rules for the Immigrant in the U.S.," which spells out in great detail how illegal aliens should avoid detection and deportation.[63] Particularly amusing is rule number 4, "Respect the Law," the point being to avoid coming to the attention of the police—and thus possibly face deportation—by obeying traffic laws like buckling your seat belt, not drinking and driving, obeying the speed limit, and using directional signals. But there's no suggestion that illegals should respect the *immigration* law.

But the most serious Mexican government interference comes from direct lobbying of American officials. Castañeda was described as telling a meeting of LULAC in 2002 that "by lobbying local governments in the United States, the Mexican government has managed to make it easier for illegal immigrants to live a more normal life. The Mexicans have pushed to get their citizens proper identification and access to college, he noted."[64]

One Foreign Ministry official called this "the onion approach"— "We start with the outer rings, we start with the state and local levels, because the federal government for many reasons is not focused on these issues."[65]

DOCUMENTS FOR THE UNDOCUMENTED?

Probably the most important layer of the onion has been lobbying for acceptance of the *matricula consular* (consular registration) card. For decades, consulates have issued these cards to Mexicans living in foreign countries, as a way of keeping track of their citizens abroad.[66] Whatever use these cards were to Mexicans—to simplify reentry into Mexico in lieu of a passport, for instance—they were of no use in the United States.

But after 9/11, when being able to demonstrate your identity became increasingly important, illegal aliens were in a bind. Illegals are ineligible for green cards (the document denoting lawful permanent residency) or for Social Security cards or, in most states, for driver's licenses and nondriver state IDs. This lack of identification created a number of difficulties for illegals, from the inability to open a bank account to the increased likelihood that the police would check one's immigration status as the result of a routine traffic stop, leading to deportation. This isn't a problem for legal immigrants, who, by definition, have U.S.-issued identification. Of course, from the American perspective, the reason illegals are denied ID is precisely to make it hard for them to embed themselves in a country they're not supposed to be in.

Mexico rejects the legitimacy of American immigration law and has hit on a way to circumvent it—upgrade the *matricula* cards, making them laminated photo IDs like driver's licenses, and market them to Mexican illegals. By 2007, some 3 million *matricula* cards had been issued.[67] The problem was that, while Mexican consulates are free to issue any kind of document they please to their citizens, it's of little use to illegal aliens unless it's accepted in the United States.

Thus an aggressive lobbying campaign was launched by the consulates to persuade state and local governments to accept the card as a legitimate form of ID, in an attempt to bring about a de facto partial legalization of illegal aliens.[68] The goal of Mexico's first big foray into American domestic politics was clear; in the words of Miguel Ángel Isidro, head of the consulate in Santa Ana, California, in 2002, "Eventually, this will be accepted throughout the United States."[69]

Up against the Mexican government's push for acceptance of the card was the FBI's opposition to it. In 2003, Steve McCraw, assistant director of the FBI's Office of Intelligence, told a House panel, "The Department of Justice and the FBI have concluded that the Matricula Consular is not a reliable form of identification."[70]

It was no contest—Mexico beat the FBI hands down.

The *matricula* campaign's first big success came in November 2001, when intense consular lobbying persuaded Wells Fargo Bank and the San Francisco Board of Supervisors to accept the *matricula* as an official ID. Since then, Wells Fargo has opened more than half a million accounts for illegal aliens using the *matricula*.

Further successes came from sending consular officials to personally lobby rural sheriffs, small-city council members, and banks and other businesses, so as to increase the number of jurisdictions and firms accepting the card and build a sense of momentum and inevitability about it. Already by 2004, as the Congressional Research Service has reported, the Mexican Embassy said that the *matricula consular* was accepted as an official form of ID by 377 cities, 163 counties, and 33 states, plus 178 banks and 1,180 police departments.[71] Also, 12 states recognized the card as one of the acceptable proofs of ID for a driver's license, and many telephone and utility companies, hospitals, and video stores also accepted it.

On the ground, there was nothing clandestine or behind-the-scenes about this campaign. When Los Angeles, for instance, agreed to accept the cards in May 2004, President Vicente Fox personally telephoned mayor James Hahn to thank him.[72] After Felipe Calderón was elected president in 2006, he promised to "lobby to get all U.S. states to accept Mexico's consular identification cards in order to help migrants get driver's licenses."[73] And consuls have been eager to describe their lobbying activities to journalists. Some examples:

- In Napa, California, San Francisco consul general Georgina Lagos Donde attended the city council vote recognizing the *matricula,* cheering with the audience; "I always say the hardest part is getting the first one to do it," she said, adding, "I've already been in touch with the mayors of Sonoma and Petaluma."[74]
- After the city of Oxnard, California, signaled that it would recognize the card, Consul Fernando Gamboa said, "Acceptance of the card is vital because officials are looking more closely at identification cards since 9/11," and added that he planned to lobby the cities of Ventura and Camarillo as well.[75]

- "Mexico's consul general in Detroit made the 172-mile drive across Michigan five times in just two weeks last month. Each time his mission was the same: to persuade authorities in the small city of Holland to accept Mexico's matricula consular as an ID card for Mexican immigrants."[76]

- "These days, the Mexican consul here [Indianapolis], Sergio Aguilera, drives from city to city, making his pitch. This week, he shuttled between East Chicago, where he met with the mayor, and Indianapolis, where he tried to persuade credit union executives to join the businesses that accept the card. 'In the past it was not so important,' Mr. Aguilera said. 'Now we have increased our efforts. I have been traveling like crazy, talking to mayors, police departments and city councils. We need their understanding and their support.' "[77]

- When Arizona's legislature considered a bill to bar acceptance of the *matricula,* Mexico's consul general in Phoenix, Rubén Beltrán, blasted the proposal, saying, "We are witnessing initiatives by legislators in a way that will create a divide in the community and disrupt the social cohesion of the state."[78]

- In 2002, five Hispanic California state legislators met with the Mexican consuls general of Los Angeles, Sacramento, San Diego, San Francisco, and San Jose. According to an article in the Spanish-language press, "The consuls proposed that the legislators use their positions so that the state authorities accept the Mexican Matricula Consular as a valid, generalized identification." A Foreign Ministry official told the group that the consuls and the lawmakers were "all in the same boat, and if we do not row together we are going to drown" and that the consuls and legislators "must share the same co-operation and the same commitment."[79]

- "Patricia Deluera, the Mexican consul in Utah, on Thursday denounced a bill in the state legislature that would prevent Mexican nationals from using an identification card issued by her country to obtain driver's licenses in Utah. Deluera said advocates of House Bill 109 were 'promoting hatred against Mexican people.' "[80]

- " 'The purpose of the Mexican Consulates is not necessarily to have people getting the matricula as much as it is institutions honoring the matricula,' [Salt Lake City consul Martin] Torres said. 'If, as a result, we have more Mexican nationals obtaining it, that's fine, but we're not out to get more Mexicans to come and get it. We're out to get more institutions to accept it.' Torres said he courts law enforcement agencies in the area that Salt Lake City's Mexican Consulate covers, including Utah, Idaho, Montana, and western Wyoming. 'As soon as I got here, and I've been here over a year, I started visiting different sheriffs, for example, in Idaho, familiarizing them with the matricula,' Torres said. 'Several of them are now honoring it. . . . If a person is stopped driving a vehicle and they don't have any source of ID, they go to jail,' Torres said. 'If at least they have their consulate ID, and the sheriff . . . knows about it and they honor that document, then they avoid going to jail. And that's what we want.' "[81]

Finally, as part of the Mexican government's emerging role as protector of all Hispanics in America, the consul general in New York organized a (so-far unsuccessful) effort to lobby New York City to recognize *all* consular cards, since other Latin American nations have now also started issuing them to their illegal aliens.[82] Mexico's coalition included Argentina, Bolivia, Brazil, Colombia, Chile, Ecuador, El Salvador, Guatemala, Honduras, Nicaragua, Peru, the Dominican Republic, and Venezuela.

OTHER LOBBYING

Although gaining acceptance for the *matricula* has been the chief Mexican objective in lobbying at the state and local level, other issues are also important, among them making illegal aliens eligible for driver's licenses and for in-state tuition discounts at state universities, and preventing local police and other officials from cooperating with federal immigration authorities. The goal is the same as with the *matricula*— assuming control over American immigration policy by working to embed illegal aliens into America's institutions. Some examples from the past few years:

- When he was consul general in Atlanta, Teodoro Maus "publicly criticized ordinances regulating day laborers in Chamblee, Marietta and Roswell and attacked a Norcross ordinance requiring businesses to display signs in English. Maus also has criticized proposals in the General Assembly and decried a ruling from the Georgia Supreme Court in a worker's compensation case that limited the amount of money the state would send to relatives of a legal Mexican immigrant killed in a construction accident here."[83]
- Denver consul Leticia Calzada went so far as to suggest a tourism boycott of Colorado until its legislature and governor approved in-state tuition and driver's licenses for illegal aliens. This was meddling so brazen that Governor Bill Owens issued a formal protest, eventually leading to her removal in a "routine" round of retirements.[84]
- The Hispanic California lawmakers who met with several of the state's Mexican consuls regarding the *matricula* (see page 74) had apparently come to see Mexican involvement in American politics as so routine that in 2004 they beseeched members of the Mexican Senate to lobby Governor Arnold Schwarzenegger to sign a bill giving illegals driver's licenses. "Assemblywoman Cindy Montanez, from the San Fernando Valley, said that it is vital for Mexico to ask Schwarzenegger to approve this legislation 'so that he would know that not only people of California, but an entire country is asking that he sign the bill.' "[85]
- Mexico gave an Ohtli Award, its highest civilian honor, to Texas State Representative Miguel "Mike" Wise, "in part for his work in trying to secure driver's licenses for undocumented workers."[86]
- In Minnesota, "a representative of the Consulate General of Mexico in Chicago joined several other panelists last week in supporting a proposed ordinance that would officially restrict Richfield city employees from asking about immigration status in most cases. . . . Passing an ordinance in Richfield would send a message to other cities in

Minnesota, [consulate representative Joyce Graciela] Stellick said. 'Good things spread like wildfire,' she said."[87]

- The Mexican consul general in Denver sought to neuter a new law prohibiting "sanctuary" cities (where municipal employees are prohibited from communicating with federal immigration authorities) by writing to the governor, attorney general, and Denver's mayor "asking for a better interpretation of the law to prevent government workers or law enforcement officers from 'carrying out their own agenda.'" He objected to the law because he feared it would result in racial profiling of Hispanics.[88]

MEXICAN INVOLVEMENT IN U.S. ELECTIONS

Not content with lobbying legislators, Mexican officials have also gotten involved in elections, although so far only on ballot questions. The two major examples were Proposition 187 in California in 1994 and Arizona's Proposition 200 in 2004. Both measures sought to limit taxpayer-funded government services provided to illegal aliens, and both measures were approved handily by voters.

The acrimonious fight over Proposition 187 was the first major assertion by Mexico of a right to participate in American domestic politics. At that early stage in the expansion of Mexico's sovereignty into the United States, Orwellian doublespeak was still needed: According to Deputy Foreign Minister Andrés Rozental, "Without interfering with the United States, the government of Mexico will work actively to prevent the passage of the anti-immigration initiative 187."[89]

This had begun months before the election, when Rozental publicly announced his government's "commitment to work closely" with those opposed to the proposition.[90] Nor was this merely a vague expression of opposition; Rozental was explicit about the nature of his country's political activism: "Mexico will participate with organizations, associations and human rights groups to bring down this proposition. We have media campaign strategies to inform the entire California electorate of the contributions that Mexicans have made and continue to make to this state, so that no one will go away with the idea that we are responsible for the costs and problems of the state."[91] Among other things, this took the form of Mexico's ten consulates in California setting up telephone hotlines to register opposition to the ballot measure and sending out thousands of letters urging voters to reject it as "discriminatory."[92] In addition, Rozental pledged that if the measure passed, the Mexican government would supply attorneys for a legal challenge in American courts.[93]

After some Americans wrote to the Mexican government objecting to this assault on American sovereignty, Foreign Minister Tello answered that since Americans were among the poll watchers observing its elections earlier that year, "you must accept a similar involvement, especially when the immediate interests of your neighbor are so evidently at stake."[94] What he did not say was that Mexico, far from having its sovereignty restricted, actually *exercised* its sovereignty, since the invitation to poll watchers was an attempt to promote Mexico's own national interest—i.e., to help reform its notoriously corrupt elections.

Nor was the nature of Mexico's critique of Proposition 187 that of a respectful friend. President Salinas said, "Mexico affirms rejection of this xenophobic campaign, and will continue to act in defense of the labor and human rights of our migrant workers."[95] The Foreign Ministry's director of consular affairs, Eduardo Ibarrola, referred to the measure, promoted by Governor Pete Wilson, as "the racist proposal of a demagogue."[96] But Deputy Foreign Minister Rozental reached the *reductio ad Hitlerum* when he said, "It's so reminiscent of what happened in other parts of the world and at other times in history. It's not unlike what happened in Germany in the 1930s or Yugoslavia in the '80s. I won't say it's blatant 'ethnic cleansing,' but it's certainly an across-theboard hysteria."[97]

Even though California's voters overwhelmingly approved Proposition 187, the Mexican government got the last laugh. After Governor Gray Davis arranged through political sleight of hand to kill the measure in 1999, the speaker of the lower house of the state legislature, Antonio Villaraigosa (who later became mayor of Los Angeles), during a visit to Mexico, publicly thanked the Mexican president for having overturned the will of California's electorate. The headline of the front-page *Los Angeles Times* story on August 4, 1999, says it all: "Zedillo Key to End of Prop. 187, Villaraigosa Says."

Ten years after Proposition 187, Arizona debated Proposition 200, which would not only have denied most government services to illegal aliens, but also would have required proof of citizenship to register to vote and proof of identity to cast a vote. The Mexican government worked against this ballot measure as well, though in a lower-profile way. The Foreign Ministry instructed consulates in Arizona to "keep in contact with state and local officials, elected officials that oppose the measure and social organizations in order to follow up on the process by which the corresponding legal institutions could review the constitutionality of the proposition, while strictly adhering to the applicable legal measures."[98] More directly, the Mexican consulate worked with local Hispanic leaders to raise nearly $2 million to fight the ballot initiative.[99]

When the ballot measure won (with the backing of nearly half of Mexican American voters), an injunction was issued to prevent its implementation. After the injunction was lifted, Mexico again denounced it, saying, "The Foreign Relations Secretariat reiterates its complete rejection of this reform that constitutes a measure fostering discriminatory actions based on an ethnic profile and which can generate an adverse climate for the Mexican community established in that state."[100] Later, when asked about Mexico's response to the new law, Foreign Minister Ernesto Derbez said, "We are seeking all the legal opportunities that exist, first using the legal capacities of the United States itself and . . . if that does not work, bringing it to international tribunals."[101] But Derbez was clear in his stance that Mexico has a right to joint sovereignty over people of Mexican origin, whatever their citizenship, whether they like it or not; in commenting on the high level of support for Proposition 200 among American voters of Mexican origin, he said, "It's sad, and it gives an idea of how we have to work to educate even *our own Mexican-Americans* about why it is important that these proposals are not accepted [emphasis added]."

COURTS

Mexico has learned the lesson that in America, if you lose in the legislature or the voting booth, go to court. Threats by Mexico of lawsuits accompanied the campaigns against Propositions 187 and 200, though it's not clear how involved Mexico was in the legal action.

More recently, President George W. Bush announced that he was sending a small number of National Guard troops to assist the Border Patrol in a support role (surveillance, construction, and transportation). This assertion of America's sovereignty—limited and superficial though it was—so alarmed the Mexican government that it again threatened to sue: Foreign Minister Derbez told a Mexico City radio station that "if we see the National Guard starting to directly participate in detaining people . . . we would immediately start filing lawsuits through our consulates."[102]

Mexico has even threatened to sue a private citizen whose conduct—within the United States—it disapproved of. In Arizona in 2005, Army reservist Patrick Haab held seven illegal aliens at gunpoint until the Border Patrol arrived, and was not prosecuted because of the state's citizen's-arrest law. The decision by prosecutors not to file charges so outraged the Mexican government that it explored the possibility of a lawsuit against Haab personally. "The lawyers are analyzing the best ways to do it," said a Foreign Ministry spokesman, and discussed the lawsuit with a Los Angeles–based human-rights group, most likely the Center for Human Rights and Constitutional Law, which Mexico has used elsewhere (see page 81).[103]

But Mexico hasn't been all bluster; it has actually followed through on earlier lawsuit threats, its consular network becoming an ongoing player in America's domestic judicial system. The Mexican government organized, paid for, and was a party to lawsuits alleging discrimination against Mexican workers (and Hispanic workers in general, including native-born Americans) by DeCoster Egg Farms in Maine; the legal action began in 1998 and continued for a number of years.[104] A settlement was announced in 2002 at a press conference at the Mexican embassy in Washington. The embassy spokesman, former Boston consul Carlos Rico, said the lawsuit was the first ever against an American company by a foreign government on behalf of its citizens. "The implications are enormous," he said. "If forced to, the Mexican government will again test U.S. courts to protect our workers anywhere in this country against the universal sting of discrimination."[105]

The Mexican government has indeed continued to function as an advocate in our judicial system. In 2004, according to the *Washington Times,* it "encouraged thousands of Mexican nationals, including many illegal aliens, who worked as janitors for California's largest supermarket chains to join a class-action lawsuit demanding millions of dollars in additional pay."[106] Rather than serve as a plaintiff in this lawsuit, the Mexican government let MALDEF take the lead, and instead, "A network of Mexican consulate offices in the United States and throughout Mexico has offered to locate eligible workers in both countries."

And in Arizona in 2006, after Andrew Thomas, district attorney for Phoenix, interpreted a new state antismuggling law to permit prosecution of illegal aliens for conspiracy to smuggle themselves, the Mexican consulate again sprang into action. It recruited Peter Schey, an open-borders crusader of long standing and head of the Center for Human Rights and Constitutional Law in Los Angeles, to coordinate the legal assault on the new policy. As Mr. Thomas said, "You have a foreign government coming in and trying to organize the defense efforts of criminal defendants in an attempt to attack the coyote law, and in fact, attack the right of any state in the nation, effectively, to pass anything meaningful to stop illegal immigration. That is an extraordinary act. And I'm not aware of a parallel to this in our history."[107]

In a similar legal challenge to America's sovereignty, the Mexican consulate in Boston recruited a New Hampshire law firm to challenge the use of that state's trespassing law to arrest illegal aliens, as two local police departments in the state were doing. The defense attorney refused to say whether she was being paid by the consulate—meaning it's almost certain she was.[108] The consul general in Boston attended one of the hearings and remarked, "The concern is that we are dealing in a state court with matters that belong to a federal level," without being asked by the reporter how such a "concern" could possibly be Mexico's business.[109]

STREET PROTESTS

When it can't win in American legislatures or voting booths or courtrooms, the Mexican government endorses the Latin American tradition of "direct action"—taking to the streets. Since 2003, street protests have forced the resignation of two presidents in Ecuador and one in Bolivia. In Mexico, after the close presidential election in 2006, the loser, populist Andrés Manuel López Obrador, organized massive protests in the capital alleging fraud, even though Mexican and international observers said the election was clean.

Several months before that presidential election, the Mexican government supported the huge marches in American cities in which Mexican illegal aliens and their supporters insisted that the American people comply with their demands. Mexico's support is especially ironic, considering that noncitizens are strictly barred from engaging in any form of political activity in Mexico itself. The U.S. State Department advice page for American travelers to Mexico says, "The Mexican Constitution prohibits political activities by foreigners, and such actions may result in detention and/or deportation. Travelers should avoid political demonstrations and other activities that might be deemed political by the Mexican authorities."[110]

Nor is this an empty threat; in 2002, Mexico's immigration service summarily deported seventeen American college students and their professor for marching in Mexico City's annual May Day parade. The next day, their bus was pulled over by armed federal police, they were hustled to the airport and given expulsion orders to sign before being put on a plane to Los Angeles. As Mexico's consul in Seattle said later, "According to the Mexican Constitution, the political rights are for the Mexicans."[111]

The Mexican government does not hold the reciprocal view—that in America, political rights are for the Americans. Although the primary drivers of the 2006 illegal-alien marches were Spanish-language radio DJs, unions, and the Catholic Church hierarchy, the Mexican government did not keep its distance. The Web site of the Institute for Mexicans Abroad—a bureau within the Foreign Ministry—posted a contact list prepared by the Mexican Embassy in Washington of the pro-illegal-alien demonstrations planned for April 10, 2006, complete with thirteen pages of names, phone numbers, and e-mail addresses of march organizers in each city for those who wanted to participate. This official government document began this way: "On April 10, 2006, immigrants and their allies are continuing historic mobilizations in Washington, DC, and multiple cities to oppose the harsh and unworkable HR 4437 and demand real immigration reform that is comprehensive, respects civil rights, reunites families, protects workers, and offers a path to citizenship for the current undocumented and future immigrants to the US."[112]

After those marches, Mexico's Undersecretary of Foreign Affairs Lourdes Aranda said, "The public expressions of support for the contributions made by immigrants . . . should be taken into account" as Congress considers immigration legislation.[113]

CRIMINAL JUSTICE

Much of the preceding litany of Mexican government interference in American governance relates to immigration policy, or rather to Mexico's successful efforts at preventing American immigration law from being enforced, so as to permit continued massive illegal immigration.

But the logic of joint sovereignty means that Mexico's involvement in internal American affairs will inevitably expand beyond matters relating to immigration and border control into all areas of government activity that could affect Hispanics—which is to say nearly all areas of government activity. One such area is criminal justice.

The research on immigrants and crime is inconclusive, but it appears that immigrants themselves are somewhat less likely to be criminals than natives, but their children are more likely. For instance, one study found that among men of Salvadoran and Guatemalan origin, ages eighteen to thirty-nine, the rate of incarceration for the native born was nearly six times higher than for the foreign born; among Mexicans, eight times higher; among Indians, nine times higher; and among Vietnamese, twelve times higher.[114] The value of such studies is limited because of flaws in the data, but whatever the facts, the presence of millions of poor, poorly educated, young foreign men means many of them will have trouble with the law.

The vehicle for the expansion of Mexico's sovereignty into this area is the Vienna Convention on Consular Relations referred to earlier. Article 36 of the Vienna Convention requires that foreigners who are arrested must be informed of their right to contact their consulate. This could be called the *"Midnight Express"* provision of the convention and is very much in our national interest—we certainly want one of our fellow citizens who is sent to a Turkish (or Mexican) jail to be able to contact the nearest American consulate.

But in the context of massive, one-sided immigration, Article 36 creates the preconditions for the loss of sovereignty. Americans living in Mexico (as opposed to drunken college students on brief visits) are relatively small in number, older, educated, and prosperous—all factors ensuring that their encounters with the Mexican criminal justice system are infrequent and thus that American consular involvement in such matters is minimal. Mexicans living in the United States, on the other hand, are very large in number, young, male, poor, and poorly educated—all factors pointing to extensive contact with the police and thus extensive consular involvement.

Some of these encounters are specifically immigration-related— i.e., arrests of illegal aliens by the Border Patrol. Here, the Mexican government demands, and receives, privileges far beyond those required by the convention. Consular staff, for instance, are given offices inside Border Patrol facilities and are informed about ongoing investigations and about the location of American civilians participating in border-watch activities.[115]

But at least Mexico doesn't claim that the Border Patrol is barred from patrolling the border. The situation is different with regard to local police. When El Paso County, Texas, sheriff's deputies arrested illegal aliens in a series of raids, the consulate objected, a spokesman saying, "It's not a criminal matter; it's a labor issue. These people (immigrants) are not criminals."[116] The consulate sought to dictate even the timing of police activity: "If they (sheriff's officials) want to do joint operations with the Border Patrol, that's fine. But in most of these cases, they arrive before the Border Patrol."

The Mexican government had a bigger impact in another case in Texas. When Edwards County deputy Gilmer Hernandez fired at the tires of a fleeing smuggling vehicle that had attempted to run him over, a bullet fragment ricocheted and caused a minor injury to one of the illegal aliens inside. State authorities recommended against prosecution of the deputy, but the Mexican consulate in Eagle Pass wrote a letter to the FBI and others demanding punishment, and within days the matter was taken over by the U.S. Department of Justice. Hernandez was convicted of violating the civil rights of the illegal alien. As Texas representative Ted Poe, a former judge, put it, "The Mexican government arrogantly demanded prosecution and our federal government succumbed to the pressure."[117]

Even away from the border, the Mexican government works to prevent local police enforcement of the immigration law. In 2005, for instance, the Mexican consul in Detroit wrote a threatening letter to the sheriff in Lima, Ohio, after it was reported that the sheriff was training his deputies to recognize fraudulent IDs used by illegal aliens and was forming a work group to examine crimes by illegal aliens.[118]

But Mexico's involvement spreads well beyond immigration-related issues. Most of the activity surrounds appeals of the death penalty for noncitizens, where attorneys often argue for a lesser sentence because the defendant was allegedly not informed in a timely manner of his right to contact his consulate. Mexico has been aggressive in this regard because it has stopped applying the death penalty in its own courts and now seeks to impose that decision on us. Mexico does this in two ways.

First, it refuses to extradite suspects who face the death penalty (or even, for a time, those facing life imprisonment); this is a legitimate exercise of its sovereignty, though not the act of a friendly nation.

The second way Mexico attempts to impose its criminal-justice preferences on us is to use Article 36 of the Vienna Convention to argue that it is illegal to execute criminals who were not informed in a timely manner of their right to contact their consulate. When requirements of a treaty like the Vienna Convention are not satisfied, countries are supposed to pursue diplomatic and political solutions, but Mexico is seeking to bend American law to its will by making consular notification a basic human right applicable to specific individuals, rather than a political agreement among governments. In fact, Mexico has argued before American courts and the World Court "for an automatic rule that statements taken from foreign defendants before they are informed of their right of consular notification should be suppressed," according to the State Department's legal adviser.[119] So far, Mexico has not prevailed; the U.S. Supreme Court said in 2006 that the exclusionary rule, by which evidence is thrown out if a suspect has not been read his Miranda warning, does not apply in cases when a suspect has not been advised of his right to consular notification.[120]

But the Mexican government will be relentless in its pursuit of control over our criminal-justice system. It established the Mexican Capital Legal Assistance Program in 2000, run by an attorney in Minneapolis, whose goal is to defend Mexicans charged in capital crimes.[121] Some consulates have twenty-four-hour phone numbers for police to call to inform them when a Mexican has been arrested.[122] In fact, Mexico's consul general in 2000 said that his government's position is that American police are *required* to inform the consulate when a Mexican is arrested, rather than wait for a suspect to request such notification.[123]

The Mexican government is even working to get in on the ground floor of law enforcement by taking part in the training of American police recruits. In 1995, the Mexican consulate in Los Angeles began a program to send Los Angeles Police Department officers to Mexico for language and cultural-sensitivity training. First, officers attended lectures at the Mexican consulate on topics such as "the plight of the Mexican immigrant to the United States." In the words of the deputy chief of the police department, "Every instructor talked about [the] plight of immigrants, even during the language time. They said these people are going to stay here and need to be included in community policing efforts."[124] In Texas also, the Mexican consulate conducts training classes for the police.[125] And at the other end of the criminal justice system, the Mexican government is running Spanish classes in California's prisons.[126]

Barring an end to mass immigration, the trajectory is clear. The Miranda warning will be extended to include consular notification; Mexican consular officials will start asking for, and receiving, offices in police stations and prisons throughout the Southwest and in big cities elsewhere; and consular representatives will oversee the conduct of police, prison guards, prosecutors, and judges in cases involving Hispanic defendants. None of this will necessarily have anything to do with immigration law, but it will further expand the new system of joint sovereignty.

SCHOOLS

Another such area is public education. Of course, Mexico is happy for us to pay for the education of illegal-alien children—open-borders lawyer Peter Schey (whom the Mexican government used to bring the 2006 lawsuit in Arizona) was responsible for *Plyler v. Doe,* the 1982 case in which the Supreme Court decided that states had to educate illegal-alien children until Congress said otherwise. Even low-skilled *legal* aliens don't pay anything like the taxes needed to defray the costs of public schools for their children.

But just because American taxpayers are picking up the tab doesn't mean that Mexico doesn't want to make sure it has a hand in education policy. In the words of a 1998 *National Review* article, "Mexico directly influences U.S. education policy at every level of government, making the assimilation of Hispanics in the United States that much more difficult."[127]

One of the ways the Mexican government does this is through aggressive support for bilingual education; it has donated thousands of dollars to the National Association of Bilingual Education and was the recipient of the group's 1997 Presidential Award in appreciation for its support of the organization's efforts.[128] And in California, where voters ended bilingual education for most public-school students, the Mexican consulates have helped parents in some districts get waivers allowing bilingual instruction to continue. As one consulate spokesman said, "It's important to have both Spanish and English in the classroom because the children are young, still creating their identities at this age."[129]

More broadly, the Mexican consular network has distributed hundreds of thousands of Mexican textbooks to districts across the country and imported Mexican teachers to work in American schools. In 2005 alone, the Mexican consulate gave the Los Angeles Unified School District nearly a hundred thousand textbooks for 1,500 schools.[130] Since the initiative began in the early 1990s, the total number of books sent to U.S. schools likely numbers in the millions.

The textbooks are not just intended to help students retain the Spanish language, as problematic as that might be for assimilation. There are books (in Spanish) on subjects such as math, science, geography, and Mexican history. The history textbooks, the same ones used in Mexico's schools, are naturally designed to foster Mexican patriotism: They refer to America's flag as "the enemy flag" in the discussion of the Mexican War and celebrate Mexico's patriotic symbols. "We love our country because it is ours," the book says.[131] The presence of such textbooks in American public schools is another example of the expansion of Mexico's sovereignty.

The role of consulates in inculcating Mexican nationalism in American children isn't confined to words on a page. In Salinas, California, for instance, the consul general responsible for the area organized a Mexican Flag Day ceremony at a public school, promoting Mexican patriotism among American children.[132] And in Aurora, Colorado, the Denver consulate helped set up an alternative public school for Spanish-speaking teenagers, where Mexican history would also be taught.[133]

OTHER LAWS

Mexico is also expanding its sovereignty in the area of labor protections. Consulates around the country work as intermediaries between regional offices of the U.S. Department of Labor and Hispanic workers. Building on efforts that had started at the local level, the U.S. Labor Department and the Mexican Foreign Ministry in July 2004 signed a joint declaration formally incorporating the Mexican government into the enforcement of American occupational-safety and wage-and-hour laws.[134] In the words of a press release announcing a specific arrangement in Atlanta, "Bi-lingual consulate employees have been trained by the U.S. Labor Department to screen calls and connect workers with appropriate department staff for assistance."[135]

Mexican interference has become so brazen, because of U.S. government inaction and encouragement, that consuls have even criticized the enforcement of local fire and safety codes. The consul general in New York, for instance, blasted a local government in Long Island for evicting dozens of illegal aliens living in overcrowded single-family homes turned into flophouses. The illegal aliens "have rights regardless of whether they are documented or undocumented," the consul said. "We will do everything we can to make sure those rights are protected."[136]

OUR PROBLEM, NOT MEXICO'S

If mass immigration is not discontinued, the preceding overview of Mexican meddling will be only the beginning. A quote from former foreign minister Jorge Castañeda described Mexico's policy with regard to American freedom of action around the world, but could just as well have been describing Mexico's goals within the United States: "I like very much the metaphor of Gulliver, of ensnaring the giant. Tying it up, with nails, with thread, with 20,000 nets that bog it down: these nets being norms, principles, resolutions, agreements, and bilateral, regional and international covenants."[137]

But, like Gulliver, we can only be tied down if we are asleep. It's hard to blame Lilliputian Mexico for trying to gain control over us—it's natural for a state to try to expand its sovereignty to areas where its people are expanding. The problem is that *we* permit it. As with the other incompatibilities between mass immigration and modern society, the problem is less the immigrants than it is us.

Reinforcing that point is the fact that this concern is not necessarily specific to Mexico. During the 2007 debate over the Senate amnesty bill, for instance, Ireland's foreign minister made it clear that he also thought America's immigration policy was not a matter of domestic policy but one that foreign governments like his had a voice in: "I can assure all undocumented Irish in the United States that this government will continue to battle hard to achieve residency status. The campaign to secure reform must go on."[138]

Italy in the past took a similar view of the intersection of immigration and American sovereignty. As John Fonte writes, "Italian government policies (circa 1900s–1930s) paralleled those of the Mexican government (1990s–2000s)—both attempted to maintain the allegiance of their emigrants who lived in the United States, supported dual nationality, and tried to use their former compatriots as political leverage upon the United States." Or, as Benito Mussolini said, "My order is that an Italian citizen must remain an Italian citizen, no matter in what land he lives, even to the seventh generation."[139]

Even if all Mexican (or even Latin) immigration stopped tomorrow, but immigration from China or Pakistan or Ukraine picked up the slack at the same unprecedented levels, we'd have similar problems. Identity politics would still exist, and elites among those immigrant groups would promote existing resentments against the United States (or against the West or Christendom) as a way of fostering group solidarity and alienation from the receiving society, and the governments of those countries would insinuate themselves into our domestic politics. We would have Chinese consuls threatening county sheriffs, Pakistani consuls shaping our public-school curricula, or Ukrainian consuls trying to sway elections.

Trying to turn America's elite away from the dangers of multiculturalism and postnationalism is a long-term project that may yet fail. There have been brief flares of resistance to the immigration-driven encroachments on our sovereignty, from congressmen Tom Tancredo and (the late) Charlie Norwood, for instance, and from some local officials (though not from our State Department, which has developed a corporate culture of post-Americanism).

But interestingly, these defenses of American sovereignty have come exclusively from supporters of tough restrictions on illegal immigration and curbs on legal immigration. It should theoretically be possible for one to be an outspoken supporter of mass immigration, even increased immigration, but still ferociously defend America's sovereignty against assault by immigrant-sending countries. But in the real world, there are no such people, at least not in positions of authority. All prominent supporters of mass immigration—Republican and Democrat—ignore the loss of American sovereignty caused by immigration, or downplay it, or even applaud it.

This should tell us something. In a modern society there are two choices: mass immigration accompanied by a progressive loss of sovereignty, or protection of sovereignty through limits on immigration.

CHAPTER 3

National Security: Safety in Lower Numbers

M odern America faces a unique security challenge. Advances in communications, transportation, and weapons technology make it relatively easy for enemies to get access to our home territory and stage spectacular and deadly attacks. In other words, under modern conditions, the "home front" is no longer a metaphor. As President Bush said in 2003, "Our country is a battlefield in the first war of the 21st century."[1]

This new reality makes immigration a central issue in national security. In the opening words of the 9/11 Commission's staff report on the topic, "It is perhaps obvious to state that terrorists cannot plan and carry out attacks in the United States if they are unable to enter the country."[2] No matter the weapon or delivery system—hijacked airliners, shipping containers, suitcase nukes, anthrax spores—people are needed to carry out the attacks. And those people have to enter and operate in the United States, often for an extended period of time. In a very real sense, the most dangerous weapons of our enemies are not inanimate objects at all, but rather the terrorists or saboteurs themselves—especially in the case of suicide attackers. Thus, keeping foreign terrorists out and keeping them off balance or apprehending them if they do get in are security imperatives.

This modern security challenge represents another example of our having outgrown mass immigration, which undermines our security in two ways: First, it overwhelms our administrative capacity to screen out enemies or locate and remove them if they're already here. A particularly outrageous example of this conflict: In 2003, Immigration and Naturalization Service (INS) contract workers at a service center in Southern California were charged with coping with the ongoing tsunami of paperwork by shredding immigration documents in order to wipe out a ninety-thousand-document backlog there. After two months of shredding, the backlog was wiped out, but they kept shredding as new mail came in to ensure that the backlog didn't return.[3]

The second conflict with national security stems from the fact that, by creating large, constantly refreshed immigrant communities, mass immigration provides enemy operatives with the sea within which they can swim as fish (to paraphrase Mao). In other words, immigrant communities unintentionally—but unavoidably—offer terrorists and saboteurs cover and safe haven. We've already seen this phenomenon from Lackawanna, New York, to Lodi, California, from Paterson, New Jersey, to San Diego—and as mass immigration continues, we will encounter more and more examples.

Like the other aspects of immigration, neither of these security concerns—workload or safe haven—is a function of changes in the immigrants themselves, compared to earlier waves. Instead, it is irreversible changes in our society that make these issues we cannot ignore.

HOME FRONT

The concept of the home front was developed during World War I and became widespread in World War II, the goal being to motivate the civilian population of nations involved in total war. The sense of solidarity with soldiers on the real fronts helped impel civilians to increase economic output, buy war bonds, conserve and recycle resources, and generally reconcile them to privation and rationing.

But in the wake of 9/11, that limited meaning no longer applies. As Deputy Secretary of Defense Paul Wolfowitz said a year after the attacks:

> Fifty years ago, when we said, "home front," we were referring to citizens back home doing their part to support the war front. Since last September, however, the home front has become a battlefront every bit as real as any we've known before.[4]

The emergence of our home territory as a genuine war front is part of what scholars call asymmetric or fourth-generation warfare, where technologically inferior countries or groups use unconventional tactics against stronger opponents.[5] Asymmetric war includes guerrilla fighting and terrorism and has been around for a long time; we've been at the receiving end of such tactics in al Qaeda's pre-9/11 assaults on our interests in the Middle East and in the fighting in Iraq.

But with the spectacular success of the 9/11 attacks (reinforced by the subsequent bombings in London, Madrid, and elsewhere), the holy grail of asymmetric warfare has become mass-casualty attacks on civilians in our homeland. In the words of an al Qaeda spokesman, "We have the right to kill 4 million Americans—2 million of them children—and to exile twice as many and wound and cripple hundreds of thousands. Furthermore, it is our right to fight them with chemical and biological weapons, so as to afflict them with the fatal maladies that have afflicted the Muslims because of the [Americans'] chemical and biological weapons."[6]

This is a new experience for us. Because of the Atlantic and Pacific oceans, no foreign army has been able to strike at the United States itself since the War of 1812, other than the Japanese attack on Pearl Harbor. After that, all Japan was able to do was launch a handful of inconsequential attacks on the West Coast, briefly hold two of the Aleutian Islands in Alaska, and send some balloon bombs floating over the Pacific to explode in the United States, only one of which caused any casualties.

German efforts against our homeland in World War II were even less significant. Two teams of saboteurs were dropped off in Florida and New York by submarine in 1942, with orders to destroy utilities and transportation links. They were all quickly arrested and accomplished nothing.[7]

But even at that time, authorities understood the link between immigration and what we now call homeland security. The old Immigration and Naturalization Service, for instance, was part of the Department of Labor until 1940, reflecting the sense that immigration's primary impact was on the workforce. As war approached, it was moved to the Justice Department, specifically because of fears that spies and saboteurs would use the immigration process to penetrate our defenses and use immigrant communities for cover and support. It was also during World War II and the beginning of the Cold War that other security elements of immigration law were put into place, such as registration of aliens and exclusion of aliens who expressed support for totalitarian ideology.[8]

Though not unfounded, these early fears of the security threat represented by immigration sometimes proved to be exaggerated, leading to overreactions, like the violence against German Americans during World War I and the wholesale internment of Japanese aliens and Japanese Americans living on the West Coast during World War II.

But under modern conditions, things have changed radically, and what may once have been exaggerated fears are now all too real. While modern technology has hugely strengthened the conventional military power of developed countries, it has also made asymmetric attacks easier to pull off. Quick and inexpensive communications and transportation make it easier for enemies to send operatives to the United States, gather information, send instructions, and coordinate attacks. In the words of the Pentagon's Quadrennial Defense Review, "Geographic insularity no longer confers security for the country."[9]

Also, modern weapons pack more punch, and potential targets are bigger prizes. Weapons of mass destruction are a modern phenomenon, allowing a small vial of a pathogen or toxin, or a suitcase-sized nuclear or radiological bomb, to wreak havoc unimaginable in the past. Even conventional explosives are more powerful and portable than ever before, easily fitting into a shoe or a Thermos. Likewise, there's a difference in kind, not just in scale, between, say, driving a carriage into the ground floor of a wood-frame building and flying an airplane into a skyscraper or nuclear power plant.

This new kind of security threat faced by modern America does not come only from terrorist groups. For instance, American policy makers now must factor in the likelihood that Iran has a network of agents and sympathizers in place among the 350,000 Iranian immigrants living in the United States. The awareness of such a threat is not new; during the Iran hostage crisis in 1979 and in the wake of violent demonstrations by Iranian students in the United States itself, the Carter administration ordered the INS to deport Iranian students who had violated the terms of their visas. The INS was forced to admit it had no idea how many there were, or where they were, or if they were still studying. The INS didn't get a full count until after the hostage crisis had ended; it concluded that more than 10 percent of the 64,000 Iranian students were illegal aliens but was able to deport only a few hundred of them.[10]

NOT JUST ARABS

But whether it's terrorist groups or hostile governments, radical Islam is the chief source of today's security concerns related to immigration. Is the solution then simply to keep out Muslims? In other words, perhaps today's immigration/security connection is a peculiarity of the war on terrorism and not part of a broader phenomenon as this book suggests. There is a certain amount of sympathy for this view; a 2002 poll found that "combating international terrorism by restricting immigration from Arab and Muslim countries" was favored by 79 percent of the public and by 40 percent of people described as leaders.[11] Likewise, in the wake of another catastrophic attack, organizations claiming to speak for Hispanic and Asian immigrants would quickly discard past claims of solidarity and throw the Muslims from the train, as it were, in an attempt to preserve continued access to the United States for their preferred groups.

Focusing on Muslims in airport security or in selecting surveillance targets may well make sense, but it is at best a short-term expedient—triage, if you will—and cannot work as the basis for a long-term immigration/security strategy. Such a narrow interpretation of the security threat posed by immigration has two problems: First, barring all arrivals from Muslim-majority countries would be of limited benefit in fighting radical Islam, because it is a crude tool, keeping out Middle Eastern non-Muslims, but admitting Muslims from elsewhere. About a quarter of today's immigrants from the Middle East are not Muslims at all, radical or otherwise—including Jews from Iran, Assyrians from Iraq, Armenians from Lebanon, and Copts from Egypt.[12] Meanwhile, such nation-specific bars would fail to keep out many people who *are* radical Muslims. Even before 9/11, visa applicants from Muslim countries formally listed by the State Department as sponsors of terrorism (Iran, Iraq, Libya, Sudan, Syria) had faced closer scrutiny—so the 9/11 hijackers didn't come from those countries but instead came from Muslim countries *not* on the official list of terrorist sponsors. Since 9/11, we've made it harder for potential immigrants from the rest of the Islamic world, meaning that we may see terrorists coming from non-Muslim-majority countries that are home to large and radicalized Muslim minorities—the Philippines, India, China, or Russia.

In fact, the FBI in 2002 warned of just such a development with regard to Russian citizens. Because of increased scrutiny of visitors from Muslim nations, al Qaeda is said to have discussed hijacking a plane using "Muslim extremists of non-Arabic appearance," specifically "Chechen Muslims affiliated with al Qaeda, but already present in the United States."[13]

But even if we were to bar everyone from Russia, the Philippines, and other countries with indigenous Muslim minorities, terrorists could continue to come from the Muslim communities of Western Europe (as did Zacarias Moussaoui, for instance)—and this is especially problematic, since visas are not currently required for visitors from these countries. As terrorism expert Robert Leiken has written, "European Muslim recruits can form the al Qaeda cells most apt to plot a course in the United States. The second-generation terrorists speak European languages, handle computers, surf the internet, exchange e-mail, and are familiar with post-industrial infrastructures and customs. Unlikely to be watchlisted, the new mujahideen not only navigate a modern society but can enter the United States freely."[14]

The only targeted approach that might conceivably work in this regard would be to bar people of the Islamic faith, whatever their nominal citizenship. Although Congress has clear constitutional authority to do this—it has plenary power over all matters related to immigration and naturalization—its political impossibility is obvious. Besides, how would we accurately determine the religion of prospective visitors and immigrants?

FUTURE WARS

But there is a second, bigger, problem with the narrow "keep out the Muslims" approach: The security threat that mass immigration represents for modern America isn't confined to radical Islam. Because of modern technological advances, *all* enemies we will face in the future will inevitably consider attacks on the American homeland as part of their war planning. And, as the Iran example above demonstrated, most countries with which the United States could see itself at war at some point in the future already have large and growing immigrant populations here. This is different from past intersections between immigration and foreign conflicts; then, immigration was often a *consequence* of foreign involvement, as we saw with the creation of large immigrant communities of Hungarians, Cubans, Vietnamese, Salvadorans, and Ethiopians during the Cold War (and even earlier, Filipinos and Puerto Ricans in the wake of the Spanish-American War). But today, the immigrant communities are already here and represent a serious vulnerability in future wars:

- Even after the planned drawdown of U.S. troops in South Korea, scheduled to be completed in 2008, there will still be 25,000 American soldiers left, intended to deter **North Korea** from restarting the war that ended with a cease-fire in 1953. North Korea claims to have already developed nuclear weapons and is aggressively threatening its neighbors and the United States with missile launches. Though the nearly 700,000 Korean immigrants here came from South Korea, there can be little doubt that the Communist regime in the north has a network of agents already in place among them. And given both the North Korean government's long history of bizarre behavior and the certainty of its demise if the war were to restart, it seems likely that it would attempt to wreak as much destruction as possible within the United States before it was defeated.

- Communist **China** has often been compared to pre–World War I Germany, an assertive rising force seeking to change existing power arrangements and expand its sphere of influence at the expense of the United States. What's more, it insists on its right to rule Taiwan, something the United States opposes except in the unlikely event that the people of Taiwan peaceably agree. War with China is by no means a certainty, but it is clearly possible, and the nearly 1.9 million Chinese immigrants throughout the United States, including a major presence in high-tech industries, represent a deep sea for Beijing's fish to swim in. China's espionage agencies have already jumped in, and while spying is different from actual attacks, the patterns are likely to be the same. According to a joint FBI/CIA report, "When approaching an individual of Chinese origin, the Chinese intelligence services attempt to secure his or her cooperation by playing on this shared ancestry."[15] The attempts are at least sometimes successful; in the words of a recent article on the prosecution of an immigrant spy ring, Chinese espionage "depends on a multitude of relative amateurs: Chinese students and visiting scientists, plus people of Chinese heritage living in the US."[16]

- **Colombia** is America's major source of cocaine, revenue from which funds both leftist rebels and right-wing paramilitary groups, who have been fighting both the government and each other for forty years. The United States is deeply involved in shoring up the central government, and despite signs of progress, Colombia was still ranked in the top category of the Failed States Index in 2006.[17] It is by no means inconceivable that the United States could be drawn into a war in Colombia if the central government were to be in danger of collapse. It's unlikely that many of the nearly half-million Colombian immigrants in the United States harbor sympathy for the leftist FARC guerrilla group, but their communities would nonetheless serve as a base of operations for FARC attacks in the United States in the event of war.

The very existence of these and other large immigrant communities constrains America's freedom of action, as policy makers must factor in the possibility of enemy attacks behind our lines—a concern that would shrink in importance over time with curbs on immigration. Although the Bush administration's National Strategy for Homeland Security in 2002 certainly didn't call for curbs on immigration, it did capture our dilemma:

> Our great power leaves these enemies with few conventional options for doing us harm. One such option is to take advantage of our freedom and openness by secretly inserting terrorists into our country to attack our homeland. Homeland security seeks to deny this avenue of attack to our enemies and thus to provide a secure foundation for America's ongoing global engagement.[18]

The point is not that reduced immigration would necessarily free America to pursue dreams of empire (or "ongoing global engagement," if you prefer), but rather that the potential for attacks on the homeland—a potential substantially shaped by immigration—limits our foreign-policy options and makes us more vulnerable to our enemies.

THREE LAYERS OF SECURITY

Modern immigration undermines our security both by overwhelming our ability to screen and track aliens and by creating host communities where enemy operatives can embed themselves. Let's examine these two aspects in more detail, starting with the first. How is our system of immigration control overwhelmed by excessive numbers?

Despite the fact that the home front is now a real war front, it's not the military that has the lead role, due to the new character of the threat. It's true that the Pentagon established the Northern Command in the wake of 9/11 "to provide command and control of Department of Defense (DoD) homeland defense efforts and to coordinate military assistance to civil authorities,"[19] just as Israel set up a Home Front Command in 1992, in the wake of attacks on its own civilian population centers during the first Gulf War. But the chief burden of homeland defense is borne by agencies commonly seen as civilian entities—the State Department's Bureau of Consular Affairs (which issues visas) and the immigration components of the Department of Homeland Security (DHS).

That our security hinges partly on the effectiveness of these civilian immigration agencies is hard to deny. An analysis of the immigration histories of the forty-eight foreign-born al Qaeda operatives who committed crimes in the United States from 1993 to 2001 (including the 9/11 hijackers) found that nearly every element of the immigration system had been penetrated by the enemy.[20] Of the forty-eight, one third were here on various temporary visas, another third were legal residents or naturalized citizens, one fourth were illegal aliens, and the remainder were former illegal aliens with pending asylum applications. Nearly half of the total had, at some point or another, violated existing immigration laws. Another examination of ninety-four foreign-born terrorists from al Qaeda, Hamas, Hezbollah, and other groups found that about two thirds (fifty-nine) had committed immigration violations prior to or in conjunction with taking part in terrorist activity, and some had multiple violations.[21]

In other words, because terrorists so frequently violate ordinary immigration laws, strict enforcement of those laws can have significant security benefits: keeping out operatives who mean to harm us; making it much more difficult for terrorists and other asymmetric warriors to operate here; and ensnaring some of those already living here, thus disrupting conspiracies and providing subjects for interrogation. This is in addition to measures specifically focused on security, such as improving the watch lists used to screen out potentially dangerous aliens.

The immigration-control network has three layers of defense: first overseas, then at the border, and finally, in the interior of the country. Each one is faced with massive, unmanageable demand, which causes overwhelmed bureaucrats to wave people through without sufficient scrutiny, and permits widespread fraud. A century ago, how effectively aliens were screened may not have mattered much—there just wasn't much a small band of anarchists, say, could have done, given the primitive nature of communications, transportation, and weapons technology. But today's volume of immigration simply cannot be subjected to the level of scrutiny that's necessary in the modern security environment.

Part of what makes mass immigration so inappropriate in this context is the mismatch between our modern system of immigration regulation and the primitive state of document security in most of the countries immigrants and visitors come from. In the past, when it didn't much matter whether you were who you claimed to be, a handwritten baptismal certificate, say, might have been adequate identification. And in any case, forgery was much more difficult before photocopiers and computers.

Today, we actually need to know who the applicant for admission really is, so we can search through security databases and also ensure compliance with the many requirements of the various visa categories and immigration benefits, such as proof of a family relationship or ownership of a home or graduation from high school. In a modern system of immigration regulation, such documentation is more important than before but is also much easier to fake, meaning that intensive efforts must be devoted to uncovering fraud—day in, day out, forever—making the proper adjudication of visa or immigration applications much more labor-intensive and time-consuming than ever before.

HOMELAND SECURITY BEGINS ABROAD

The first of the three layers in our immigration-control network is manned by the visa officers working for the State Department in our consulates abroad. In the words of the State Department's inspector general, visas "must be considered as a part of a larger process beginning with the visa process and continuing through the admission of aliens to the United States and tracking them while they remain in this country."[22] Consular officers screen applicants for both immigrant and nonimmigrant visas (the latter for students, tourists, and others claiming that they intend to go home).

"Until the events of September 11, the visa process was seldom considered a major element of national security,"[23] according to the same inspector general's report. That has changed; DHS Undersecretary Asa Hutchinson described the visa process as "forward-based defense" against terrorists and criminals.[24] Another writer has called visa officers "America's other Border Patrol."[25]

The visa filter is especially important because the closer an alien comes to the United States, the more difficult it is, practically speaking, to keep him out. It's easiest to reject a potential visitor or immigrant who is still living abroad. Once a foreigner has driven or flown all the way to an American airport or land crossing, it's harder to turn him away, although the immigration inspector theoretically has a free hand to do so. Most difficult of all is finding and removing people who've actually been admitted; at that point, not only is there no specific check point where aliens can be screened, but even the most superficial connections with American citizens or institutions can lead to noisy protests against enforcement of the law.

In 2005, about 800 visa officers issued about 6 million visas to foreigners, an average of about 7,500 visas per officer, roughly one every fifteen minutes. Visa applicants undergo a computerized background

check against various federal government watch lists, and are sometimes interviewed to try to determine if they truly qualify for the visa
and whether they are lying about their identity, their family relation-
ships, or their destination in the United States, and whether the supporting documents presented (a local birth certificate or high school
diploma, for instance) are forgeries. Because of the massive numbers of
permanent and temporary visas allowed by current law, officers seldom
have more than a few minutes to decide a case, leading to huge failure
rates. Perhaps 4 million people have entered the United States with
temporary visas and remained to become illegal aliens, plus a large but
unknown number who used fraud to obtain permanent immigrant
visas.

Supporters of loose borders and mass immigration claim that there's
nothing really wrong with the visa system, usually pointing to flawed
intelligence as the most important security shortcoming that needs to
be addressed. Mary Ryan, for example, former head of the Bureau of
Consular Affairs, testified to the 9/11 Commission:

> Even under the best immigration controls, most of the
> September 11 terrorists would still be admitted to the
> United States today . . . because they had no criminal
> records, or known terrorist connections, and had not
> been identified by intelligence methods for special
> scrutiny.[26]

This is simply untrue, both for the hijackers and for earlier al Qaeda
operatives in the United States. A normal level of visa scrutiny, in fact,
would have excluded almost all the hijackers. Investigative reporter Joel
Mowbray acquired copies of fifteen of the nineteen hijackers' visa applications (the other four had already been destroyed by the State Department), and every application was incomplete or contained obviously
inadequate or absurd answers. This led all the half-dozen current and
former consular officers consulted by the reporter to conclude that every one of the applications should have been rejected.[27]

Even if the applications had been properly prepared, many of the hijackers, including Mohamed Atta and several others, should have been rejected because they were young, single, and had little income—precisely the kind of person likely to overstay his visa and become an illegal alien, completely apart from any terrorist connections. And not coincidentally, those least likely to overstay their visas—mature people with family, property, and other commitments in their home countries—are also least likely to commit acts of terrorism.

When the immigration law has been properly applied, it actually *has* bolstered security. Ramzi Binalshibh, for instance, one of the candidates for the label of twentieth hijacker, was rejected four times for a visa, not because of concerns about terrorism but rather, according to a U.S. embassy source, "for the most ordinary of reasons, the same reasons most people are refused"—that is, he was thought likely to overstay his visa and become an illegal alien.[28]

WINKING AT FRAUD

But even if applicants appear qualified on the surface, there's the deeper problem of fraud. As the State Department's deputy inspector general has said, referring to visas and passports: "Fraud in travel documents is a systemic challenge for the Department in consular work."[29] Unfortunately, fraud is more often than not viewed by the State Department as an embarrassing obstacle to issuing a visa, rather than an offense against the United States. The degree to which State Department practice winks at lying by visa applicants would be comical, were it not so serious.

The Immigration and Nationality Act (INA) says, "Any alien who, by fraud or willfully misrepresenting a material fact, seeks to procure (or has sought to procure or has procured) a visa, other documentation, or admission into the United States or other benefit provided under this Act is inadmissible."[30] In other words, if an applicant lies about something that would affect the visa-issuing decision (as opposed to something like, say, his favorite color), then that alien is to be permanently barred from the United States. This conveys very clearly the seriousness with which Congress intends the visa process to be taken.

Unfortunately, the State Department doesn't take it seriously at all. The *Foreign Affairs Manual,* which instructs visa officers on how to interpret the law, makes clear that this provision of the law should not be applied except in the most extreme circumstances.[31] The relevant part of the manual begins with a quote from Harry Truman's Commission on Immigration and Naturalization, which essentially says that foreigners have a right to come to the United States:

> Shutting off the opportunity to come to the United States actually is a crushing deprivation to many prospective immigrants. Very often it destroys the hopes and aspirations of a lifetime, and it frequently operates not only against the individual immediately but also bears heavily upon his family in and out of the United States.

The manual continues by instructing visa officers that, if the foreign applicant has lied but admits his lie in a "timely" fashion, it must be ignored. What's more, the concept of lying about a "material fact" is interpreted as narrowly as possible; in the words of the manual, "Materiality does not rest on the simple moral premise that an alien has lied, but must be measured pragmatically in the context of the individual case as to whether the misrepresentation was of direct and objective significance to the proper resolution of the alien's application for a visa." In other words, materiality depends on what the meaning of "lie" is. What's more, if the temporary visa holder, once in the United States, does anything suggesting that he intends to stay permanently (i.e., gets a job, enrolls in school, or gets married), his lies will again be ignored, so long as these actions happened more than sixty days after entering the country.

As a former Foreign Service officer has noted, "Compare this with the penalty for a misrepresentation to, say, the IRS, and one begins to realize the distortion of U.S. immigration law as administered by the State Department."[32]

This customer-service mind-set, which still typifies the State Department's visa management, is perhaps best exemplified by the trademark expression of Thomas P. Furey, consul general in Riyadh, Saudi Arabia, when the 9/11 hijackers were granted permission to come to the United States: "People gotta have their visas!"[33] This effectively inverts the meaning of the law regarding applicants for temporary visas, which explicitly states that the burden is on the foreign applicant to prove he's not going to become an illegal alien; instead, all too often the de facto burden is on the visa officer to prove why an applicant should be turned down.

When particular visa categories have been examined, the level of fraud has been stunning. A look at the religious-worker visa, for instance, found that more than one third of the applications audited by investigators were based on fraudulent information, and fraud was particularly widespread in applications from Muslim countries.[34] According to testimony presented to Congress, a random selection of L-1 visa petitions (for intra-company transferees) in southern China found only two out of ten were bona fide.[35] The same overview of fraud reported that 40 percent of P-3 visas in New Delhi (for artists and entertainers) contained information that was not credible. Also, 45 percent of H-1B visas (for computer programmers and other skilled workers) in Madras, India, were found to be fraudulent.

A 2002 assessment of the Bureau of Consular Affairs' (CA) management of the visa process is unfortunately still true:

> The post-September 11 era should have witnessed immediate and dramatic changes in CA's direction of the visa process. This has not happened. A fundamental readjustment by Department leadership regarding visa issuance and denial has not taken place. The Department still does not fully appreciate the consular function as part of a coordinated national effort to manage

border security and implement the INA, both to prevent the travel of those who might present risks to the
United States and its citizens and also to facilitate legitimate travel.[36]

Nevertheless, there have been some improvements since 9/11—DHS
now has nominal oversight over the visa process, and there have been
increases in consular personnel, better national-security training, and
new antifraud efforts.[37] In addition, other administrative changes are
clearly needed—for instance, more serious efforts at ending the customer-
service culture in the management of the visa process, which may only
be possible by transferring the entire process to DHS, so as to separate it
from the State Department's institutional bias toward currying favor
with foreign governments.

But the problem cannot be satisfactorily addressed by such administrative measures. Even massive staffing increases—beyond anything that is
actually feasible—would not be able to ensure the proper vetting of applicants at the current level of admissions. And even the staff increases that
have taken place are not what they seem, since many of the new Foreign
Service officers are replacing locally hired foreign staff, who never should
have been allowed to be involved in the visa process in the first place.

Moreover, the "product line" needs to be trimmed; the dozens of
immigrant and nonimmigrant visa categories, each with various subcategories, all with different and increasingly complex requirements,
make it impossible to run a secure and efficient visa process.

The only way we will ever be able to have a visa system appropriate
to our modern security needs will be to reduce the immigrant and
nonimmigrant visa workload that the officers need to assess. Even the
State Department recognizes the trade-off between the number of visas
processed and the quality of the visa decisions (i.e., ensuring that ineligible applicants are refused). One cable sent to consular posts said,
"Quality decisions can make the process less efficient, and, in the context of declining staff, posts have often been forced to choose efficiency
over quality."[38] One way the cable sought to increase efficiency was to

require consular officers to approve a larger portion of nonimmigrant visas without conducting interviews, precisely the opposite of the kind of heightened scrutiny that modern conditions demand.

Without a permanent cut in the workload, even the improvements now underway will be eroded as time passes—whatever new leeway that visa officers have in saying no will become increasingly restricted because the institutional pressures are always to satisfy the perceived constituents (foreign governments and citizens, the higher education industry and big business, and immigration lawyers), rather than the immigration system's *actual* constituents, the American people.

DISORDER AT THE BORDER

"The stated mission of immigration inspectors is to 'control and guard the boundaries and border of the United States against the illegal entry of aliens.'"[39] In fact, the border is the last physical checkpoint an alien crosses before being admitted to the United States. And the overload here is even greater than at the visa section.

About 180 million foreigners were admitted to the United States as nonimmigrants in 2004—and that's only an estimate, because more than three quarters were Mexicans and Canadians, whose entry is not recorded.[40] In addition, about 169 million Americans and 75 million green card holders returned from abroad through the same ports of entry. (All these numbers include individuals who entered more than once as they crossed back and forth across the border.) Of the 32 million entries by foreigners that were actually recorded in 2005, about 24 million were tourists and nearly 5 million were business travelers.

And in between the ports of entry, more than 1.1 million illegal aliens were arrested by the Border Patrol trying to sneak in without passing through inspection.

This massive workload has led to the same response at the borders as in the visa offices overseas—the fatalistic acceptance of massive lawbreaking by a demoralized bureaucracy. The 9/11 Commission staff report on immigration said that before the attacks, "The culture at the airports was one of travel facilitation and lax enforcement, with the exception of programs to interdict drug couriers and known criminals."[41] One aspect of this was a 1991 mandate from Congress that passengers of every flight from abroad be cleared through immigration and customs within forty-five minutes, no matter what, forcing inspectors at many airports to limit screening of foreigners to one minute each. Even 9/11 caused this to be altered only slightly, with Congress in 2002 changing the mandate so that instead of simply requiring lines to be cleared within forty-five minutes, now Congress requires staff levels to be such that passengers be cleared within forty-five minutes.[42]

What's more, the post-9/11 takeover of the immigration inspectors by the Customs Service as part of the creation of the Department of Homeland Security (to form U.S. Customs and Border Protection, or CBP) has resulted in a downgrading of immigration concerns. One report highlights the "lack of immigration expertise in CBP, both at headquarters and in the field," a truly alarming development given the importance of border screening to security.[43]

As a result, overwhelmed inspectors are simply unable to do their jobs properly. A 2006 report from Detroit, referring to the busiest crossing on the entire northern border, said that "U.S. and Canadian inspectors on the Ambassador Bridge and elsewhere say they are routinely told by supervisors to wave vehicles through checkpoints without scrutiny to satisfy commercial interests."[44] The report describes "lane flushing," in which cars and trucks are sent through the inspection points en masse, unexamined, if lines get too long.

Airports experience a similar process. When the inspectors' computers are down, foreign visitors are simply permitted to enter the country without a computerized check against the various watch lists, because to do otherwise would force people to wait and prompt complaints from the airlines.

A different response to the overload is on exhibit at the southern border, where Mexicans are issued a Border Crossing Card (colloquially known as a "laser visa") for short local trips to shop or visit relatives.

These machine-readable cards, issued by the State Department's visa officers, are now equipped with various high-tech characteristics, including digitized fingerprints, to ensure that they are legitimate and are being used by the people they were issued to. *But they are almost never scanned,* because doing so would slow down traffic.[45] The bearers simply hold the cards up to the border inspectors as they pass quickly into the United States, with only the tiny proportion pulled aside for closer scrutiny rather than having their cards scanned. This is an invitation to massive fraud—both the use of fake cards and the use of genuine cards by other people, who often mail them back to the person they rented them from after securing easy passage across the border.

And this is not a minor weakness. Fully half of all nonimmigrant entries by foreigners into the United States are Mexicans using a Border Crossing Card.

People claiming to be American citizens are also given only cursory checks because of this overload and because of the overall climate shaped by the overload, which prioritizes speed of passage over security. One study found that federal undercover agents "successfully entered the United States using fictitious driver's licenses and other bogus documentation through nine land ports of entry on the northern and southern borders. CBP officers never questioned the authenticity of the counterfeit documents presented at any of the nine crossings."[46]

The work of the Border Patrol is very different from that of immigration inspectors—rather than assessing the bona fides of each successive person in line, border agents are tasked with stopping anyone and anything from trying to sneak across between ports of entry. Nonetheless, the massive numbers have elicited a similar response. To begin with, virtually all of the roughly 1 million Mexican illegal aliens caught at the border are given what is known as voluntary return—they agree not to clog up the court system in exchange for not being formally deported, which would mean they'd be detained and barred from returning legally for a period of years. Instead, by accepting voluntary return, the illegal is able to turn right around in Mexico and try again, often within minutes of being released. In effect, border enforcement has turned into a version of the old Soviet joke—"we pretend to work and they pretend to pay us"—in which the Border Patrol pretends to enforce the law and the illegal aliens pretend to be punished.

But voluntary return at the border applies only to Mexican illegals; Mexico won't take back citizens of other countries who passed through on their way to sneak into the United States. In 2005, non-Mexican illegals caught on the Mexican border (known as OTMs, for "other than Mexican") accounted for about one in eight arrests. They were mostly Central Americans, with a smattering of other nationalities from around the world. This was a big jump from previous years, and it elicited a predictable nonenforcement response—since there wasn't enough room, under current spending priorities, to detain them all until they were processed for return to their home countries, most were simply let in to the country with a summons asking them to return in a few weeks for a deportation hearing. Of course, few returned. This "catch and release" policy was not addressed by the Bush administration until media coverage and congressional outrage forced a response.

Failures caused by overload at the border have had real-world security consequences. For instance, Lafi Taisir Mufleh Khalil, one of the conspirators in the aborted 1997 Brooklyn subway plot, arrived with a C-1 transit visa—essentially for those changing planes in the United States and continuing elsewhere—but upon his arrival at New York's Kennedy Airport (the nation's busiest international airport), the immigration inspector incorrectly treated him as a tourist, enabling him to stay legally for six months while planning the attack.[47]

September 11 hijacker Mohamed Atta is another example of failure caused by overload. The immigration inspector in Miami (another of the nation's busiest international airports) who screened his return to the United States from Spain in January 2001 said "he knew that if he took more time than 45 seconds to determine a visitor's admissibility or if he made too many referrals to secondary inspection, he could receive a poor performance appraisal."[48] Nonetheless, he noticed that Atta did not have the required visa for flight school and referred him to secondary inspection for further scrutiny. There, despite his lack of the proper document and despite his having overstayed his visa during his previous visit, he was nonetheless admitted. Steven Camarota noted the impact here of overload not just at the border but in immigration policy overall: "The scale of illegal immigration creates a tacit acceptance by law enforcement, policymakers, and even the INS itself. For example, it was far easier for an immigration inspector to allow Mohamed Atta back into the country even though he overstayed his visa in January 2001 knowing that there have been millions of overstayed visas in the past decade and policymakers had done nothing about it."[49]

Around the same time that Atta was improperly admitted in Miami, Hezbollah operative Mahmoud Kourani was successfully smuggled from Mexico in a hidden car compartment, probably through the world's busiest land border crossing, one near San Diego.[50] Kourani is now in prison. His federal indictment said he was a "member, fighter, recruiter and fund-raiser for Hezbollah" and was trained in "weaponry, spy craft and counterintelligence in Lebanon and Iran," and that his activities were overseen by his brother, Hezbollah's chief of military security for southern Lebanon.

Failures due to overload along the border between ports of entry have also had security consequences. Gazi Ibrahim Abu Mezer, for example, who was part of the plot to bomb the Brooklyn subway, was actually caught by the Border Patrol three times trying to sneak in from Canada. Though that part of the enforcement process actually worked, the Canadians wouldn't take him back after the third time he was apprehended and, because of a lack of detention space, the Border Patrol was forced to simply release him into the United States pending a deportation hearing.

But where conventional immigration enforcement has been allowed to proceed, it has successfully screened out terrorists at the border. For instance, an attentive border inspector in Washington State stopped Algerian terrorist Ahmed Ressam because of his nervous behavior, and a search of his car uncovered a trunk full of explosives, intended for an attack on Los Angeles International Airport.

Likewise, Mohamed Mani Ahmad al-Kahtani, another of the twentieth-hijacker candidates, was turned away by an airport inspector in Orlando. The initial inspector was uneasy enough because of his demeanor that she referred him to secondary inspection, where a veteran colleague took his time screening Kahtani. After an hour and a half of questioning, he was turned away because he had no return ticket and limited funds, and responded to questioning "in an arrogant and threatening manner."[51] Overload at the border makes it very difficult for inspectors to engage in this kind of intensive scrutiny.

CHECK-IN/CHECK-OUT

As with visa processing, there have been improvements in border management since 9/11. Most notable is the development of US-VISIT (the United States Visitor and Immigrant Status Indicator Technology program), intended to be a comprehensive entry/exit tracking system for foreigners coming to the United States, using fingerprint scanning and photographs. Congress first mandated such a system in 1996, after the first World Trade Center attack, but "the development of a system was delayed for years, partly because the immigration agency saw no easy way to achieve these objectives without unacceptably slowing the flow of visitors and commerce, but also because of heavy lobbying against the project from border communities."[52]

After 9/11, some of this opposition was overcome. The 9/11 Commission lent its weight, saying in its final report that "funding and completing a biometrics-based entry-exit system is an essential investment in our national security."[53] The system is now in place at all ports of entry—*but only a fraction of travelers are checked.* Even with the 2006 announcement that green-card holders returning from overseas trips would be enrolled in the system, a majority of foreigners will still be exempt, including virtually all Mexicans and Canadians. What's more, the *exit-recording* part of the system (which is vital for knowing who is still in the country after their permission expires) is not scheduled to be fully implemented even at airports until the end of 2008, with no more than a promise that "the Department of Homeland Security will continue to explore effective and cost-efficient means of establishing biometric exit requirements at land border crossings."[54]

Despite well-publicized successes in keeping out some bad guys, the decision to exempt most foreign visitors and not to move ahead with the check-out portion of the system "severely undermines the program and risks transforming this potentially critical national security tool into a high-tech Potemkin Village."[55]

Another new initiative to improve border security is the Western Hemisphere Travel Initiative (WHTI), which will require that Americans and foreigners entering the United States from neighboring countries have a passport. In the past, Americans returning from Mexico, Canada, or the Caribbean, and Canadians coming for short visits, could enter with merely a driver's license or no identification at all.

Far from being a substitute for lowering immigrant and nonimmigrant numbers, these two important initiatives—US-VISIT and WHTI—are important *reasons* for lowering numbers. The volume of human traffic across the borders is constantly invoked by politicians, businesses, and bureaucrats as arguments against these vital measures. But the completion of these measures is, as the 9/11 Commission noted, essential for our security. Therefore, we must do what we can to reduce the overload at the border in order for US-VISIT and WHTI to be successfully implemented. This is in addition to the higher levels of spending and manpower that will be needed to run a modern border-management system.

At visa offices, reducing numbers is easier, because we can simply eliminate visa categories, tighten standards, punish liars, and turn down more people. But cutting the workload at the border, to accommodate the needs of the modern security environment, isn't quite as easy. Americans and lawful permanent residents (green-card holders) have every right to come and go. Likewise, America can benefit from legitimate tourists and business travelers who really do go home when they've finished their visits—though how many we admit and under what conditions is, like immigration in general, a prudential question subject to cost/benefit analysis, not a matter to be decided by ideological or religious imperatives, as open-borders proponents would have it.

The area where numbers can be reduced most may well be the place where such reductions would do the most good in restoring control over the system—on the southern border. Three quarters of all legal entries to the United States are by land, and three quarters of land crossings are from Mexico. The reason for this huge flow is the parasitic nature of Mexico's border communities—they exist only because of their proximity to the United States, to take advantage of the arbitrage that's possible where a third-world country butts up against the first world. This is completely different from communities on the Canadian border, which are geographic accidents and little different from elsewhere in Canada, because the border marks the meeting point of two modern, first-world countries.

The examples of such arbitrage on the Mexican border are numerous: Mexican commuters living cheaply in Mexico but earning American wages on this side of the border; American retailers attracting Mexican shoppers dissatisfied with third-world inefficiency and lack of selection; and American college students looking for cheap liquor and lax standards. Before NAFTA, the parasitic nature of the border was promoted by federal law; Mexican border factories known as maquiladoras or twin plants were allowed to import parts from companies on the American side of the line, assemble products from them, and reexport those products northward without tariffs, artificially encouraging the growth of manufacturing in the formerly desolate border areas. This drew millions of people away from their homes in central Mexico and closer to the United States, prompting huge increases in traffic across the border, legal and illegal, that simply would not have happened without government intervention.

For instance, while the city of San Diego grew nearly 70-fold during the twentieth century, its sister city on the Mexican side, Tijuana, is about 5,000 times larger that it had been in 1900. Likewise with the other border towns; historian David Lorey compiled population numbers through 1990 that show Calexico, California, growing 23-fold but

Mexicali across the border growing 949-fold.[56] El Paso was 32 times larger than in 1900, but Ciudad Juárez was 96 times larger. And while Laredo grew 9-fold, Nuevo Laredo grew 33-fold. All of them exploded solely because of the existence of the border, and all are many times larger than their counterparts on the American side of the line (with the exception of San Diego, which has an economy not dependent on the border), because the relationship is not symbiotic but rather parasitic— the benefits of the border mainly go to communities on the Mexican side.

The final chapter will outline policy recommendations in more detail, but there are a number of practical steps that can contribute to developing a modern border-control system by significantly reducing traffic across the Mexican border. In the short term, this can be done by applying much higher standards for the issuance and use of Border Crossing Cards, whose users account for fully half of temporary foreign visitors to the United States. In the longer term, the way to limit the parasitic traffic across the Mexican border is to limit development there, through federal purchase of land potentially subject to development as part of a broader plan to develop a border security zone stretching the length of the border, giving the Border Patrol an uninterrupted swath of land from the Gulf of Mexico to the Pacific where it can do its job without impediment.

Reducing the number of people trying to sneak in between ports of entry has been the subject of extensive debate in the media and Congress, and is addressed in the final chapter. But the two most important means of doing this are physical barriers and interior enforcement; the first makes it harder to get across, while the second makes it less attractive to try in the first place.

INSIDE GAME

The third layer of immigration security is inside the country, and here, too, mass immigration overwhelms the proper administration of the law.

This is obvious with regard to conventional enforcement measures. With so many illegal aliens already here, the immigration enforcement bureaucracy simply goes through the motions of doing its job, without even attempting to reduce illegal immigration. The occasional arrest of an illegal-alien child molester is widely trumpeted, for instance, but no real effort is made to find, say, the 4 million people who have overstayed their visas.

But for the purposes of this discussion, it's important to understand how the bureaucracy is also overloaded by excessive *legal* immigration, which is caused exclusively by Congress.

The security consequences of adjudicating the legal status of aliens inside the country are hard to overestimate. While it might seem that terrorists need only get physical access to the United States, by means legal or illegal, the reality is more complicated. As a former counsel to the 9/11 Commission has written, "Once within U.S. borders, terrorists seek to stay. Doing so with the appearance of legality helps ensure long-term operational stability."[57]

In other words, simply getting into the country usually isn't enough for terrorists or other alien attackers; for all but the most trivial actions, they need to stay here for some time to plan and organize their operations. That means they need somewhere to live, a way to get around, some kind of cover story, a job or school enrollment, and often a source of funds.

So potential attackers need to acquire, retain, and perhaps upgrade their immigration status in order to successfully carry out their schemes. The 9/11 Commission staff report on immigration specifically noted this: "Evidence indicates that Mohamed Atta, the September 11 ringleader, was acutely aware of his immigration status, tried to remain in the United States legally, and *aggressively pursued enhanced immigration status for himself and others* [emphasis added]."[58]

This highlights the vital security function not only of the Bureau of Immigration and Customs Enforcement (ICE), but also of U.S. Citizenship and Immigration Services (USCIS), which processes applications for green cards and employment authorization documents, for citizenship, and for other immigration benefits. It is vital to our security that the immigration bureaucracy approach each successive interaction with an alien as an opportunity to screen out terrorists and other undesirables.

To understand how this works, imagine access to our society as a ladder or a staircase; at the bottom are foreigners outside the United States, and at the top are immigrants who have become naturalized citizens.[59] Visas and border control are very important, because they help keep terrorists from getting into the country in the first place. But simply getting into the United States isn't enough; each step up the ladder—illegal alien, then short-term visitor, long-term visitor, permanent resident, and U.S. citizen—affords a terrorist and others additional opportunities to harm us.

If a foreigner abroad is at the bottom of this figurative ladder, the next step up is an illegal alien. A terrorist here illegally obviously has the ability to attack us, because of his physical presence, but his lack of legal status limits his freedom of action. Even before 9/11, when it was even easier than today to be an illegal alien, there were still certain risks when getting a job, applying for a driver's license, being stopped by a police officer, and so forth.

Zacarias Moussaoui demonstrates some of the limitations of illegal status. As a French citizen, he was able to visit the United States for up to ninety days without a visa through the Visa Waiver Program; but after his ninety days passed, he became an illegal alien. That's why the INS was able to take him into custody when his erratic behavior at flight school attracted unfavorable attention. Anything an illegal-alien terrorist does that attracts attention might get him arrested.

This is not necessarily the case for a terrorist who's made it to the next step up the ladder—possession of legal status through a short-term temporary visa, such as for a tourist or business traveler. This is better than being an illegal alien, of course. But the short duration of such a visit (at least the short time before the visitor turns into an illegal alien) and the limits on exiting and reentering the country (and the ban on legal employment) make it difficult for a short-term visa holder to engage in extensive conspiracies. The constraints of short-term visas are evident from the fact that the 9/11 terrorists on still-valid short-term visas were merely the "muscle"—they assisted in the attacks but arrived in the United States relatively late and had little role in planning or preparation. The actual organizers, such as Hani Hanjour, Nawaf al-Hamzi, and Mohamed Atta, ended up overstaying their short-term visas at some point, because the amount of time required to plan and organize the attacks exceeded their allotted stay.

To organize a conspiracy, then, it's helpful to take the next step up the ladder—to long-term but still temporary (nonimmigrant) status, such as a student or employment visa, an Employment Authorization Document (which permits an alien to work while an application for permanent residence winds its way through the adjudication process), or an asylum application (which allows the applicant to remain until his case is decided). A terrorist with long-term nonimmigrant status can remain here legally for years, affording more time to organize attacks, though still constrained by limits on the ability to reenter the country after leaving. Atta and fellow 9/11 pilot Marwan al-Shehhi, for instance, applied to adjust their status from short-term tourists to longer-term vocational students for precisely this reason; as simple tourists, they couldn't legally go to flight school, get the training they needed to stage their attacks, and coordinate the activities of other terrorists.

Even more attractive for potential terrorists is the next rung up the ladder—lawful permanent residence (a green card), which affords almost complete freedom of action without most of the restrictions that encumber visitors, not to mention illegal aliens. A 2005 study of a large group of terrorists in the United States found that twenty-three of ninety-four applied for green cards, of whom sixteen were approved.[60] Consider the case of Mahmud Abouhalima, one of the leaders of the first World Trade Center bombing, who became a legal resident after falsely claiming to be an agricultural worker, allowing him to qualify for a green card as part of the big illegal-alien amnesty passed by Congress in 1986. It was only after he became a permanent resident that he was able to come and go freely and make several trips to Afghanistan, where he received the terrorist training he ultimately used in the 1993 attack. Had he been prevented from receiving a green card, he would not have been able to leave the United States and then return as a trained terrorist. His receipt of a green card thus greatly facilitated his terrorism and was an important factor in al Qaeda's ability to stage the attack.

The final step is citizenship, the ultimate immigration status for terrorists. As a naturalized U.S. citizen, an immigrant becomes an American, able to work at any job, precluded from deportation, and enjoying full constitutional protections. In the same 2005 study mentioned above, twenty-one of ninety-four terrorists applied for citizenship, all but one of them successfully.[61] The recruitment of naturalized citizens is a conscious al Qaeda strategy. The *San Francisco Chronicle* quoted an Arabic-language newspaper account of a confession by naturalized citizen Khalid Abu-al-Dahab, who has been described as a one-man communications hub for al Qaeda, for whom he shuttled money and fake passports to terrorists around the world from his California apartment. According to the *Chronicle*, "Dahab said bin Laden was eager to recruit American citizens of Middle Eastern descent."[62] When Dahab and fellow terrorist and naturalized citizen Ali Mohamed (a U.S. army veteran and author of al Qaeda's terrorist handbook) traveled to Afghanistan in the mid-1990s to report on their efforts to recruit American citizens, "bin Laden praised their efforts and emphasized the necessity of recruiting as many Muslims with American citizenship as possible into the organization."

MORE OVERLOAD

Every time a foreign citizen within the United States tries to take another step up the ladder toward citizenship, the immigration officer assessing the application needs to approach his task with America's security foremost in mind.

Unfortunately, massive overload makes this impossible. In 2005, USCIS received 6.3 million applications for fifty different kinds of immigration benefits and adjudicated 7.5 million applications.[63] On any given day, USCIS processes 30,000 applications, conducts 135,000 national security background checks, answers 82,000 telephone inquiries, and more.[64]

The immigration bureaucracy is so utterly overwhelmed by this tsunami of immigration that even DHS Secretary Michael Chertoff was forced to concede that "parts of the system have nearly collapsed under the weight of numbers."[65]

Some examples of such collapse would be amusing if they weren't so serious. In 2002, it was reported that the INS had stored away in underground limestone vaults some 2 million documents that had been filed by immigrants but subsequently forgotten by the agency.[66] In the words of an INS spokesman, "The field offices weren't sure what to do with all of the documents they had not been able to look through, and they were a bit overwhelmed by the unprecedented growth" in immigration.

This, like the shredding story at beginning of this chapter, is an extreme example, of course. It would be easy to blame this sort of thing on a few bad apples or even on bureaucrats in general, denouncing them as clock-watching time-servers, too lazy or stupid to do their jobs—a charge that politicians and the media make with some regularity.

The reality is different. However necessary it is to improve tracking of applications and oversight of staff, the real problem is systemic, the result of excessively high levels of immigration. In the words of one government report, "It would be impossible for USCIS to verify all of the key information or interview all individuals related to the millions of applications it adjudicates each year—approximately 7.5 million applications in fiscal year 2005—without seriously compromising its service-related objectives."[67]

This overload has distorted the very organizational culture of USCIS (just as at the visa section, border inspection booths, and the Border Patrol), resulting in a situation in which "staff are rewarded for the timely handling of petitions rather than for careful scrutiny of their merits," in the words of another government report.[68] Michael Maxwell, former director of the Office of Security and Investigations at

USCIS, elaborated on this point in 2006 congressional testimony: "USCIS District Offices and Service Centers are holding competitions and offering a variety of rewards, including cash bonuses, time off, movie tickets, and gift certificates, to employees and/or teams of employees with the fastest processing times. The quality of processing is not a factor; only the quantity of closed applications matters, and it is important to note that it takes a lot less time to approve an application than to deny one, since denials require written justifications and, often, appeals."[69]

The bureaucratic frenzy to churn out approvals at ever-increasing rates has led one processing center to adopt a dangerous innovation; as Maxwell writes: "It appears that the Texas Service Center has developed an 'auto-adjudication' system that can process I-765s [the application for an Employment Authorization Document] from start to finish without any human involvement at all. In other words, there is no point in the process when a USCIS employee actually examines the supporting documentation to look for signs of fraud. Instead, the I-765 application is processed automatically when the underlying application for LPR status has been sitting on the shelf for 90 days."[70]

This emphasis on speed rather than security comes from the very top; politicians from both parties constantly press for faster and faster adjudication. For example, then-governor George W. Bush made a high-profile pledge during the 2000 presidential campaign to cut waiting times to less than six months.[71]

The inevitable result, as elsewhere in the immigration system, is massive fraud, though you wouldn't know it from the surreal denials by management. Emilio Gonzalez, for instance, head of USCIS, said on CNN, "Obviously if people are of the opinion that there is rampant fraud in this agency, I would like to disabuse them of that."[72]

In fact, "rampant"—along with "pervasive"—is precisely the word government investigators used to describe fraud in USCIS, with one official estimating that 20 to 30 percent of all applications involved fraud.[73] The report said, in its understated fashion, that "the goal of providing immigration benefits in a timely manner to those who are legally entitled to them may conflict with the goal of preserving the integrity of the legal immigration system."

Another government report found that because of widespread fraud, "a number of individuals linked to a hostile foreign power's intelligence service were found to have been employed as temporary alien workers on military research."[74] What's more, "organized crime groups have used sophisticated immigration fraud schemes, such as creating shell companies, to bring in aliens ostensibly as employees of these companies."

The Department of Labor found that this kind of employment fraud was very widespread. Part of the application process for certain work visas is "labor certification," a process conducted by the Department of Labor to determine if there are qualified American workers willing to take a job at a certain wage. An analysis of this process in 2004 found that the *majority* of applications had false information.[75]

One way that overload directly creates fraud is in the issuance of Employment Authorization Documents (EAD) which are given to certain aliens who are not lawful permanent residents (green-card holders) but are nonetheless permitted to work. As a way of coping with the overload caused by excessive immigration, these documents are automatically given to anyone whose application for permanent residence takes longer than ninety days to process (i.e., virtually all applicants). And the very issuance of these documents adds to the overload, since they account for fully one quarter of applications processed by USCIS. With an EAD, the alien can get a legitimate Social Security card, a driver's license, and often permission to travel abroad (known as Advance Parole). This is why "many individuals apply for permanent residency fraudulently simply to obtain a valid temporary work authorization document."[76] It doesn't matter whether USCIS eventually rejects the green-card application, because the fraudulent applicant has already got what he wanted and has embedded himself in our society.

The connection between this massive fraud and national security is acknowledged even by the immigration bureaucracy. USCIS has established an Office of Fraud Detection and National Security, whose dual mission is explained this way: "While the connection between immigration fraud and national security is palpable, the line that divides them is not always as clean. An analysis of the immigration history of the terrorists involved in the 9/11 plots reveals that all of them committed some form of immigration fraud. It is not, therefore, unreasonable to assume that those that threaten the national security of this country today may seek to evade our immigration laws through fraud. The nexus between national security and fraud becomes much clearer in the wake of 9/11."[77]

This new awareness of the importance of fraud comes none too soon. A 2006 Congressional Research Service analysis found a sustained, long-term decline in fraud investigations—a 43 percent decline in work hours devoted to investigating fraud from 1986 to 2003, resulting in an astounding 88 percent drop in the number of completed fraud cases—over a time period when the immigrant population roughly doubled.[78] Likewise, immigration-fraud prosecutions fell by nearly half from 1992 to 2003.

Even vetting immigration applications specifically for security reasons (as opposed to generic fraud) has fallen victim to overload. Checking applicants against security databases is constantly highlighted as the high-tech way to reconcile security with massive immigration, the only issue being whether the intelligence used to compile these watch lists is reliable enough.

But even with the best intelligence and all the computing power that modern technology can provide, the watch-list system cannot cope with today's level of immigration. In 2004, USCIS conducted more than 27 million checks against the Interagency Border Inspection System (IBIS) database. Adjudicators have to check an average of 3.7 names per application, including maiden names and names of dependents covered under the application.[79] The same year they also did 1.9 million fingerprint checks and 1.5 million name checks with the FBI. Adjudicators also check the internal DHS databases for prior immigration history. What's more, every time a name check results in a hit, the adjudicator has to do an average of 5.4 *additional* database checks to verify that the hit was actually on the applicant in question. To complicate things further, much of the background check process is (and must always be) heavily reliant on names and documents, often from foreign countries and sometimes from low-quality photocopies, with names transliterated into English in a variety of ways.

It's not too much to say that an arithmetical increase in immigration results in a geometric increase in the effort needed to screen the immigrants.

And because of that, the error rate in background checks is extraordinarily high. A quality-assurance study of security checks done on the applications processed by USCIS in 2004 found security-check errors in 12 percent of applications for Temporary Protected Status, 15 percent of green-card replacement applications, 64 percent of refugee applications, and a whopping 96 percent of Advance Parole applications.[80]

At one major processing center, some 75 percent of the names on immigration benefit applications that triggered watch-list hits over a period of four years were not properly checked.[81] As one official at the processing center said, "What happened was, customer service took first priority and national security was secondary." Another official concurred: "The real problem is the push to get the backlog completed by October, and adjudicators are processing applications so fast that there is no time for thorough background checks."

And such error rates presume that the name check was conducted in the first place. Former USCIS security official Michael Maxwell testified that fully 20 percent—or 1.5 million—of the applications processed by USCIS in 2005 did not go through the automated background-check process at all.[82] What's more, if those name-check requests that are sent to the FBI or the CIA don't receive a response from those agencies within forty days, "the application or petition shall be processed on the assumption that the results of the request are negative," i.e., adjudicators are simply to *assume* that the alien is not a threat and go ahead with the application.[83]

At every step in the immigration process, overload undermines our attempts at improving security. We are asking the impossible of our federal workers—overseas, at the border, and inside the country—when we demand thorough screening of an unprecedented and rapidly growing volume of immigration. In fact, the more we modernize our immigration system, the more glaring is the incompatibility with the old-fashioned paper documents from third-world countries that must be examined and vetted by hand. Unlike telephone traffic, for instance, which has been able to grow exponentially because human operators have been replaced by automated switches, immigration processing cannot grow in the same way, because it must always be processed by human beings. We have nonetheless pretended that we can automate ourselves out of this problem, and the result has been a dangerously insecure immigration system. Any effort to fix this must include reductions in immigration.

FISH IN THE SEA

But even if there were a magical way of resolving the problem of administrative overload, the second security vulnerability of mass immigration would remain: Large, constantly refreshed communities of foreigners provide cover and incubation for attackers. In today's world of cheap and easy communications and transportation, immigrant communities, however unwittingly, fit Mao's observation regarding China's war with Japan: "The people are like water and the army is like fish."

President Bush used a different image in his address to the joint session of Congress after the 9/11 attacks, when he said, "Al Qaeda is to terror what the Mafia is to crime."[84] The comparison is instructive. During the great wave of immigration around the turn of the century, and for some time after immigration was stopped in the 1920s, law enforcement had very little luck in penetrating the Mafia. This was because immigrants lived in enclaves with limited knowledge of English, were suspicious of government institutions, and clung to Old World prejudices and attitudes like omertà, the Sicilian code of silence.

But with the end of mass immigration, the assimilation of Italian immigrants and their children accelerated, and the offspring of the immigrants developed (because they were inculcated with) a sense of genuine membership and ownership in America—what John Fonte of the Hudson Institute calls "patriotic assimilation." It was this process that drained the water within which the Mafia had been able to swim, allowing law enforcement to do its job more effectively and eventually cripple the Mafia.

Anthropologist Francis Ianni described this process thirty years ago: "An era of Italo-American crime seems to be passing in large measure due to the changing character of the Italo-American community," including "the disappearance of the kinship model on which such [Mafia] families are based."[85] Ianni continued, "After three generations of acculturation, this powerful pattern of organization is finally losing its hold on Italo-Americans generally—and on the crime families as well." In the same way, reductions in immigration will promote more rapid assimilation in Muslim (and other) immigrant communities and thus make it harder for terrorists (and other attackers) to operate there—harder to find cover, harder to recruit sympathizers, harder to raise funds.

That this is a problem in Muslim immigrant communities is beyond dispute. A *New York Times* reporter wrote shortly after the 9/11 attacks that there are many reasons that Islamic terrorists use Germany as a base, "among them the fact that the terrorists could blend into a society with a large Muslim population and more foreigners than any other in Europe."[86]

This also applies in our own country. Another report observed about Paterson, New Jersey, "The [9/11] hijackers' stay here also shows how, in an area that speaks many languages and keeps absorbing immigrants, a few young men with no apparent means of support and no furniture can settle in for months without drawing attention."[87]

The chief intelligence officer for the DHS was explicit on this point: "As previous attacks indicate, overseas extremists do not operate in a vacuum and are often linked with criminal and smuggling networks—usually connected with resident populations from their countries of origin."[88]

Nor is the role of the immigrant community entirely passive. Two of the 9/11 hijackers—Nawaf Alhazmi and Khalid Almihdhar—had been embraced by the Muslim immigrant community in San Diego. As the *Washington Post* noted, "From their arrival here in late 1999 until they departed a few months before the 9/11 attacks, Alhazmi and Almihdhar repeatedly enlisted help from San Diego's mosques and established members of its Islamic community. The terrorists leaned on them to find housing, open a bank account, obtain car insurance—even, at one point, get a job."[89]

And even worse than the role immigrant enclaves play in simply shielding terrorists is their role in recruiting and incubating new ones. One disturbing example comes from Lackawanna, New York, where six Yemeni Americans—five of them born in the United States to immigrant parents and raised in an immigrant community—were arrested in 2002 for operating an al Qaeda terrorist sleeper cell. The six arrested men traveled to Pakistan in 2001, ostensibly for religious training but actually to go to an al Qaeda terrorist training camp in Afghanistan; all are serving prison terms for providing material support to terrorism. The seventh member of the cell (a naturalized American citizen) did not return after training in Afghanistan, was later jailed in Yemen, and escaped from prison there in 2006. The ringleader of the cell, yet another American citizen, was killed in Yemen by the CIA in 2002.

The community that bred this cell is intimately shaped by immigration. As the local paper reported:

> This is a piece of ethnic America where the Arabic-speaking Al-Jazeera television station is beamed in from Qatar through satellite dishes to Yemenite-American homes; where young children answer "Salaam" when the cell phone rings, while older children travel to the Middle East to meet their future husband or wife; where soccer moms don't seem to exist, and where girls don't get to play soccer—or, as some would say, football.[90]

In the decade ending in 2005, more than eighteen thousand Yemenis immigrated legally to the United States. In Lackawanna itself, the Arab population ballooned by 175 percent during the 1990s. The median household income in the Yemeni neighborhood is 20 percent lower than in Lackawanna as a whole.

A report at the time of the Lackawanna arrests said there were likely more such groups among undigested immigrant communities: "Federal officials say privately that there could be dozens of similar cells across the country, together posing a grave danger to national security. They believe that such cells tend to be concentrated in communities with large Arab populations, such as Detroit."[91]

One such example came to light in 2005 when five men in the Pakistani community of Lodi, California—three visa-overstaying illegal aliens plus a naturalized citizen and his native-born son—were arrested by federal authorities on terrorism-related charges. Lodi's is an insular immigrant community like that in Lackawanna—an estimated 80 percent of the two thousand or so Lodi Pakistanis do not speak English, women are not permitted even to attend the local mosque, and a large portion of the girls are not permitted by their families to attend school, studying instead at home.[92] Ongoing immigration ensures continuing attachment to backward practices. As one report related:

> Women may be isolated, partly because of language. They could improve their English if they could go to adult school, but they don't go because it would require them to come into contact with men. There is a class for English as a second language at Heritage School, but since it is publicly funded, the law prohibits officials from excluding men from the class. Husbands and fathers in traditional homes object if classes are co-ed, and would not allow their women to attend.[93]

The 2000 census found more than 200,000 Pakistani immigrants living in the United States, and from 2000 through 2005, more than 81,000 more became new legal permanent residents.

Of course, Muslim immigrant communities are not alone in exhibiting characteristics that may shield or even incubate criminality. For instance, as criminologist Ko-lin Chin has written, "The isolation of the Chinese community, the inability of American law enforcement authorities to penetrate the Chinese criminal underworld, and the reluctance of Chinese victims to come forward for help all conspire to enable Chinese gangs to endure."[94] And the solution is the same for these other ethnic groups, as well. William Kleinknecht, author of *The New Ethnic Mobs,* notes, "If the mass immigration of Chinese should come to a halt, the Chinese gangster may disappear in a blaze of assimilation after a couple of decades."[95]

The idea of any connection between immigration and terrorism has been dismissed by many policy makers and activists. Former INS commissioner James Ziglar, for instance, piously observed that "We're not talking about immigration, we're talking about evil."[96] Elsewhere Ziglar even employed the "then the terrorists will win" cliché, saying, "If, in response to the events of September 11, we engage in excess and shut out what has made America great, then we will have given the terrorists a far greater victory than they could have hoped to achieve."[97]

After 9/11, groups lobbying in favor of mass immigration rushed to make the same point. Cecilia Muñoz of the National Council of La Raza gamely averred, "There's no relationship between immigration and terrorism."[98] And Jeanne Butterfield, executive director of the American Immigration Lawyers Association (and former head of the Marxist Palestine Solidarity Committee), echoed this denial of reality: "I don't think the events of last week can be attributed to the failure of our immigration laws."[99]

And indeed, to argue that cuts in the level of immigration are necessary for homeland security might appear opportunistic, like agricultural lobbyists exploiting 9/11 to argue for farm subsidies by peddling the idea of "food security." After all, it's only Muslim fanatics who are trying to murder our children, not Mexican dishwashers or Filipino nurses.

But it's clear that under modern conditions of asymmetric warfare, mass immigration itself represents a significant security threat, both by overwhelming our ability to filter out undesirables and by constantly refreshing the immigrant communities that serve as havens for malefactors. While there is no question that other security measures are also needed—such as improved intelligence gathering overseas, greater cooperation with foreign governments, and military operations—without cuts in both permanent and temporary immigration, we are leaving ourselves open to the enemy.

CHAPTER 4

Economy: Cheap Labor Versus Modern America

The key to the economic facet of the conflict between mass immigration and modern society is the fact that immigration floods the job market with low-skilled workers, creating what economists call a slack, or loose, labor market. This results in a buyer's market for labor, where employers can pick and choose among workers rather than having to compete with one another to attract and keep staff.

This has two major implications for the economy: First, a loose labor market reduces the bargaining power of workers compared to employers, resulting in lower earnings and less opportunity for advancement for the poorest and most marginal of Americans. And second, by artificially keeping wages lower than they would be otherwise, mass immigration reduces the incentives for more-efficient use of labor, slowing the natural progress of mechanization and other productivity increases in the low-wage industries where immigrants are concentrated.

In other words, while immigration certainly increases the overall size of our economy, it subverts the widely shared economic goals of a modern society: a large middle class open to all, working in high-wage, knowledge-intensive, and capital-intensive jobs exhibiting growing labor productivity and avoiding too skewed a distribution of income.

This is not to say that a dramatically lower level of immigration would create a permanently tight labor market. The business cycle would continue to alternate between expansion and slowdown, as it always has. But with less immigration, the job market would be tighter for longer during an expansion and would not be as loose for as long during a recession.

What's more, lower levels of immigration would not serve as a magic solution to poverty and the economic marginalization of the less-educated and others; there are other factors contributing to these problems, including technological change, discrimination, increased trade, and cultural dysfunction among some of the poor. But mass immigration is a significant contributor to the problems of the economically marginal as well as an impediment to the long-term competitive position of industries that use cheap immigrant labor—and since it is the result of federal policy (either through legal immigration or through the deliberate decision not to curtail illegal immigration), it is something we as a nation actually have the power to change.

ECONOMIC CHANGE

Immigration has always added workers to the economy, of course, but today is different because our economy has changed dramatically since the end of the first great immigration wave. When millions of Irish and Germans and Scandinavians and Italians and Jews and Slavs crossed the Atlantic, America was still settling vast swathes of empty land and undergoing the titanic process of industrialization. A century ago, what economists call the primary sector of the economy (farming, fishing, and so on) still employed more Americans than any other, as it had everywhere since the dawn of humankind. Today, only 2 percent of our workforce occupies itself in this way. Meanwhile, we've passed through the industrial phase of economic development and entered the postindustrial era, with the tertiary sector (the service industry overall) employing fully 80 percent of working Americans, and the percentage is climbing.

This change in our economy has had many effects. Union membership, for instance, has declined substantially; in 2005, only one out of twelve workers nationwide belonged to a union, and only about one out of thirteen private-sector workers was unionized.[1] This compares to nearly one third of the workforce during the two decades after World War II.[2]

The change from the old manufacturing economy has also made education much more important than in the past. A century ago, people with little education could find work to support their families and advance economically, but this is much more difficult today, as less-educated workers are steadily falling behind the more educated. For instance, as late as 1979, college graduates earned only 43 percent more than high school graduates, but by 1995, they earned 84 percent more.[3]

Both as a cause and effect of these changes in the economy, the educational attainment of Americans has increased significantly. Nearly a quarter of American adults had fewer than five years of schooling in 1910; now, less than 2 percent do. Likewise, the percentage who had completed high school increased sixfold, from about 13 percent of the total to 84 percent. And the percentage of college graduates increased tenfold, from 2.7 percent of American adults to 27 percent. Another way to look at it is that in 1900, only a little more than 10 percent of high-school-age children were actually enrolled in school; in 2001, nearly 95 percent were.

Into this twenty-first-century economy we have resumed the importation of what amounts to nineteenth-century foreign labor. Between 1980 and 2000, immigration increased the number of workers in the United States by nearly 10 percent and the number of high school dropouts by 20 percent, causing what economists call a supply shock—a sudden infusion of a particular resource (in this case, labor, especially low-skilled labor).[4] And this shock to the labor market is likely to continue indefinitely, barring a change in federal policy; from 2000 to 2005, 8 million more immigrants arrived, the majority of them with no education beyond high school.[5]

The contrast with American workers is stark: Only about 8 percent of native-born workers today have less than a high-school education, but almost 30 percent of immigrant workers do. What's more, while immigrants account for about 15 percent of all workers, they make up nearly 40 percent of workers lacking a high-school degree, resulting in an artificially bloated low-skilled labor force.

This gap between native and immigrant skills has been growing as the economy and society have modernized. In 1960, immigrant men were only about 25 percent more likely to be high-school dropouts than native-born men; by 1998, after the huge wave of low-skilled immigration, immigrants were nearly *four times* more likely to be dropouts.[6] Of course, the process of modernization has been going on everywhere, so the proportion of immigrants who lack a high-school education has also been falling over the years, but much more slowly than among Americans, causing the gap to widen.

AN OPPORTUNITY SOCIETY?

In his second inaugural address, President Ronald Reagan said, "Let us resolve that we the people will build an American opportunity society in which all of us—white and black, rich and poor, young and old—will go forward together arm in arm." Most of us, regardless of political affiliation, aspire to such a vision of an America where people can better themselves through their own exertions, a basic element of our self-image as Americans, and one that contains a good deal of truth.

But mass immigration subverts the efforts of precisely those for whom economic self-improvement is most difficult and most urgent— all those at the margins of today's mainstream economy, who often have little to offer but their labor and who constitute the pool of potential takers of relatively low-wage jobs. This mainly means low-skilled workers, high-school dropouts, and those with only a high-school education, who would be the main substitutes for immigrant labor.

Because education is the key to advancement in a modern economy, common sense would suggest that our least-educated countrymen are also the poorest. The data bear this out: The average annual income of an American adult without a high-school degree is only about one-fourth that of a person with more than a high-school degree; an American who has finished high school but gone no further earns slightly more than half of what his counterpart with education beyond high school earns. Because of this, Americans with a high-school degree or less make up two thirds of adults in poverty. The long-term concerns are also serious—nearly half of all children in households headed by a native-born American are dependent on a worker with a high-school degree or less.[7]

Although much of the economic analysis of immigration rightly looks at its effects on Americans with relatively little schooling, it's important to note that those at the margins of the economy include more than just high-school dropouts. Those harmed by artificially loose labor markets include a disproportionate share of blacks and Hispanics and American Indians, as well as the young and the old seeking part-time work, mothers of young children looking for flexible jobs, the physically and mentally handicapped, ex-convicts attempting to build new lives, recovering addicts, and even earlier immigrants.

What all such people have in common is some degree of reluctance by employers to hire them—in some cases for invidious reasons, such as racial bias, and in other cases for perfectly rational reasons, such as a desire not to have to adjust the flow of work to suit the vacation plans of college students. But in all these cases, the attractiveness of nonmainstream American job seekers is reduced by the mass immigration of what President Bush calls "willing workers"—strangers from abroad whose superabundance relieves employers of the economic need to bid for workers by offering higher wages and better working conditions, and also of the need to accommodate those who are, for whatever reason, seen by employers as less desirable.

Sociologist William Julius Wilson, in his study of inner-city Chicago, describes a loose labor market as one where "employers are—and indeed, can afford to be—more selective in recruiting and in granting promotions. They overemphasize job prerequisites and exaggerate the value of experience. In such an economic climate, disadvantaged minorities suffer disproportionately and the level of employer discrimination rises."[8]

REDUCING WAGES

The effect of the ongoing surge of immigration on the income of low-skilled Americans is a textbook case of supply and demand. In fact, in his famous textbook, economist Paul Samuelson wrote specifically about the pre-1965 tight-border policies: "By keeping labor supply down, immigration policy tends to keep wages high." He stated the basic principle: "Limitation of the supply of any grade of labor relative to all other productive factors can be expected to raise its wage rate; an increase in supply will, other things being equal, tend to depress wage rates."[9]

The National Research Council, in a wide-ranging study of immigration, concluded that in economic terms, immigration "harms workers who are substitutes for immigrants while benefiting workers who are complements to immigrants."[10] In other words, since immigrants are disproportionately low skilled, it is low-skilled American workers who see their wages drop as immigrants expand the pool of people competing for jobs appropriate to their skill level. The NRC report estimated that immigration was responsible for nearly half the decline in wages of high-school dropouts between 1980 and 1994. At the same time, higher-skilled workers may gain, as the services that low-skilled workers provide (like lawn-mowing or valet parking) become cheaper and as the high skilled can specialize more.

In fact, immigration's overall economic benefit to Americans already here (as opposed to the simple increase in the total size of the economy) comes specifically from lowering the wages of American workers who compete with the immigrants. The National Research Council found that Americans as a whole received an economic benefit of between $1 billion and $10 billion per year from immigration, a tiny amount in what was, at the time of the report, an $8 trillion economy. But this small net economic benefit arises from the redistribution of wealth away from the poor and toward the rest of society; the report found that the poorest tenth of American workers (high-school dropouts who compete with immigrants) suffer a 5 percent cut in wages because of immigration, which is then redistributed to the rest of the American workforce, making the average person with at least a high-school education a minuscule two tenths of 1 percent richer.

In other words, immigration takes a figurative pound of flesh from one low-skilled American worker, who already has little to spare, and then slices it thinly among nine other better-educated Americans, who are more prosperous to begin with, giving each of them a barely noticeable benefit. And of course, even that small benefit is swamped by the extra cost in government services generated by low-skilled immigration, as discussed in the next chapter.

More recent research has found a quite pronounced loss to native-born American workers. Harvard economist George Borjas has found that the immigration wave of the 1980s and 1990s caused a drop in the annual earnings of all categories of American workers, including a 3.6 percent drop for male college graduates and a 7.4 percent drop for male high-school dropouts.[11] Lest these numbers seem small, Borjas calculates that immigration reduced the average American high-school dropout's income in 2000 by about $1,800, while the American college graduate saw his salary reduced by $2,600.

Since education is not distributed evenly among Americans, some groups of American workers will experience a disproportionately large effect from immigration. Borjas found that the immigrant influx from 1980 to 2000 caused the annual wages of native-born white workers overall to fall 3.5 percent, but those of black workers fell 4.5 percent, and the wages of native-born Hispanic workers fell 5 percent.[12] As he writes: "The adverse impact of immigration, therefore, is largest for the most disadvantaged native-born minorities."

JOB DISPLACEMENT

But the loose labor market created by immigration doesn't just reduce the wages paid to low-skilled American workers—it also makes it less likely they will be hired in the first place and more likely they will drop out of the job market altogether.

Of course, there is no simple, one-to-one relationship between the arrival of immigrants and job losses for Americans. But the evidence is piling up that immigration does indeed crowd out American workers. A recent analysis has found that during the first half of this decade, almost all the net increase in jobs for working-age adults went to immigrants, despite the fact that the native born accounted for the large majority of the increase in the working-age population.[13] Over this period, from 2000 to 2005, the number of adult immigrant workers with a high-school education or less increased by 1.6 million, while unemployment among similarly educated Americans grew by nearly 1 million, and an additional 1.5 million such Americans left the labor force altogether (i.e., stopped even looking for work). This wasn't just coincidence; the fall in the proportion of low-skilled Americans working was greatest in precisely those states with the biggest growth in the immigrant population, while unemployment among the native born in immigrant-heavy job categories was 10 percent, double the overall national rate.

The connection between immigration and the decline in employment is especially clear in the case of black Americans. Much field research has shown that employers prefer to hire immigrants over black Americans. Two scholars who studied the interaction of blacks and immigrants in New York have written:

> Native-born applicants are at a disadvantage compared to legal immigrants in securing entry-level work. In fact, even though central Harlem residents are nearly all African American, recent immigrants have a higher probability of being hired for Harlem's fast-food jobs than anyone else. Interviews with employers suggest

that they believe immigrants are easier to manage in
part because they come from countries where $4.25 an
hour represents a king's ransom. Whether or not employers are right about the tractability of immigrants,
such attitudes make it harder for the native-born to
obtain low-wage jobs.[14]

William Julius Wilson found the same thing in his study of inner-city
Chicago; Hispanics, he wrote, "continue to funnel into manufacturing
because employers prefer Hispanics over blacks and they like to hire by
referrals from current employees, which Hispanics can readily furnish,
being already embedded in migration networks."[15]

The exodus of black men from the labor market has been dramatic.
From 1960 to 2000, the employment rate for black men (the proportion
of black men not in jail who are actually holding jobs) fell significantly,
from about 90 percent to 76 percent (the employment rate for white
men fell much less, from 96 percent to 91 percent).[16] The drop in employment for black high-school dropouts was even more dramatic,
from 89 percent to 56 percent (the decline for white dropouts was from
94 percent to 76 percent). In other words, nearly half of black American
men with less than a high-school education are not working.

There were a variety of reasons for this huge drop in the employment of black men: the explosion in illegitimate births, racial discrimination, the loss of manufacturing jobs, the spread of welfare dependency,
the shift of economic activity out of the inner city, increased drug use
and criminality, and other factors. But economists have confirmed the
field studies of sociologists in finding that immigration contributes significantly to the reduction in black employment. A 2006 paper by Harvard economist George Borjas and two colleagues found that one third
of the decline in the employment rate of black male high-school dropouts between 1980 and 2000 was due to immigration (in addition to
about 10 percent of the increase in the proportion of them in prison). As
the authors write, "As immigrants disproportionately increased the supply of workers in a particular skill group, we find a reduction in the

wage of black workers in that group, a reduction in the employment rate, and a corresponding increase in the incarceration rate."[17]

If immigration caused one third of the decline in black men's employment, then of course two thirds of it was caused by other factors. Wilson found a variety of concerns expressed by Chicago employers (including black employers) about hiring inner-city black men: "Employer comments about inner-city black males revealed a wide range of complaints, including assertions that they procrastinate, are lazy, belligerent, and dangerous, have high rates of tardiness and absenteeism, carry employment histories with many job turnovers, and frequently fail to pass drug screening tests."[18] Whether or not employers exaggerate these concerns, and whatever other factors are involved, it's undoubtedly true, as Borjas and his colleagues wrote, "We would have witnessed much of the decline in black employment and the concurrent increase in black incarceration rates even if there had been no immigration in the past few decades."[19]

But the ability of government to effect change in many of the areas of concern is limited; huge expenditures have not halted the decline of urban schools, for instance, while other problems are the bailiwick of society rather than government. Immigration, however, is one important area where government *can* make a difference, increasing incentives for constructive work by preventing mass immigration from artificially flooding the job market with low-skilled workers.

Inner-city black men are not the only ones being displaced from the job market by immigration. Young Americans are obviously also natural candidates for entry-level jobs—students looking for summer or part-time jobs, or recent entrants to the job market (whatever their level of education) who still do not have much work experience. Researchers at Northeastern University have concluded, "It appears that employers are substituting new immigrant workers for young native-born workers. The estimated sizes of these displacement effects were frequently quite large."[20]

These researchers found that between 2000 and 2005, the number of young (ages 16 to 34) native-born American men who were employed fell by 1.7 million, while the number of new male immigrant workers grew by 1.9 million. This was not because there were fewer young American men, but rather because "the ability of the nation's teen and young adult (20–24) population to become employed has deteriorated badly over the past five years."[21]

ECONOMIC PROGRESS BY IMMIGRANTS

In addition to native-born minorities, young workers, and others, a final group of people marginal to the economy is harmed by ongoing mass immigration into a modern economy: earlier immigrants. As management theorist Peter Drucker wrote, "Immigrants have a mismatch of skills: They are qualified for yesterday's jobs, which are the kinds of jobs that are going away."[22]

Over the entire course of this new wave of immigration that started in the 1960s, the immigrant population has been doing steadily worse relative to Americans; in other words, although immigrants increase their earnings during their time in the United States, the gap between their earnings and those of the native born has been steadily growing for decades. For instance, while immigrant men earned slightly more than their native-born counterparts in 1960, by 1998 they earned fully one quarter less.[23] Another way to look at this is to note that in 1970, the percentage of immigrants and native born who lived in or near poverty (double the official poverty level or less) was the same, at about 35 percent. The mismatch between immigrant skills and the needs of a modern economy has caused a gap to develop and grow steadily, until in 2005, when the total of the poor and near-poor among Americans had fallen to 29 percent, the poor and near-poor accounted for fully 45 percent of the immigrant population.[24]

Of course, maybe the widespread poverty we see in the immigrant population is just a statistical illusion; that is, maybe because there are lots of recent immigrants (who are unfamiliar with America and know little English), they skew the averages and make the trends look bad even for long-term immigrants. If this were true, then the trends for long-term immigrants would be different.

But they're not. We can see this by comparing the native born to established immigrants, those here between ten and twenty years, thus long enough to learn the ropes in their new country, but not so long that they'd be retired and earning less. Such a comparison shows a steady deterioration in the position of these established immigrants, both in the proportion living in poverty or near-poverty and in the proportion owning their homes.[25] In other words, each successive group of immigrants, even after decades of living here, is falling further and further behind the American mainstream.

George Borjas found the same thing when looking at successive groups of young male immigrants and how each did over time.[26] Those who arrived in the late 1950s started somewhat behind their American counterparts, but by 1970 actually had higher incomes. The group that came in the late 1960s started somewhat further behind the American average (partly because the American average had by then increased), and made slower progress, never quite catching up. Those who arrived in the late 1970s started even further behind the native born, and closed some of the gap, but not as much as those who came before them. And those who came in the late 1980s not only started even *further* behind the native born than their predecessors, but they didn't catch up at all during the 1990s, instead seeing the gap between their incomes and those of the mainstream get even wider. As Borjas puts it, "the waves of immigrants who made up the Second Great Migration had lower starting wages *and* lower rates of economic assimilation."[27]

The story of immigrant economic progress doesn't end with the immigrants themselves, of course; perhaps the more important question is whether the *descendants* of the original immigrants do better over time and catch up with the mainstream. Here, too, the mismatch between mass immigration and modern society is making itself felt. Borjas has found that the children of immigrants (the second generation) tend to advance their economic standing relative to the mainstream (Americans of the third generation and later) by five or ten percentage points.[28] The problem is that as each successive group of immigrants is more and more out of sync with the needs of a dynamic modern economy, they are starting life in America further behind the mainstream—so their children, although doing better than their parents, are doing less well in relation to the rest of America. Borjas found that the typical second-generation man in 1940 earned about 18 percent more than other native-born workers; that advantage shrank to about 15 percent among the second generation working in 1970, and to 6 percent in 2000.

This evidence of a growing mismatch bodes ill for the children of today's immigrants, since the wages of the immigrant parents in 2000 were some 20 percent behind the mainstream. If the pattern holds, then the children of today's immigrants will never catch up, still having in the year 2030 incomes 10 to 15 percent *below* the average for other native-born Americans.

And even this unhappy projection of immigrant advancement over the generations may be too optimistic, because it assumes that the same economic and other conditions apply now as in the past. But, as Borjas notes, the social mobility we saw in the twentieth century "was shaped by unique historical events and by social and economic circumstances that may be difficult to replicate in the future."[29] But the one circumstance we *can* replicate is the low level of immigration that prevailed during the middle of the twentieth century, thus tightening the labor market for all low-skilled workers, including the immigrants already here. As Borjas put it, "This moratorium could have provided a 'breathing period' that may have fueled immigrant social mobility by cutting off the supply of new workers to ethnic enclaves, and by reducing the economic and social contacts between the immigrants and the various countries of origin."[30]

INCOME INEQUALITY

In addition to the harmful economic consequences for particular groups of people, mass immigration affects society as a whole by swelling the ranks of the poor, thinning out the middle class, and transferring wealth to the already wealthy. In other words, mass immigration increases economic inequality.

Income inequality is not in itself a bad thing. In the tenth Federalist Paper, James Madison traced its source to "different and unequal faculties of acquiring property," and accepted it as simply a part of the human condition that had to be accommodated. Americans have long shown a greater tolerance for income inequality than people elsewhere because, unlike most other nations, the sin of envy manifests itself in Americans more usually as an aspiration for personal advancement rather than a leveling desire to bring others down. As the *Economist* magazine put it, "Whereas Europeans fret about the way the economic pie is divided, Americans want to join the rich, not soak them."[31] In other words, Americans have generally—and correctly—placed more stock in equality of opportunity than equality of result.

Likewise, the actual measures of economic inequality often exaggerate the problem.[32] They do not take account of noncash benefits for the poor, which amount to a transfer of hundreds of billions of dollars in assistance for health care, food, and housing from the top half of earners (who are the source of virtually all tax revenues) to the bottom half. Also, the distribution of income is skewed by the fact that those at the top simply work more hours than those at the bottom.

Nevertheless, as President Bush has said, "The fact is that income inequality is real; it's been rising for more than 25 years."[33] This steady growth in income inequality cannot safely be dismissed. Tocqueville noted the importance of "the general equality of condition among the people" in shaping both the government and civil society in the United States. While perfect equality of result is neither possible nor desirable, too great a degree of inequality can give rise to social dysfunction. Research has found that greater economic inequality is related to less social trust and civic engagement, less political participation, higher crime, and worse health.[34]

And inequality has unquestionably been growing during the course of this latest wave of mass immigration. One measure of inequality is the Gini coefficient, which ranges from a value of 0 (perfect income equality, where each 1 percent of the population earns exactly 1 percent of total national income) to a value of 1 (perfect *in*equality, where one person earns all the income, and everyone else has zero income). So, the bigger the number, the greater the inequality. By this measure, the United States has seen its traditionally high degree of income inequality grow further; Census Bureau figures show the Gini coefficient climbing steadily from .399 in 1967 to .466 in 2001.[35]

This may not seem like much, but it means that there was a significant increase in the share of the nation's income that went to the top earners. The highest-earning fifth of the population went from receiving about 44 percent of all income in 1967 to more than 50 percent in 2001, while the top 5 percent of households went from 17.5 percent of all income to more than 22 percent. All other groups saw their share of national income decline.[36] The reason this happened is that the real after-tax income of the poorest one fifth of Americans rose by 9 percent between 1979 and 2004, while that of the richest one fifth rose by 69 percent, and that of the top 1 percent rose by fully 176 percent.[37]

Interestingly, the graph tracking the share of national income going to the top 1 percent of the population follows very closely the graph showing the foreign-born share of the population—both are high in the 1910s and 1920s, then fall steadily until about 1970, and then start rising steadily.

Overlapping graphs don't prove anything in themselves. There's a variety of factors that contribute to increased income inequality, most of them manifestations of the modern world—such as growing international trade and outsourcing, technological change, and postindustrial economic restructuring.

But if modern society is bound to experience some increase in economic inequality from unavoidable causes, there is all the more reason not to exacerbate that trend through an optional federal policy of mass immigration. And yet that is precisely what we're doing; in the words of a scholar from the liberal Brookings Institution, "It seems likely that immigrants are contributing to widening income inequality in the United States."[38] It could not be otherwise, given that mass immigration "benefits high-skilled workers and the owners of capital but not low-skilled workers or those who do not own capital."[39]

Between 1989 and 1997, immigration and children born to immigrants accounted for 75 percent of the increase in the poverty population.[40] This has led to a situation in which immigrants and their native-born young children accounted for 23 percent—nearly one in four—of all the people in the United States living in poverty in 2005, thus swelling the number of people at the bottom of the income distribution. And children with immigrant mothers account for fully 27 percent of all children in poverty.

In California, the state most heavily affected by the current immigration wave, real wages for the top tenth of male workers grew 13 percent from 1969 to 1997, while the bottom quarter saw its real wages fall 40 percent during the same period. The Public Policy Institute of California found that the leading causes of this phenomenon were the increasing share of immigrants in the workforce and falling wages for less-educated men (a phenomenon itself partly caused, as we have seen, by an abundance of low-skilled immigrant labor).[41]

Looking at growing inequality from another angle also shows the impact of immigration. Although the concept of the middle class is extraordinarily broad and hard to pin down, an examination of the 1990 and 2000 censuses demonstrates a link between mass immigration and a declining percentage of middle-income households.[42] All the states in the study experienced a decline in the percentage of middle-income families during the 1990s, but the decline was largest for states with the greatest increase in immigration. The same was true for metropolitan areas—more immigration equals a smaller middle class; over the 1990s, the metro areas with the largest share of immigrants in the population saw the proportion of low-income households (those in or near poverty) increase, while the low-immigration metro areas saw their low-income shares decrease. So, while other factors also play a part, immigration is an important reason for increased income polarization.

One need not be a socialist to sense that the growing, immigration-induced gap between rich and poor, approaching the stratospheric levels of income inequality seen in Brazil and Mexico, is moving us away from the kind of society modern America aspires to. In this regard, Michael Lind has written that mass immigration contributes to the "Brazilianization" of our society and has noted the "striking dependence on immigrant menials by the families of the upper-middle and upper classes, whose lifestyle could not be sustained without a supporting cast of deferential helots."[43] Though we're not quite there yet, mass immigration under modern conditions is actually moving us *backward,* toward a master-servant, plantation-style economy, more reminiscent of the antebellum South or today's Persian Gulf sheikhdoms than of the middle-class commercial republic we imagine ourselves to inhabit.

SLOWING INNOVATION

The preceding discussion focused on the impact of mass immigration on workers—how it reduces their wages and crowds them out of the job market, and causes increased inequality. But is an artificially bloated low-wage labor market at least good for business? Spokesmen for the U.S. Chamber of Commerce, the National Restaurant Association, the California Farm Bureau, and others would have you believe the answer is yes, and in the short term, that's likely to be the case. Employer organizations spend enormous resources lobbying the government to import a "reserve army of labor," to use Marx's phrase, so that they can hold down their labor costs and avoid unionization.

But in the longer run, the superabundance of cheap labor harms the future competitiveness of industries where the immigrants are most heavily concentrated. The entire history of economic development— starting with the first ape-man to pick up a stick—is a story of increasing the productivity of labor, so each worker is able to create more and more output.

But capital will be substituted for labor only when the price of labor rises, something the federal government's mass-immigration program is specifically intended to prevent. A 2001 report by the Federal Reserve

Bank of Boston highlights this problem by warning that a new wave of low-skilled immigrants over the course of this century may slow growth in U.S. productivity.[44] By artificially holding down the natural process of wage growth in labor-intensive industries, mass immigration thus serves as a kind of subsidy for low-wage, low-productivity ways of doing business, retarding technological progress and productivity growth. In effect, mass illegal immigration is an unintentional, but very real, Luddite force in our economy.

Germany experienced the same thing when it imported large numbers of Turkish and Yugoslav workers in the 1950s and 1960s; as two of the foremost scholars of immigration have written, "Economists began reporting that the program was slowing investments in automation and mechanization, so that 'Japan [was] getting robots while Germany [got] Turks.'"[45]

That this is so should not be a surprise. Julian Simon, in his 1981 classic, *The Ultimate Resource,* wrote about how scarcity leads to innovation:

> It is all-important to recognize that discoveries of improved methods and of substitute products are not just luck. They happen in response to scarcity—a rise in cost. Even after a discovery is made, there is a good chance that it will not be put into operation until there is need for it due to rising cost. This point is important: Scarcity and technological advance are not two unrelated competitors in a Malthusian race; rather, each influences the other.[46]

This is true for copper or oil, and just as true for labor—as wages have risen over the generations, innovators have devised new ways of substituting capital for labor, increasing productivity to the benefit of all. The reverse is also true; the artificial superabundance of a resource will tend to remove much of the incentive for innovation.

Stagnating innovation caused by mass immigration is perhaps most apparent in the most immigrant-dependent activity—the harvest of fresh fruit and vegetables. Academic researchers have warned about the long-term viability of the industry: "New technologies and mechanization appear to offer the only solution to significantly reduce production costs and maintain competitiveness," write three prominent agricultural economists.[47] But immigration is an obstacle to adoption of such technologies, according to Orachos Napasintuwong, an economist at the University of Florida: Because of "the augmentation of labor supply through unauthorized foreign workers . . . the incentive for new labor-saving technologies is reduced from what it would be in the absence of international labor mobility."[48]

It wasn't always this way. The period from 1960 to 1975 was a time of considerable agricultural mechanization, precisely because it was a period of relative scarcity of agricultural labor, roughly from the end of the Bracero program, which imported Mexican farmworkers, to the beginning of the mass illegal immigration we are still experiencing today.[49] During hearings on the proposed termination of the Bracero program in the early 1960s, California farmers claimed that "the use of braceros is absolutely essential to the survival of the tomato industry." But Congress ended the program anyway, causing harvest mechanization to accelerate; as a result, the production of tomatoes grown for processing (juice, sauce, and so forth) actually *quintupled,* demand for harvest labor dropped 89 percent, and the real price of tomato products fell.[50]

But a continuing increase in the acreage and number of crops harvested mechanically did not materialize as expected, in large part because the supply of workers grew artificially large due to the growing illegal immigration wave that the federal government was unwilling to stop.

An example of a productivity improvement that "will not be put into operation until there is need for it due to rising cost," in Simon's words, is in raisin grapes.[51] The production of raisins in California's Central Valley is one of the most labor-intensive activities in North

America. Conventional methods require bunches of grapes to be cut by hand, manually placed on trays for drying, manually turned, and manually collected.

But starting in the 1950s in Australia (where the climate was suitable but there was no large supply of foreign farm labor), farmers were compelled by circumstances to develop a labor-saving method called dried-on-the-vine (DOV) production. This involves growing the grapevines on trellises, then, when the grapes are ready, cutting the base of the vine instead of cutting each bunch of grapes individually. This new method radically reduces labor demand at harvest time and increases yield per acre by up to 200 percent. But this high-productivity, innovative method of production has spread very slowly in the United States because the mass availability of foreign workers has served as a disincentive to farmers to make the necessary capital investment. In fact, fully half a century after their invention, DOV methods are still used for less than a third of California's raisin crop.

And it's not just raisins. Florida citrus farmers have belatedly come to realize that they can never drive down their labor costs enough to match producers in the third world; as the *New York Times* writes, "Facing increased competition from Brazil and a glut of oranges on world markets, alarmed growers here have been turning to labor-saving technology as their best hope for survival."[52] Mass immigration enabled farmers to avoid making such a commitment for many years, meaning that in 2006, only about 5 percent of Florida's orange groves used mechanical harvesting.[53]

Florida's sugar cane harvest is a good example of how farming modernizes when immigrant labor is no longer cheap.[54] In the 1930s, Eleanor Roosevelt decried the working conditions endured by sugar harvesters—using a machete, bending at the waist, dealing with heat, mosquitoes, and snakes—which had changed little since the Middle Ages. It was so bad that in 1942, U.S. Sugar was actually indicted on federal charges of slavery because of its treatment of black American cane-cutters.

As a result, the sugar companies began to import West Indians through a federal guest worker visa program. But starting in the 1980s, the industry was hit by a persistent wave of lawsuits filed on behalf of farmworkers whose contracts had been violated by their employers, contracts that guaranteed a certain level of pay along with housing and transportation. Despite years of farmers' claims that it was impossible to mechanize the harvest of sugar cane, these lawsuits raised the real cost of employing the foreign labor so much that the farmers finally concluded that it would be more profitable to mechanize than to honor all the legally required terms of the farmworker contracts. So, by the 1997–98 growing season, U.S. Sugar, the biggest producer, harvested 100 percent of its cane by machine, resulting in increased productivity, plus higher wages and more civilized working conditions for the remaining harvesters.

The threat to the continued competitiveness of U.S. agriculture posed by mass immigration doesn't come just from the inability to compete on the basis of wages with third-world countries; there is also the danger that the slowing of technological innovation brought about by artificial infusions of labor will allow our economic competitors in other *developed* countries to leap ahead of us. This is perhaps most disturbing in the field of robotic harvesting.[55] Automated picking of fruits and vegetables by a robotic system is the third wave of agricultural mechanization (after labor aids, which facilitate harvesting work but don't reduce labor demand, and labor-saving machines, which improve productivity and reduce labor needs). The development of viable robotic harvesting technologies is still in its infancy, but great progress is being made. Unfortunately, because of the mass availability of alien labor in the United States, the European Union is well ahead of us in bringing this potentially revolutionary technology to market.

Mass immigration's role in retarding economic modernization is not confined to agriculture, which is, after all, very different from the rest of the economy. Other parts of the economy experience the same phenomenon of a scarcity of low-skilled labor yielding innovation, while a surfeit yields stagnation. An example of the latter: A 1995 report on Southern California's apparel industry warned of the danger to the industry of reliance on cheap immigrant labor:

> While a large, low-cost labor pool has been a boon to apparel production in the past, overreliance on relatively low-cost sources of labor may now cost the industry dearly. The fact is, southern California has fallen behind both domestic and international competitors, *even some of its lowest-labor-cost competitors,* in applying the array of production and communications technologies available to the industry (such as computer aided design and electronic data interchange).[56]

As with agriculture, the limited academic inquiry that has been made into manufacturing has found that mass immigration is slowing the spread of labor-saving technology. An economist at the Federal Reserve Bank of Philadelphia has written that "plants in areas experiencing faster less-skilled relative labor supply growth adopted automation technology more slowly, both overall and relative to expectations, and even de-adoption was not uncommon," adding that the effect was even stronger when the growth in less-skilled labor came specifically from immigration.[57] That's *deadoption*—some factories actually *stopped using* labor-saving technology once immigration drove down the price of labor sufficiently. A purer example cannot be found of the conflict between mass immigration and the goals of a modern society.

Home construction is another field in which modernization is slowed by mass immigration. The form this modernization takes is modular construction. Modular, or prefab, homes are manufactured in pieces in the controlled environment of a factory, protected from the weather and meeting exact specifications. The modules are then trucked to the building site and assembled and finished off, resulting in a much higher-quality product than a "stick-built" home (one constructed from scratch on-site), and one that is completed faster with much less labor.

Technological advances mean that such buildings are nothing like the trailer homes of the past, and the methods can be used even for luxury residences. According to Gopal Ahluwalia, director of research at the National Association of Home Builders, "In the long run, we'll see a move toward homes built in factories."[58]

But the home-building industry has moved very slowly to embrace this transformative technology. According to a 2002 report from the Massachusetts Institute of Technology, "The housing industry is fragmented, resistant to change, labor intensive, inefficient, unresponsive, and wary of new processes and technologies" and "is far behind other industries in the adoption of new process and technology innovations."[59] As a result, only 3 percent of new homes are built using modular construction.

The demand that does exist among builders for modular construction is driven by labor costs. As one modular home manufacturer put it, "With our systems, it's almost always about labor when we sign up a new builder."[60] But although labor costs have been increasing, they're lower than they would be otherwise—because of mass immigration. In the words of one building magazine, "Immigrant labor has for years seemed like a bottomless cornucopia of workers."[61]

Even in the service sector, there is enormous potential for labor-saving measures that have been rendered less attractive because of the artificial glut of cheap foreign labor. After all, immigrants were not imported to pump gas, so now Americans pump their own gas, aided by technology that lets buyers pay at the pump—thus there are fewer attendants but more gas stations, and customers get in and out faster than before. Likewise with bank tellers, many of whose routine functions are now performed by ATMs, and telephone operators, most of whom were long ago replaced by automated switches.

There are plenty of other innovations in the service sector that would spread more quickly if the low-skilled labor market were tightened through lower levels of immigration: Continuous-batch or "tunnel" washing machines can reduce labor demand for hotels, restaurants can install ordering kiosks, movie theaters can use ATM-style devices to sell tickets, the retail industry can adopt increasingly sophisticated vending machines as an alternative to hiring more immigrant clerks.

As science fiction as it might seem, many Veterans Administration hospitals are now using mobile robots to ferry medicines from their pharmacies to various nurse's stations, eliminating the need for workers to perform that task.[62] And devices like automatic vacuum cleaners, lawn mowers, and pool cleaners are increasingly available to consumers.

These last examples point to perhaps the greatest competitive threat from mass illegal immigration: its inhibiting effect on the development and spread of robotics. Japan's society is aging much more rapidly than our own because of its much lower birthrate, but it has decided not to import large numbers of foreign workers, investing instead in robots. Media coverage of this development has focused on cute robotic pets, but this is no laughing matter—Toyota in 2006 announced a major initiative to augment workers with robots at all its Japanese plants, robots much more sophisticated than the thousands of less-advanced devices it already uses for hazardous jobs like welding and painting.[63] And the automaking giant plans to start retail sales of household robots by 2010, which the firm expects to become one of its major business units.[64] Without a change in immigration policy, we run the risk of future observers noting that "Japan got robots while America got Mexicans."

Historian Otis Graham tied together the impact of mass immigration on American competitiveness and on its workforce: "The U.S. can either evolve towards a high-technology economy with a labor force of constantly advancing productivity, wage levels, and skills, or it can drift towards a low technology, low-skill, and low-wage economy, marked by widespread job instability and growing income disparity. Immigration policy will be important to the outcome."[65]

WHAT ABOUT SKILLED WORKERS?

Assuming all this is true, why not just import lots of skilled workers instead? Perhaps our immigration problems would be solved if we didn't reduce the numbers but simply reoriented policy to select only educated people, essentially ending Mexican immigration, and replacing it with an increased flow of Chinese and Indians.

Many critics of current immigration policy take this approach, some suggesting a point system for selecting future immigrants, a version of which was included in the ill-fated Senate amnesty bill of 2007. Such an arrangement, used in Canada and Australia for a portion of their immigrant flows, would award points to prospective immigrants based on various characteristics, such as educational attainment, occupation, and knowledge of the destination country's language. Any applicant who exceeded a minimum number of points, say 70 out of 100, would be granted an immigrant visa.

While the specifics of an immigration policy consistent with the goals and characteristics of modern America will be outlined in the final chapter, it's necessary to spell out here why mass immigration of skilled foreigners would also be incompatible with our modern society.

First, in a practical sense, the less skilled are more likely to want to leave their home countries in search of job opportunities than the skilled, so that continued high levels of skilled immigration are unsustainable. People who can expect a bigger jump in their income and a greater improvement in their overall standard of living naturally have more to gain from moving abroad.

Research confirms that the less-educated see a much larger increase in their earnings because of immigration. A project called the New Immigrant Survey looked at a sample of people receiving green cards (i.e., becoming lawful permanent residents) and found that those who had never been illegal aliens were more educated and more likely to speak English than those who had been illegal aliens at some point in the past (one out of five of the new legal immigrants had been illegal at one time). Compared to the last job they held in their native country, men in the more educated group saw a significant 52 percent increase in their income. But those men in the less-educated group enjoyed a huge 175 percent increase, almost tripling their incomes after immigration.[66]

Germany learned of the finite demand for immigration among the highly skilled. During the 1950s and 1960s, it imported huge numbers of unskilled Turkish and Balkan workers. But when it launched an immigration initiative in 2000 to attract only high-skilled immigrants, the 20,000 available slots for foreign computer specialists were never all used, even after the government repeatedly extended the program.[67]

DEPENDS WHAT THE MEANING OF "SKILLED" IS

The second thing to keep in mind is that "skilled" means something very different now than it did in the past. A century ago, simply screening out illiterates notably increased the educational level of the immigration flow; an immigrant who had actually graduated from high school would have been more educated than the vast majority of Americans.

The whole context has changed today. Only 8 percent of native-born Americans are high-school dropouts (compared to 30 percent of immigrants), while nearly 30 percent of the native born have a bachelor's degree or higher (compared to about 27 percent of the foreign born). Because the average American is much more educated than before, the standards for judging the educational level of immigrants must also be increased.

This is important because the economic benefit from immigration, such as it is, comes from the difference between the skills of immigrants and the skills of natives: as noted earlier, those against whom immigrants compete for jobs lose, while the rest benefit, and the difference between the amount lost and the amount gained is the net economic benefit to the country. Currently, the benefit is small and comes at the expense of the most vulnerable of our countrymen and of future innovation, and in any case is swamped by the education and social-welfare costs incurred by the government because of low-skilled immigration.

But an immigration program targeted at selecting skilled immigrants would have to result in an immigration flow that was dramatically different—i.e., dramatically *more* skilled than native-born Americans—

because if the immigrants' educational profile ends up being the same as that of Americans, their presence will increase the size of the economy, but it won't yield any economic benefit to the country. In the words of the National Research Council report, "It is only because immigrants and native workers differ from one another that immigration yields a net national gain. These differences between natives and immigrants, which may well be a legitimate source of concern about the ability of immigrants to assimilate socially and culturally [referring here to low-skilled immigration], are the very reasons why the nation gains economically from immigration."[68]

So if 30 percent of Americans have at least a bachelor's degree, then to create a benefit for the economy, new immigrants would need to have an average level of education that was much, *much* higher—say 60 or 80 percent of them having at least a bachelor's degree. But this would be virtually impossible, because a large part of the immigration flow must always consist of people admitted regardless of their skills—spouses and minor children of American citizens, for instance, as well as refugees, not to mention the spouses and minor children of the skilled immigrants themselves, whose educational attainment is not a factor in their admission. So, in order for the total immigration flow to make up for these groups who are not selected for their skills and still have a sufficiently high average level of education to create a meaningful net economic benefit for the nation, the number of skilled immigrants admitted would have to be huge, beyond anything world demand for immigration to the United States could ever sustain—there just aren't that many millions of PhDs in the third world.

What's more, a policy of mass skilled immigration that sought to benefit the nation as a whole would have to be careful to admit only people who brought what economists call their "human capital" with them—i.e., people who had already completed their education. Much of today's skilled immigration is made up of people who acquire their education *here*—foreign students who arrive without a college degree or with only a bachelor's degree, to make use of our very heavily subsidized system of higher education, and who later finagle a way to stay permanently. Under current law, the various employment-based immigration categories are where education and job skills are taken into account; in 2005, nearly 90 percent of the immigrants awarded permanent residency under these categories already lived here, many (perhaps most—the government won't say) having originally entered as students enrolling at our universities.

And the subsidies received by all students, even those paying full tuition, are huge. The average subsidy, using data from the mid-1990s, was more than $8,000 per student per year, covering only one third of the cost of higher education; at top-tier schools, the subsidy can amount to as much as $50,000.[69] This subsidy is paid by American taxpayers and American alumni. In the 2005–2006 school year, there were about 565,000 foreign students at American colleges[70] (these are foreigners admitted on a student visa, not immigrants who go to college after moving here)—at an average subsidy of $8,000, that would represent an outlay by Americans of more than $4.5 billion to subsidize the education of foreign students. A subsidy of that size is, in Borjas's words, "sufficiently large to outweigh any of the productivity benefits that foreign students presumably impart on the nation."[71]

A third concern related to mass skilled immigration is that even if it were possible to generate a sustained, highly educated flow from abroad, it would reduce the incentives to improve America's educational system and even cause distortions in it. A century ago, industry needed warm bodies to man the factories, and no institutional infrastructure is needed to create those. But a postindustrial economy requires an extensive educational system to prepare future workers—elementary and high schools, community colleges, private technical schools, and colleges and universities. The problems in our schools need little elaboration: inner-city schools that fail to impart even the skills for functional literacy, American students lagging behind those in other countries in almost every subject, universities wasting students' energies on frivolous and absurd topics.

But with mass skilled immigration, what incentive would there be for American business, the single most important interest group in local, state, and federal politics, to work for improvements in our educational system? The point is not which reforms are most appropriate—maybe enhanced school choice is an answer, or maybe more money and training for teachers, or maybe other things entirely. But if business is able to count on continuing mass immigration to fill its skilled positions, then it loses its stake in the success of America's educational system. And nothing is guaranteed to bring about the continued decline of American schools more certainly than the indifference of business to the outcome.

Borjas explores the hypothetical case of mass skilled immigration and comes to some troublesome conclusions about its distorting effects on educational choices. He calculates that after a decade and a half of admitting 1 million college graduates a year, the wages of native-born college graduates would be reduced by 15 percent.[72] And since the financial payoff would be so much smaller from the time and money invested in getting a college degree (plus the lost income you could have earned, had you been working), he estimates enrollment in college by American young people would plunge by 15 to 30 percent, with the largest drops among the most disadvantaged students. The logical conclusion of such an immigration policy would be that attending college would become a "job Americans won't do."

Borjas adds a final point about college graduates seeing their wages cut by 15 percent that should end any consideration of mass skilled immigration: "It is also worth adding that such a wage cut would make it difficult, if not impossible, to muster much political support for an immigration policy that admitted one million skilled workers annually."[73]

NOT BY BREAD ALONE

But stepping back from these economic arguments against a policy of mass skilled immigration, it's necessary to note that immigration cannot be judged solely by its effects on wages and employment. Different kinds of immigration will clash with different aspects of modern America, explored by the different chapters in this book. English-speaking immigrants, for instance, may present less of an assimilation burden because they already know the language; immigrants from distant countries may present less of a challenge to our sovereignty than those from nearby countries; and at a given level of education, illegal immigrants impose fewer costs on taxpayers than legal immigrants, because they are not eligible for most government programs.

So it is with educated immigrants. They would, for instance, likely be a net plus for government coffers. Despite the fact that educated immigrants are much more likely than educated Americans to be uninsured and use welfare,[74] the fact remains that they have much higher incomes than uneducated immigrants and thus pay more in taxes and use fewer government services. The National Research Council estimated that the average lifetime fiscal impact of an immigrant with more than a high-school education would be $105,000.[75]

But mass skilled immigration presents other challenges. This book's chapter on demography, for instance, decries the social-engineering aspect of federal immigration policy—overturning the American people's revealed preference in the modern era for a slower-growing population. This is true whether or not the immigrants have college degrees.

Likewise, most of the concerns outlined in the chapter on national security focus on the overall level of immigration, regardless of educational attainment. In fact, one issue not explored in that chapter is that high levels of skilled immigration sponsored by the high-tech industry may represent a special threat to America's security. As former defense secretary Donald Rumsfeld put it, "Because we're so dependent on satellites, we're so dependent on information technologies, the most advanced nation in the world almost becomes the most vulnerable to attacks against those systems."[76] The vulnerability created by the nexus of skilled immigration and this advanced technology has already been exploited for purposes of espionage,[77] making sabotage in time of war that much more likely. Note that this is a problem specific to modern conditions—importing foreign talent in the nineteenth century to improve cannon-making, for instance, simply could not have presented the same problems.

Most important, perhaps, is the assimilation challenge that would be posed by mass skilled immigration. This may seem like an odd concern; after all, educated immigrants are more likely to know English, or at least have a greater likelihood to pick it up, than uneducated immigrants. Likewise, educated immigrants are, almost by definition, more likely to find relatively well-paying jobs that will allow them to settle into the home-owning, middle-class mainstream of American society.

But while speaking English and getting a job are important first steps to assimilation, they are not sufficient for the development of the deep emotional and psychological attachments that this book's chapter on the subject calls patriotic assimilation. There are a couple of reasons that educated immigrants may actually pose a *greater* challenge for patriotic assimilation than the uneducated. The first is that they have greater resources to take advantage of the modern opportunities to live a transnational lifestyle—to live simultaneously in two (or more) countries at the same time. This means their ties (and their children's ties) to the old country are less likely to atrophy, making it less likely that their affections and attachments will end up being redirected to their new country.

Two scholars who have examined a survey of new immigrants put it this way: "The picture that emerges from this analysis is of a fluid and dynamic global market for human capital in which the bearers of skills, education, and abilities seek to maximize earnings in the short term while retaining little commitment to any particular society or national labor market over the longer term."[78] Another study found that "regardless of nationality, transnational immigrant organizations' members are older, better-established, and possess above-average levels of education. . . ."[79]

The survey of new immigrants suggests a second assimilation-related concern about educated immigrants: "Those with high earnings and U.S. property ownership are actually *less likely* to intend ever naturalizing; and those with high levels of education are least likely to express satisfaction with the United States, and for this reason both are groups of people less likely to plan [on] becoming U.S. citizens or settling permanently."[80]

In other words, the more educated and the more prosperous are less likely to want to commit to any one nation, including this one. This is related to, but a little different from, the first issue; it's not just a question of flitting about in "a fluid and dynamic global market for human capital," but instead a sense that the immigrants don't feel the need to join America because they already belong to something else.

This second concern relates to how the immigrants identify themselves—specifically, whether they come here already in possession of a fully formed national identity. While humans have always seen themselves as belonging to one or another kind of community, the development of national identity is a modern phenomenon. Philosopher Ernest Gellner, for instance, specifically ties nationalism to the needs of a modern, industrial society.[81] The idea that national identity needs to be cultivated and developed comes out in the famous aphorism related to the unification of Italy in 1861: "We have made Italy, now we must make Italians." What Italians, or any other national community, are made out of is people who have a wide variety of subnational or prenational attachments—people who think of themselves mainly in terms of different regions or religious communities or tribal groups.

When we talk of patriotic assimilation, we mean cultivating in immigrants an American national identity. But this can be much more difficult to accomplish in the case of those newcomers who *already* have a national identity than for those who arrive here not yet having developed one, still seeing themselves in terms of tribe or clan. And it is precisely the more educated immigrants who are more likely to have acquired an alternate sense of national identity in their home countries, because they are products of modern urban life and have already made their way through a modern educational system.

We actually have some experience with this in our history. One indicator of having been "nationalized" is knowledge of the nation's standard language, often artificially constructed from one of the many dialects spoken by the prenational peasantry. Immigrants from Italy, for instance, started coming here in large numbers when the project of making Italians was still a work in progress. Though Italy's schools taught the standardized version of the Italian language, based mainly on the dialect of Tuscany, and educated people in Italy all knew this version of the language, those who immigrated to the United States generally had little education and thus little exposure to the nationalizing influence of Italy's schools. The result: "In the United States, immigrants from one area of Italy could not understand their new neighbors from another area; they were reduced to speaking a mixture of the little standard Italian they knew, combined with words from one or another of the dialects and from English."[82] This linguistic arrangement—the development of an Italian American dialect—represented an important fact: Many immigrants from Italy went straight from being Sicilians or Calabrians to being Italian Americans, without ever having actually been Italians, at least not in any emotional or psychological sense, and this happened precisely *because* they were uneducated.

We clearly saw the contrast between prenational and nationalized immigrants when refugees from various nations in central and eastern Europe came here after World War II, joining immigrant communities that had seen few newcomers in a generation. The older communities had been established by pre–World War I immigrants from peasant backgrounds with little education, often speaking rural dialects; for them and their American-born children, their Hungarianness or Lithuanianness was mainly a matter of folk traditions, distinctive cuisine, and religious affiliations. Because such expressions of ethnic heritage did not constitute a modern national identity, they did not pose too much of an obstacle to the immigrants and their children developing a strong sense of American national identity, especially in the context of strong pressures for Americanization from the broader society.

But the post–World War II refugees were much more likely to be educated, urbanized, and thus nationalized—possessing a fully formed national identity, which many were not ready to discard for a new one. One example: "The earlier immigrants had been chiefly peasants unaware of the Belorussian heritage, but the post-1945 immigrants were predominantly professionals, artisans, and skilled workers. Moreover, because these new immigrants had been educated during the national renaissance in both Soviet Belorussia and Poland, they were fully aware of their Belorussian identity."[83]

It was the same with Serbs: "The earlier settlers had been illiterate or barely literate peasants, with rarely more than four years of elementary education. The postwar newcomers were often graduates of high schools, technical schools, and even universities, and their literary Serbian contrasted with the peasant dialects of the earlier settlers." The result? "Now, in a fundamental way, the process of Americanization has been interrupted."[84]

This concern over immigrants who have already gone through the process of modernization and have a competing national identity is today no longer limited to the educated. As modernization has spread around the world, governments even in less-developed countries have successfully used the media and the schools to shape their people's attachments and impart to them a modern national consciousness. But among many of the uneducated, the process remains incomplete; there are probably still many peasants in India, for instance, or Guatemalan highlanders who lack any modern sense of national identity. But there are few such people among the educated, urban classes who would be the source of any hypothetical scheme of mass skilled immigration.

CHAPTER 5

Government Spending

The conflict between mass immigration and modern America may be most evident when studying government services. The combined spending by federal, state, and local governments accounts for almost one third of our total economy, a figure many times larger than during prior waves of immigration. This includes welfare spending, of course, but also spending on schools, roads, criminal justice, and other tax-supported activities.

The problem this poses was summed up by Nobel Prize–winning economist Milton Friedman: "It's just obvious that you can't have free immigration and a welfare state."[1]

Importing millions of poor people with large families means that, by definition, they will pay relatively little in taxes but make heavy use of government services. This is true not because of any moral defect in the immigrants or any meaningful differences between today's immigrants and those of the past. Instead, it is *we* who have changed—our modern society embraces a larger role for government, expecting it to underwrite a broad system of social provision for the poor, education for the young, support for the elderly, a large portion of the nation's medical care, and many other functions.

There is no way to avoid this conflict between mass immigration and the functions of modern government—the welfare state and other aspects of big government are inherent to modern society. Efforts to trim government and make welfare policy less morally problematic may well succeed to some degree; the 1996 welfare reform, for instance, is generally acknowledged to have been a success, and perhaps other such measures are possible.

But whatever measures we might take in the future to limit the size and scope of government, big government in some form or another is never going away. As one welfare scholar has put it, "Transfer or redistribution policies are a pervasive, if not predominant, government activity in all modern societies."[2] And that means that mass immigration can never stop being a drain on public coffers.

The fiscal threat that immigration now poses did not exist in earlier eras, when government was much smaller. In 1901, for instance, the entire federal budget totaled $525 million, equivalent to about $13.5 billion in 2006 dollars.[3] By 2006, the nation's population had quadrupled, but the federal budget reached $2.7 *trillion*, 200 times larger, in real terms, than in 1901.[4]

That means that a century ago, during the previous wave of mass immigration, the federal government spent roughly $178 a year per American, in today's dollars, while today it spends about $9,000—a fifty-fold increase in the amount of government per person.

This huge growth in government is apparent in other statistics as well. For instance, federal spending accounted for less than 3 percent of the economy in 1900 but grew to 20.1 percent in 2005. Government has also grown at the state and local levels; the combined spending of all levels of government—federal, state, and local—has grown from about 8 percent of the total economy in 1900 to 31 percent in 2005.[5]

WELFARE

A large part of this growth in government has been the development of the welfare state—the extensive system of government support for the poor. There was no welfare state during prior waves of mass immigration—in fact, it wasn't until well after the end of the last great wave of immigration in 1924 that the institutions of the welfare state began to develop.

As the late journalist Richard Estrada put it, "From the late 1920s through the mid-1960s, the period when the welfare state went from swaddling clothes to its Sunday best, the levels of immigration were virtually negligible. Today, they are at their highest levels in U.S. history."[6]

The Social Security Act of 1935 established old-age pensions (what we usually mean when we talk about Social Security), as well as unemployment assistance and Aid to Families with Dependent Children (which was renamed in 1996 as Temporary Assistance to Needy Families, or TANF). The current Food Stamp program was established in 1964. Medicare and Medicaid were established in 1965. The Child Nutrition Act of 1966 created the WIC program, short for the Special Supplemental Nutrition Program for Women, Infants and Children. Then in 1974 came Supplemental Security Income (SSI) for the indigent elderly, blind, and disabled.

Whatever concerns many conservatives have with these New Deal and Great Society programs, the costs of some of them would have remained more manageable had the poor population not increased. Instead, the United States saw a surge in immigration, mainly of poor and unskilled people with big families. That makes them just like the immigrants of the past, of course, but also just the kind of people this new welfare system was designed to subsidize.

The low level of education among immigrants is clear. In 2005, about 30 percent of all immigrants in the workforce lacked a high-school education, nearly quadruple the rate for native-born Americans.[7] Well over half (55 percent) had no more than a high school diploma. The largest immigrant group by far—Mexicans—had the lowest levels of education, with 62 percent of working-age Mexican immigrants having less than a high-school education, and only 5 percent having a college degree.[8]

In a modern economy, people with very little education generally earn very low wages, with limited opportunities for advancement, and this holds true for immigrants. In 2005, immigrants were nearly half again as likely to be in poverty than natives—17 percent of immigrants had incomes below the official poverty line (about $20,000 for a family of four), compared with 12 percent of native-born Americans.[9] When immigrants' U.S.-born young children are added (which makes sense, since they live in the same household), the immigrant poverty rate is more than 18 percent.

Nearly half of immigrant households—45 percent—were in or near poverty, meaning their income was below 200 percent of the poverty level, compared with 29 percent of native-headed households. The near-poverty benchmark is important because people whose incomes are below that level generally don't pay federal income taxes and are usually eligible for means-tested welfare programs.

Mexicans—the largest and least-educated immigrant group—are also the poorest, with nearly two thirds living in or near poverty and more than one in four actually below the poverty line.

The result of this widespread immigrant poverty is widespread immigrant welfare use. Among households headed by native-born Americans, 18 percent use at least one major welfare program. That's already quite high, of course, but among immigrant-headed households, the rate is half again as high, at almost 29 percent.[10] Immigrant use of cash assistance programs[11] is only a little higher than among Americans, while the gap is larger for use of food stamps and government-owned or -subsidized housing. The biggest differences are in WIC and subsidized school lunches, which immigrants are more than twice as likely to use, and Medicaid (health insurance for the poor), which immigrants are about two thirds more likely to use.

These welfare programs combined cost federal taxpayers some $500 billion a year, most of which is for Medicaid. This is significant because it is in Medicaid—the biggest and most expensive welfare program—where the gap between immigrants and the native born is the biggest. Use of most of the other welfare programs, whether by

Americans or immigrants, is mostly in the single digits; but Medicaid is used by fully 15 percent of native-born households and an astounding 24 percent of immigrant households (and 37 percent of Mexican immigrant households).

Underlining the mismatch between mass immigration and the modern welfare system is the extraordinarily high immigrant eligibility for the Earned Income Tax Credit (EITC). The EITC is available only to people who work, and it functions as a kind of negative income tax—those who file a tax return have their EITC check calculated automatically by the IRS, based on their income and family size. In its surveys, the Census Bureau estimates whether people are eligible for the EITC, so the number of people actually receiving it is probably somewhat lower, but the figures are quite high nonetheless. More than 15 percent of native-headed households are eligible for this $30 billion program, but nearly twice as large a share (30 percent) of immigrants qualify, including fully half of Mexican-immigrant households.

The EITC was designed as a way to encourage enterprise rather than dependency among the poor. For the same reasons, the 1996 welfare-reform legislation introduced work requirements for certain programs. At the same time, other welfare programs are targeted at helping children, such as WIC, subsidized school lunches, and the State Children's Health Insurance Program (a part of Medicaid). In other words, the modern American welfare system is designed mainly to provide support for the working poor with children.

Who are immigrants but the working poor with children? Immigrants work (in 2001, almost 80 percent of immigrant households using welfare had at least one person working[12]), they're poorer than Americans (see above), and they have more children than Americans (the average immigrant woman has 2.7 children in her lifetime, versus 2.0 for native-born women). In other words, mass immigration is almost perfectly designed to overwhelm modern America's welfare system.

In the words of two welfare scholars, "This very expensive assistance to the least advantaged American families has become accepted as our mutual responsibility for one another, but it is fiscally unsustainable to apply this system of lavish income redistribution to an inflow of millions of poorly educated immigrants."[13]

HEALTH CARE

A specific aspect of assistance to the poor warrants separate treatment. The United States spent more than $2 trillion on health care in 2006, nearly half of the expenditures coming from government at all levels, including Medicare (for the elderly), Medicaid (for the poor), and other costs.[14] Health-care expenditures have been growing by more than 7 percent a year, much higher than inflation, and one of the issues this has brought to the fore is the number of people who lack medical insurance.

Universally available, high-quality medical care is an important value for a modern society, which is why the problem of the uninsured has given rise to many proposed solutions, from a single-payer, government-run system suggested by the Left to expanded "health savings accounts" offered by the Right. It's all the more curious, then, that there's little discussion of how mass immigration subverts our efforts to address this issue. In 2005, immigrants were two and half times more likely to be uninsured than the native born, almost 34 percent versus about 13 percent.[15] In other words, about one out of three immigrants in the United States has no health insurance.

If the number of immigrants were small, this might not make much difference. But because of their huge numbers, immigrants account for a large part of the uninsured problem. One in four people in the United States without health insurance is an immigrant, and among children who are uninsured, one out of three is either an immigrant or the young child of an immigrant.

And immigrants got to be such a large share of the uninsured population because they are responsible for most of its growth. Immigrants and their U.S.-born children account for nearly three quarters of the growth in the uninsured population from 1989 to 2005.[16] Over a different time period, another study found that immigrants accounted for 86 percent of the growth in the uninsured from 1998 to 2003.[17] Looking at only one portion of the immigration population, yet another study estimated that illegal aliens alone accounted for one third of the growth in the number of uninsured adults from 1980 to 2000.[18] It would not be too much to say that the crisis of the uninsured is a creation of our immigration policy.

This large population of uninsured immigrants would be even larger, of course, except that so many immigrants are on Medicaid and thus directly supported by taxpayers. In fact, nearly half (47 percent) of people in immigrant families are either uninsured or on Medicaid, nearly double the rate for native families.

The cost to taxpayers of the Medicaid program is obvious, but immigrants without any insurance at all also impose significant costs on government and on consumers. After all, even the uninsured get sick, and no modern society is going to allow them to go entirely without treatment. This treatment usually happens at emergency rooms; in the words of one recent study, emergency rooms "have become one of the nation's principal sources of care for patients with limited access to other providers, including the 45 million uninsured Americans."[19] (Actually, as we've seen, a large portion of the uninsured are noncitizens, rather than Americans.)

Taxpayers bear some of the costs incurred by the emergency departments of these "safety net" hospitals. Medicaid sends "disproportionate share hospital" payments to hospitals serving the poor, including immigrants; and in the Medicare prescription drug bill, Congress allotted payments of $250 million per year (for four years, through 2008) to the states for treatment provided to illegal aliens.[20] In addition, "A number of states also provide additional support to emergency and trauma systems through general revenues or special taxes."[21]

In California, where households headed by immigrants (legal and illegal) make up the *majority* of the uninsured,[22] emergency departments statewide lost nearly half a billion dollars in 2001–2002, up 58 percent from just two years before.[23] In Texas, where immigrant households account for nearly four in ten of the uninsured, the state's twenty-one trauma centers lost $181 million in 2001 due to unreimbursed costs.

There is no estimate of total health-care costs borne by taxpayers due to immigration overall, but there are a number of estimates regarding just illegal aliens, who represent about one third of the foreign-born population. One estimate of the cost to emergency providers of treating illegal aliens is $1.45 billion, and the cost to counties along the Mexican border nearly a quarter of a billion dollars.[24] Other state-specific estimates: nearly $600 million in uncompensated care for illegals provided by New York taxpayers in 2006;[25] in Florida in 2005, $165 million;[26] in Texas in 2004, $520 million;[27] in California in 2004, more than $1.4 billion;[28] and in Arizona in 2004, $400 million.[29]

These estimates do not include the costs of care provided to uninsured *legal* immigrants—an important point, since the main reason for immigrant poverty, and thus the lack of health insurance, is lack of education, not legal status.[30]

But not all uncompensated care is covered by government, and hospitals must thus write off a portion of the costs of treating the uninsured. Hospitals then shift these costs onto paying patients and their insurance carriers, resulting in higher premiums for those who *do* have health insurance. One report estimated that each American family with insurance through a private-sector employer paid more than nine hundred dollars extra in premiums in 2005 due to the cost of treating the uninsured.[31]

The Emergency Medical Treatment and Active Labor Act (EMTALA) requires all emergency rooms nationwide to screen and stabilize any and all comers, whether they can afford it or not—so when hospitals can no longer shift enough of the costs for uncompensated care to others, they simply close their emergency rooms. This doesn't create a direct monetary cost for consumers, but it does hold the potential to levy the ultimate tax—death—on Americans in need of emergency care. From 1993 to 2003, the number of hospitals with emergency rooms declined by 9 percent, even though the number of emergency room visits increased 26 percent, double the rate of increase in the population.[32] In Los Angeles, more than sixty hospitals have closed their emergency rooms over the past decade.[33]

A 2005 report bleakly summarized the situation: "To the degree that immigration continues to increase, it is likely that the uninsured will also continue to increase as a proportion of the population."[34]

EDUCATION

Another very costly service provided by the government is education. Total expenditures nationwide on all levels of education reached $866 billion in the 2003–2004 school year, accounting for 7.9 percent of the gross domestic product.[35] An indication of how this huge investment in education is characteristic of our modern society is seen in the fact that even as late as 1949, education spending accounted for only 3.3 percent of our GDP.

The role of immigration in increasing the cost of education is especially large because immigrant women are more likely to be in their child-bearing years, and immigrants generally have larger families. So while immigrants constitute about 12 percent of our total population, the children of immigrants (some born here, some immigrants themselves) comprise 19 percent of the school-age population (five to seventeen years old) and 21 percent of the preschool population (four and below).[36] In California, nearly half the children in both age groups are from immigrant families. While more than two thirds of these children are native born, their use of American public schools is a direct result of our immigration policy allowing their parents to enter.

Total school enrollment nationwide reached a post–Baby Boom low of 44.9 million in 1984, and is now at about 55 million.[37] This means that the 10.3 million school-age children in immigrant families account for all—100 percent—of the growth in elementary and secondary school enrollment nationwide over the past generation. Obviously this isn't the case in every school or every town or even every state. But in the nation as a whole, the surge in school enrollments is due entirely to the federal government's immigration policies.

This immigration-driven growth in enrollment has caused over-crowding at many schools. The U.S. Department of Education has found that 22 percent of public schools are overcrowded, with 8 percent of the total being overcrowded by more than 25 percent of capacity. The overcrowding is worst in precisely the kind of schools immigrant children are likely to attend: large-capacity schools in central cities, especially in the West, especially those with more than 50 percent minority enrollment, where the majority of students receive free or reduced-price school lunches (i.e., are from poor families).[38]

The education expenses incurred by this immigration-driven surge in enrollment are huge. One study, which looked at only part of the impact of immigration, found that education of illegal-alien students cost the states $12 billion a year, and when U.S.-born children of illegal aliens are added, the cost more than doubles to $28.6 billion.[39] California was estimated to have spent $7.7 billion on education for the children of illegal aliens, nearly 13 percent of the state's total education budget for 2004–2005.

And this cost estimate did not take into account the extra expense of educating immigrant students as opposed to native-born students; a study conducted some twenty-five years ago found that even then, bilingual education programs cost from $100 to $500 more per pupil, while a more recent look at California found that supplementary programs for "limited English proficient" students cost an extra $361 per student.[40] Another more recent study, of Florida, found that "ESOL [English for speakers of other languages] students cost $153 million in fiscal year 2003–04 beyond what they would have if enrolled in basic programs."[41] Across the nation, this adds up, since about 10 percent of all public-school students are considered limited English proficient, otherwise known as "English language learners."[42]

CRIMINAL JUSTICE

Total spending on justice—including police, courts, and prisons—by all levels of government was $185 billion in 2003, up more than 400 percent from 1982, a growth rate sixteen times greater than the rate of increase in the population.[43]

How much of this cost is attributable to immigration is hard to gauge. The multiplicity of jurisdictions involved means that different information is collected and tallied in different ways. In the words of a recent government report, there is "no reliable population and incarceration cost data on criminal aliens incarcerated in all state prisons and local jails."[44]

Despite the stereotype of immigrants contributing disproportionately to crime, the skimpy evidence that exists suggests that immigrants—both today and a century ago—are no more likely to be involved in crime than the native born, and perhaps less so.[45] But given that there are more than 36 million immigrants, and they are disproportionately young, single men, they will inevitably have a large presence in the criminal justice system and create large costs. This is all the more a concern, given research that finds the likelihood of an immigrant being incarcerated grows with longer residence in the United States[46] and that the U.S.-born children of immigrants are dramatically more likely to be involved in crime than their immigrant parents. For instance, native-born Hispanic male high-school dropouts are eleven times more likely to be incarcerated than their foreign-born counterparts.[47]

The costs at the federal level are easier to calculate, consisting of expenses incurred housing aliens in federal prisons plus the grants made under the State Criminal Alien Assistance Program (SCAAP), which reimburses certain states and localities for a small part of the costs they incur when incarcerating certain illegal aliens. About one quarter of federal prisoners are aliens, and when combined with the reimbursement program, the Government Accountability Office estimates they cost the federal government nearly $6 billion for 2001–2004.[48] The amount would have been larger had Congress not consistently cut the

SCAAP program, narrowing its scope (now only those illegals held four days or more can qualify) and cutting the number of cents on the dollar it reimbursed.

There are some estimates of state costs for illegal aliens; New York, for instance, was estimated to have spent $165 million,[49] Florida $60 million,[50] Texas $150 million,[51] California $1.4 billion,[52] and Arizona $80 million.[53] Large as the costs are, they include only prison costs, not jail costs (prisons hold offenders for more than one year; jails are the local facilities where people are kept for shorter periods of time), nor the costs incurred by police or the courts, nor the monetary losses suffered by the victims. At least as important is the fact that these estimates count the incarceration only of illegal aliens, not the rest of the immigrant population.

NET COSTS

Of course, all these costs might not matter if all immigrants were highly productive, earning high wages, paying large amounts in taxes, and making only modest demands on government services. Immigrants, legal and illegal, pay taxes, of course—income and payroll taxes, sales and excise taxes, property taxes (included in their rent), and many others. But given their low levels of education and consequent low incomes, and their large families and heavy use of services, it is a mathematical inevitability that today's immigrants create a burden on taxpayers—not because they're especially different from yesterday's immigrants, but because *we* are from our predecessors.

Heritage Foundation scholar Robert Rector has calculated that in 2004, low-skill immigrant households (those headed by an immigrant with less than a high-school education), paid more than $10,000 in all taxes (federal, state, and local) but received in services more than $30,000, representing a net burden on American taxpayers of nearly $20,000 per household per year.[54] In fact, he found that since the average earnings of low-skill immigrant households in that year were just under $29,000, "the average cost of government benefits and services received by these households not only exceeded the taxes paid by these households, but actually exceeded the average earned income of these households." Rector calculated the total tax burden created by such households at more than $89 billion each year. Furthermore, the average lifetime cost to the taxpayer of *each* low-skilled immigrant household is $1.2 million.

The high stakes for taxpayers are made clear by this one fact: "It takes the entire net tax payments (taxes paid minus benefits received) of one college-educated family to pay for the net benefits received by one low-skill immigrant family. Each extra low-skill immigrant family which enters the U.S. requires the taxes of one college-educated family to support it."[55]

An earlier study of this issue was *The New Americans,* a landmark 1997 report by the National Research Council.[56] Although the numbers are certainly bigger now, the report found that immigrants of all kinds (legal and illegal, high-skill and low-skill) create a net burden on government at all levels of between $11 billion and $22 billion a year, swamping the presumed net economic benefit that immigrants create (by lowering the wages of the poor) of between $1 billion and $10 billion per year. The report also calculated the costs incurred by immigrants in two very different states, California and New Jersey. The average immigrant-headed household in California used almost $3,500 more in state and local services than it paid in taxes, amounting to an extra tax burden for each native-headed household of nearly $1,200 per year. New Jersey, with a more ethnically diverse and more highly educated immigrant population, still saw the average immigrant family consume nearly $1,500 more in services than it paid in taxes, increasing the tax burden for each native-born family by more than $200 per year.

The report also estimated the lifetime cost of an immigrant based on different educational levels. It found that the average immigrant high-school dropout would cost American taxpayers a total of $89,000 over his lifetime, and that an immigrant with only a high-school degree would still cost taxpayers $31,000. An immigrant with education beyond high school, though, was estimated to create a fiscal benefit of $105,000 over his lifetime. Given the mix of immigrants the United States takes in, the report estimated a net lifetime cost to taxpayers of $3,000 per immigrant.

In addition to these real-world cost estimates, the National Research Council report also included a kind of thought experiment, projecting the net fiscal effect not only of the immigrant but also of his descendants for three hundred years into the future. Even after three centuries, the balance sheet of taxes paid versus services used for an immigrant high-school dropout and his posterity would *still* be negative, to the tune of $13,000. This mathematical game did find that other immigrants and their descendants would be a plus, adding up to a total benefit to taxpayers over a period of three hundred years of $80,000 for the average immigrant.

Although supporters of mass immigration latched onto the three-hundred-year projection's net plus for taxpayers, the report's authors warned, "It would be absurd to claim that the projections into the 23rd century are very reliable." As another scholar has written, "We cannot reasonably estimate what taxes and benefits will be even 30 years from now, let alone 300."[57]

Notwithstanding this parlor trick, the lesson of *The New Americans* is the same as Milton Friedman's—"It's just obvious that you can't have free immigration and a welfare state." Other, more narrowly focused, research has made the same point. For instance, a 2005 study found that "in Florida the net burden on state and local governments from immigrants is on the order of $2,000 per immigrant household."[58] A nationwide study looking only at illegal aliens found that they cost federal taxpayers about $10 billion more in services than they paid in taxes, and the gap is even larger at the state and local levels, since that's the source of most services used by immigrants.[59] Estimates of the net cost of illegal immigration at the state level (just for public education, health care, and incarceration) point to the same problem: a net cost to New York taxpayers of $4.5 billion in 2005; Florida, nearly $1 billion; Texas, $3.7 billion; California, nearly $9 billion; and Arizona, more than $1 billion.[60]

A final aspect of the issue of government services is different from what's been discussed above. There is a huge existing investment in public infrastructure that immigrants immediately benefit from without ever paying in to—like joining a club without a buy-in fee. These public assets—built over the years with the taxes of Americans—include roads, navigable waterways, ports, subway systems, and airports, plus things like water treatment plants and sewage systems, national parks, public beaches, and other public lands, schools, universities, and libraries, as well as government buildings and military bases.

In a smaller America with a smaller public sector, immigrants weren't inheriting quite as much when they showed up. In fact, the previous period of mass immigration in our nation's history—about one lifetime's worth of mass inflows from the late 1840s to the early 1920s—was precisely the period when our country underwent the urbanization and industrialization (which immigrants contributed massively to) that led to the creation of such a large public infrastructure in the first place. But now that America has completed that process and reached maturity, continued mass immigration simply represents a gift of billions of dollars in infrastructure to new immigrants, a kind of inheritance tax on Americans, lessening the value of their share of the public assets bequeathed them by their ancestors.

WHAT TO DO?

Given that current immigration policy ensures that immigrants will be a fiscal burden, is there a way out? Is there a way a modern nation can undertake mass immigration without soaking the taxpayer?

The most simplistic suggestion comes from utopian libertarians, whose slogan is "Immigration *sí,* welfare *no!*" In other words, if there's a problem with immigrants using welfare, the solution is to abolish welfare. In the words of libertarian journalist Tom Bethell, "a few million more 'undocumented' newcomers may just about finish off the welfare state: one more argument for an open border."[61]

Looking at the actual numbers, the Heritage Foundation estimated that "in order for the average low-skill household to be fiscally solvent (taxes paid equaling immediate benefits received), it would be necessary to eliminate Social Security and Medicare, all means-tested welfare, and to cut expenditures on public education roughly in half."[62]

Needless to say, this isn't going to happen, because despite widespread desire for reform, the American people don't want to abolish the welfare system (let alone cut education spending in half). A detailed examination of public-opinion surveys shows that Americans have embraced the idea of some kind of government system of social provision for the poor.[63] In a 1939 article accompanying a poll on public expectations of government, *Fortune* magazine wrote, "In 1929, beneficence would probably not have been accepted as a proper function of government. But today it is emphatically held desirable."

There has been no change in this view over the generations. The compilers of the survey of polls wrote, "The stability of opinion on the central issues in this debate is nothing short of astonishing." When presented with the statement "It is the responsibility of the government to take care of people who can't take care of themselves" in almost two dozen surveys from 1987 to 2001, a majority of respondents agreed in every survey, from a low of 56 percent agreement, up to 74 percent.

The "astonishing" persistence of support for some sort of welfare system demonstrates that it is an inherent part of modern society. (And pollsters don't even bother to ask the public whether they support abolition of the public schools or public highways, since the answers are obvious.) Despite wide support for work requirements, concerns about illegitimacy, and ambivalence about the effectiveness of welfare programs, the idea of abolishing the welfare system altogether is nothing more than a fantasy.

Well, if we don't abolish big government, would shrinking it break the connection between mass immigration and huge tax burdens? Again, the answer is no. Grover Norquist, one of the most active advocates for smaller government (and, improbably enough, a vocal supporter of open borders), laid out a plan in 2000 to cut the size of government's role in the economy by half in twenty-five years.[64] The success of such an extraordinarily ambitious plan would reduce government from one third of the economy to one sixth. Put aside the inconvenient fact that, nearly one third of the way along Norquist's twenty-five-year timetable, government has only gotten bigger; but if by some miracle this plan were to come to fruition, we would still have a multitrillion-dollar government sector—and Milton Friedman's basic insight would still be valid.

Perhaps instead of relying on utopian schemes to abolish government as a way of limiting the fiscal fallout of immigration, we might leave government services essentially intact but simply wall off the immigrants, denying them access. This is the heart of the idea of turning away immigrants who are likely to become a "public charge," a principle in American immigration law dating back to colonial times.[65] This principle holds that foreigners who cannot support themselves should be kept out of the country, or if already here, deported. In reality, the public-charge provision is most useful in denying people access to the United States in the first place, rather than removing those already here; some 10 percent of visa applicants are rejected on public-charge grounds, whereas during the entire decade of the 1980s, only twelve aliens were deported on those grounds.[66]

Two laws passed in 1996 sought to reinvigorate the principle that immigrants shouldn't be using welfare. The Illegal Immigration Reform and Immigrant Responsibility Act increased the qualifications to sponsor an immigrant (i.e., promising to support the immigrant if he falls on hard times, rather than letting him use welfare), and made the sponsorship agreement, called the "affidavit of support," a legally enforceable contract.

Meanwhile, the immigration-related parts of the big 1996 welfare-reform law (the Personal Responsibility and Work Opportunity Reconciliation Act) tried to limit immigrant welfare eligibility. The law kicked immigrants already here off SSI and food stamps (though that was never fully enforced), and future immigrants were barred for five years from most means-tested benefits.

Welfare reform in general appears to have worked in shrinking

some programs and encouraging work. But the immigrant-specific provisions did nothing to reduce immigrant welfare use. First of all, there
were numerous exceptions in the laws (they did not apply to refugees
and asylum recipients, for instance) and Congress almost immediately
rolled back certain provisions (eliminating the ban on SSI for immigrants here before the law's passage and allowing food stamps for the elderly, children, and the disabled). Also, many states (particularly those
where immigrants are concentrated) took up the slack, since it was a
state option to provide Medicaid and TANF to noncitizens—resulting
in nothing but a shifting of the processing of the welfare benefits from
federal to state bureaucrats. Finally, the national-origin groups most
likely to receive welfare before the law's passage saw the biggest increases
in naturalization rates after its passage, because once an immigrant at-
tains citizenship, the alien-specific welfare limits no longer apply.[67]

The result of all this was that the experiment in excluding immigrants from the modern welfare system was a failure. After briefly falling in the late 1990s, welfare use was back to 1996 levels within five
years; in 1996, 22 percent of immigrant-headed households used at least
one major welfare program, and in 2001 the figure was 23 percent.[68]
Use of TANF and food stamps did decline, to a level only a little higher
than that of the native born, but this resulted in almost no cost savings
because it was offset by higher costs for Medicaid, the biggest and most
expensive welfare program of all. Five years after welfare reform, the
number of immigrant families using welfare had actually *increased* by
750,000, accounting for 18 percent of households on welfare, up from
14 percent in 1996.

In a broader sense, it's simply out of the question for our modern
society to do what it takes to prevent fiscal costs from immigration. Immigrants don't just cross a physical border when entering the United
States; they also cross a moral border, entering a nation that will not
tolerate the kind of premodern squalor and inhumanity that is the norm
in much of the rest of the world. Are Americans prepared to allow
people to die on the hospital steps because they're foreigners? No. Are

we going to deny immigrants access to the WIC program? Say the name of the program out loud and you'll get your answer: Americans are not going to deny nutrition to women, infants, and children.

And even barring illegal-alien children from the schools makes the public uncomfortable. A 2006 *Time* magazine poll, for instance, found that only 21 percent of respondents thought illegals should be allowed to obtain government services like health care or food stamps, only 27 percent thought illegals should get driver's licenses, but fully 46 percent thought illegal alien children should be allowed to attend public schools.[69]

Walling immigrants off from government benefits once we've let them in is a fantasy. The 1996 welfare reform was a vast social experiment which taught us two things: First, welfare *can* be made less harmful to the recipient and to society; and second, fine-tuning welfare policy to limit the costs of immigration is doomed to fail.

Perhaps then the answer is amnesty? After all, if illegal aliens (the least educated and poorest part of the immigrant population) were legalized, their wages and tax payments would increase, perhaps solving our fiscal problem.

Again, no. It's true that amnesty would increase the income of illegal aliens, by perhaps 15 percent, which would translate to an increase in their average tax payments to the federal government of 77 percent as not only their incomes rose but also as more of them were paid on the books.[70] But they would remain poor—with an average household income one third below others'—and now, as legal immigrants, they would be eligible for many more government programs and less reluctant to make use of them. The result would be that an amnesty for illegal immigrants would nearly triple the fiscal burden they place on the federal budget, from $10.4 billion a year to $28.8 billion. Robert Rector of the Heritage Foundation has written that, far from saving money, an amnesty "would be the largest expansion of the welfare state in 35 years."[71]

The last option for limiting the fiscal fallout of mass immigration might be to bar the immigration of the uneducated and instead permit mass immigration only of highly educated foreigners. Were this possible, it might well be a fiscal plus; the National Research Council report found that immigrants with more than a high-school education represented a net lifetime fiscal plus of $105,000.

While there is no doubt that educated immigrants are not a fiscal burden like the uneducated, even highly educated immigrants make much heavier use of public services than comparable natives and thus are not the fiscal boon that they could be. Among those with at least a college degree, average incomes are very close—$45,000 for the native born and $42,000 for immigrants. But even at that high level of education, immigrants are still more than twice as likely as the native born to use welfare (13 percent versus 6 percent) and to be uninsured (17 percent versus 7 percent).[72]

Also, the idea of a massive flow composed exclusively of highly educated immigrants is as fantastical as the "immigration sí, welfare no" mantra. It's true that there are a significant number of highly educated immigrants—about 10 percent have graduate or professional degrees, the same proportion as among the native born. But that cannot become a mass flow, because immigrants are people who are dissatisfied with conditions in their homelands—and highly educated people are the most likely to have opportunities that would keep them in their homelands. What's more, immigration is not an atomized process, with unconnected individuals randomly seeking to move here; instead, immigration takes place through networks of family and friends, networks that are not based on education levels or work skills.

More important, the fiscal effect is only one part of the conflict between mass immigration and modern society. Different immigrants will conflict with different goals and characteristics of a modern society—the highly educated are not likely to represent a fiscal burden nor drive down the wages of the poor, but they would, for instance, still be part of the social-engineering project that uses mass immigration to artificially increase our population (see the discussion of skilled immigration in the previous chapter). Also, they might well represent a greater assimilation challenge, not because they won't learn English, but because they are far more likely than the uneducated to have acquired a fully developed, modern national consciousness in their home country—and thus are more resistant than peasants to the adoption of a new American sense of nationhood and more likely to pursue dual citizenship.

CHAPTER 6

Population

F ew people would think of America as having a government policy
regarding population. Many developing countries have tried to slow
population growth, most notoriously China with its one-child policy; at
the other extreme, the Soviet Union used to award the Mother-Hero
medal to women bearing ten or more children. The United States government, on the other hand, has never presumed to instruct Americans
on how many children they should have—nor would Americans take
kindly to such an intrusion.

But just like Communist China and the Soviet Union, the United
States *does* have a government-administered population policy—in our
case it's mass immigration. The settlement of about a million and a half
people per year from abroad—both through the legal immigration program and because the government has chosen not to enforce the laws
against illegal immigration—represents the federal government's decision that Americans aren't having enough children and that therefore
more people must be imported from abroad. As a result, immigration
and births to immigrants together account for at least two thirds of
America's population growth.

There are two reasons this immigration-driven population policy conflicts with our modern society: First, mass immigration is social engineering, an attempt by the government to undo the childbearing decisions of modern Americans and reshape the people more to its liking, directly contrary to the views of the overwhelming majority of the American people. Columnist Charles Krauthammer, for instance, makes this motivation explicit when he writes that Americans are being "saved by immigrants"—saved, in other words, by the federal government from the consequences of their own considered decisions.[1]

The second conflict is that mass immigration, by artificially adding tens of millions of people to the population, undermines a variety of modern quality-of-life objectives that are served by the slower rate of population growth that the American people have freely chosen—objectives such as less-dense living, environmental stewardship, and historic preservation.

And just like the other aspects of immigration, the source of the problem is not them, it's us—mass immigration is incompatible with modern America's demographic characteristics not because the immigrants are all that different from their predecessors, but rather because we Americans of today have made different decisions than *our* predecessors about what we want our society to be like.

SMALLER FAMILIES

One of the hallmarks of a modern society is that it has undergone the "demographic transition"—the shift from the high death rates and high birthrates that prevailed during all prior human history, first to lower death rates but continued high birthrates, and then to low death rates *and* low birth rates. A number of factors are responsible for this: advances in hygiene and medicine, radically lower infant mortality, urbanization, later age at marriage, development of contraceptives, greater access to education and employment for women, and no doubt others. In our country, the number of children the average American woman can be expected to have during her lifetime (what scholars call the total fertility rate) has fallen from about seven children in 1800 to about two today.

This drop in fertility is happening everywhere. As Ben Wattenberg has written, "Never have birth and fertility rates fallen so far, so fast, so low, for so long, in so many places, so surprisingly."[2] In fact, in most developed countries, fertility has dropped so much that the size of their populations will soon start declining, if they haven't already. Demographers calculate that, on average, each woman needs to have slightly more than two children to replace herself and the father (the extra fraction accounts for girls who die before reaching childbearing age). But all the developed countries of Europe and Asia have fertility rates below replacement level; only France, Ireland, and Iceland are even close. In Britain, the fertility rate is about 1.7 children per woman, Canada 1.6, Germany 1.4, Italy, Spain, and South Korea 1.3, Japan and the Czech Republic 1.2, and Taiwan 1.1.[3]

As the birthrates in these countries decline to unheard-of lows, the populations are aging rapidly; the Census Bureau projects that by 2030, half of Italy's population will be older than fifty-two, while in Japan, one out of every nine people will be more than eighty years old.[4] The overall population of many of these countries has already started falling and will continue to fall; Germany's population is expected to drop 10 percent between 2002 and 2050, Italy's by 13 percent, and Japan's by 21 percent.[5]

How to address these extraordinarily low birthrates, and the population decreases and rapid aging that accompany them, is for the people of these countries to decide. But the United States does not face this challenge. U.S. fertility has fallen over the years, of course, but over the past generation it has stabilized at replacement level—just above two children per woman—giving us the highest fertility rate of any developed nation. (Contrary to some claims, the falling birthrate had nothing to do with abortion laws; the fertility rate fell to replacement level by 1972, the year *before* the Supreme Court's *Roe v. Wade* decision.) There have been fluctuations—an increase during the Baby Boom and a drop to below-replacement level for a few years during the 1970s—and there will probably be more fluctuations in the future. But American fertility appears to have more or less stabilized on its own, without any meddling from the government, at the rate needed to maintain a constant population.

Contrary to widespread belief, America's relatively high fertility is not the result of immigration. An analysis of census data shows that in 2000 America's overall fertility rate was about 2.1 children per woman, while the fertility of native-born women was about 2.0.[6] In other words, the immigration of millions from abroad over the past generation raised America's fertility by one tenth of a point (actually a little less, because of rounding), meaning that most of the difference between America and the other developed countries is due not to immigration but to different choices made by native-born Americans.

There's no doubt that immigrant fertility *is* higher than that of native-born women, with illegal-alien women having an average of 3.1 children, and legal immigrants having about 2.6.[7] In fact, fertility actually goes up for most major immigrant groups when they move to the United States; for women in the top ten immigrant groups, birthrates were 33 percent higher than for their counterparts in the old country. And for the largest immigrant group, Mexicans, the birthrate jumps by more than 50 percent after immigration to the United States.

The reason that these higher fertility rates have little impact on the national rate is simple mathematics—America is already a large country, and there just aren't enough immigrants to affect this kind of statistic. Immigrant birthrates would either have to be radically higher than they are, or the number of immigrants would have to be scores of millions larger, to have any appreciable impact on the nation's overall fertility rate.

Mathematics is also the reason that immigration cannot have much effect on the nation's average age and on the future prospects for Social Security, despite much uninformed editorializing to this effect. Part of any nation's modernization is that the age structure of its population changes. In a mature nation, people live longer and fewer children are born, so the elderly share of the population increases, as does the age of the theoretical average person. In 2000, the average age in the United States was thirty-six, compared to thirty-three in 1980.[8]

But the ability of immigration to make the American population as a whole more youthful is extremely limited. First of all, immigrants as a whole are actually *older* than native-born Americans; in 2000, the average age of immigrants was 39, compared to about 35½ for the native born. This is because there are relatively few children who are immigrants and because immigrants grow older like everyone else.

Maybe people are thinking of only *recent* immigrants when they imagine that immigration can make America significantly younger. But here, again, it cannot work. From 1980 to 2000, we experienced the largest wave of immigration that our country—or any country—had ever seen. In 2000, nearly 22 million lived here who'd come over the previous twenty years, and their average age was thirty-three, almost three years younger than the native born.[9] But because America's population is already so large, and the immigrants aren't really *that* much younger than Americans, removing them from the equation has only a trivial effect—it would make America a little more than four months older.

And even if all immigrants who arrived between 1980 and 2000 *and their American-born children* were removed from the equation, the effect would still be minimal—increasing America's average age by about one year.

The reason all of this is true—mathematically inevitable, in fact—is that immigrants can never be young enough or numerous enough to make any difference in such statistics. Only by ensuring that all immigrants arrived as infants and by massively increasing their numbers beyond anything that's even possible could immigration significantly change America's age structure. Immigration has very large impacts in other areas of American society, but it cannot do much to increase fertility and lower the average age of the population at a time when the American people as a whole have already moved to a more modern demographic profile.

But maybe the average age of the population isn't the point. Boosters of mass immigration who point to its salutary demographic effects may have in mind what scholars call the dependency ratio—the proportion of working-age people (usually ages fifteen to sixty-four) compared to the total number of people dependent on them, both older and younger. Of course, there are plenty of working-age people who aren't working, as well as many people over sixty-four (though few under fifteen) who *are* working. Nonetheless, the dependency ratio is a useful way of looking at a society to see how much of its population is likely to be economically productive.

Here again, simple arithmetic ensures that immigration can have only a minimal effect on the working-age share of the population. While immigrants are certainly more likely to be of working age—82 percent versus 64 percent of the native born—the overall national rate isn't affected much by their removal. In fact, if the immigration from 1980 to 2000 had never happened—in other words, we remove all the immigrants and their children from the calculation—the working-age share of the population would fall imperceptibly from 66.2 percent to 65.9 percent.

Even the Census Bureau acknowledges, in its careful, bureaucratic fashion, that immigration is "highly inefficient" in reducing the dependency ratio over the long term.[10]

Nor, despite the frivolous commentary of many pundits, can immigrants help us avoid making reforms to Social Security. When today's workers retire, tomorrow's workers will be the ones to support them through Social Security taxes, just as the taxes paid by today's workers are supporting current retirees. The idea seems to be that we can use immigration to import tomorrow's taxpayers for Social Security.

This also is false. First of all, the Social Security Administration's projections of a large deficit in the future already include the current high levels of more than 1 million immigrants per year.[11] And their projections show that any changes in immigration—either doubling it or reducing it to zero—would have only tiny impacts on the huge Social Security system. And even the small benefit that the Social Security Administration projects to come from immigration is suspect, since the projection uses unrealistically optimistic assumptions about the earnings and tax payments of immigrants—for instance, that immigrant earnings and tax payments are the same as those of Americans from the moment they arrive here.

GROWING POPULATION

Mass immigration doesn't do much to make our country younger or more fertile, but what it *does* do is make it bigger. Immigration is the central force driving the growth in our overall population, which is increasing at a rate of almost 3 million per year. The most recent Census Bureau estimate is that America's population will reach 420 million people by 2050, up from 281 million in 2000 (and a little over 300 million now). The majority of this increase, barring a change in federal policy, will be due to immigration—both immigrants who arrived during that time and children born here to them after their arrival.

The precise effect of immigration depends on the accuracy of the Census Bureau's guesswork in projecting future population growth. Its January 2000 report used four different immigration levels to project four different population possibilities.[12] The problem is that the actual immigration levels are turning out to be between the medium and high levels used by the Census Bureau, meaning that between 2000 and 2050, new immigration (and births to those new immigrants) will artificially boost America's total population by between 76 million (in the Census Bureau's medium scenario) and 170 million (the high scenario). In other words, the federal immigration program will be responsible for the presence of between 76 million and 170 million more people in the United States by the year 2050, compared to the number who would have been here had there been no immigration at all after 2000.

A more recent fifty-year projection finds that it's likely that America's population in 2057 would be 100 million larger than it would be with no immigration.[13] This assumes today's level of net annual immigration (new arrivals minus emigration) of about 1.25 million per year, which would cause the population to grow to 458 million, as opposed to 358 million if there were no immigration between now and then. Net immigration of about three hundred thousand per year (which would be the approximate result of the policy recommendations included in the final chapter of this book) would still cause America's population to increase to 382 million in 2057, "only" 80 million above today's level, but most of it due to the decisions of individual Americans—i.e., births—rather than the federal government's immigration policies.

Of course, immigration also contributed to population growth in the past. But the America of a century ago was by today's standards essentially a third-world country with high fertility among the native born. In the first decade of the 1900s, for instance, the growth of the immigrant population accounted directly for only 20 percent of the increase in America's total population, because the higher, premodern birthrates among native-born Americans drove significant population growth regardless of immigration levels. By contrast, in the first two years of this decade, the growth of the immigrant population accounted directly for 40 percent of the total increase. This needs to be combined with births to immigrant women, which are the other part of immigration's contribution to population growth; immigrant women account for one quarter of all births in the United States.[14] The bottom line is that immigration today is responsible for at least two thirds of population growth.[15]

So what? Don't we have plenty of room? When you look at a map, sure. Our population density in 2005 was 31 people per square mile, less than the global figure of 48 people per square mile and well below the 1,064 people per square mile in Bangladesh.[16] Nor is this just a statistical trick, lumping together a lot of uninhabitable land in Alaska and the western deserts with the rest of the country—683 counties (more than one fifth of the total) actually declined in population during the 1990s.[17] So we would have no problem finding someplace to put 100 million more people.

But there are two problems. First, the American people didn't ask for 100 million more people—in fact, through the accumulation of millions of decisions that American couples have made over the past generation, we have effectively voted for a modern demographic profile and a stable or slow-growing population, not a rapidly growing one. And second, this artificial, politically induced population growth undermines many modern quality-of-life goals we have embraced—preservation of open spaces, for instance, and environmental stewardship, and protection of national parks and historic sites—as well as exacerbating many of the challenges of modern life, such as ever-longer commutes due to sprawl made possible by universal car ownership.

SOCIAL ENGINEERING

During the debate over the pivotal 1965 Immigration Act, the law that helped usher in the current immigration era, policy makers specifically rejected the idea that the proposed changes would restart mass immigration. Attorney General Robert Kennedy, for instance, wrote in the *New York Times* in 1964 that the new immigration bill then being debated "would increase the amount of authorized immigration by only a fraction."[18] His brother, Senate Immigration Subcommittee chair Edward Kennedy (a position he still holds today), assured the nation that "under the proposed bill, the present level of immigration remains substantially the same." And in 1965, new attorney general Nicholas Katzenbach testified that "this bill is not designed to increase or accelerate the numbers of newcomers permitted to come to America. Indeed, this measure provides for an increase of only a small fraction in permissible immigration."

In a textbook case of unintended consequences, the 1965 law touched off the biggest immigration wave in our history. How big? Immigration over the past four decades accounts for more than one third of *all* the people ever to move to what is now the United States, starting with the first Siberian to cross the Bering land bridge in search of game.[19]

The American people have never supported this social-engineering project. Poll after poll has shown that only a tiny minority of Americans want increased immigration, while most want cuts. A 2006 Zogby poll, for instance, found that when presented with the actual level of immigration, only 2 percent of Americans thought immigration was too low, while 66 percent thought it was too high, a result which was consistent across a variety of groups.[20]

The results were similar in another 2006 poll that specifically asked likely voters about immigration's role in population growth.[21] When informed that current immigration policies would add 100 million people to the population over the next fifty years, respondents were asked what the United States should do about the level of immigration; 64 percent wanted to reduce it, while 3 percent wanted it increased. When presented with the statement "The population increase caused by the present level of immigration will negatively impact the quality of life in America, such as causing more congestion, overcrowding and pollution," 66 percent agreed, 31 percent disagreed. And finally, respondents were asked what they thought would happen to the quality of life in their particular communities if those communities experienced the same one third increase in population that immigration would cause for the nation as a whole. Again, the results were overwhelming; 65 percent said quality of life would be worse versus only 7 percent who said it would be better.

And the fact that today's massive wave of immigration is undoing the population choices of the American people is not an accident—it's the whole point of mass immigration for many of its boosters. Ben Wattenberg, for instance, writes that "without a prospering and *demographically growing* example of liberty—America—it would be harder to pursue the continuing growth of liberty [emphasis added]."[22] In other words, if the American people prove themselves unworthy of what Wattenberg calls "the American mission to promote the global growth of individual and economic liberty within a democratic context" by not voluntarily increasing their numbers enough, then foreigners have to be imported to do the job for them.

The constant talk of using immigration to address supposed "labor shortages" is also part of this social-engineering approach. A previous chapter has addressed the incompatibility of mass immigration with the goals of a modern economy; what's important for our purposes here is that the calls by business lobbyists to address perceived labor shortages by increasing immigration (rather than allowing the domestic labor market to work) are simply another way of saying that business is dissatisfied with the performance of the American people, and wants their inadequate breeding efforts to be supplemented by imports from abroad.

This is second-guessing the American people, who have decided, through what one might call the reproductive free market, to have a stable population. Of course, few people consider national population growth when deciding whether and how many children to have, but that misses the point about how markets work. The price of a loaf of bread, for instance, isn't determined by one decision, as the advocates of central planning used to imagine; rather, the price of the bread is determined by the interaction of millions of individual decisions— many not directly related to the bread at all—by farmers, bakeries, trucking companies, grocery stores, consumers, and others, all making separate decisions based on their own situations. The price of bread that eventually arises from this accumulation of actions is neither right nor wrong, but it is the expression of the community—the "revealed preference," as economists say—at that particular time under those particular conditions.

Likewise with the reproductive free market. There is no birthrate that is objectively right or wrong, but the American people have opted, through millions of individual decisions, for a birthrate that would result in slower population growth and eventual stabilization. Who are politicians to second-guess this clear and consistent decision of the American people, a decision made even clearer by survey research showing that Americans overwhelmingly oppose the policies designed to overturn their demographic decisions?

One might object that in a democracy, the people's representatives are elected, so voters get the policies they deserve. But, as a Mexican scholar has written of the United States, "There are a handful of topics where the elites do not act in the interests of Those they govern. Of these, the most notorious is the contentious issue of immigration."[23] As quantified in the study of elite versus public opinion that was discussed in the chapter on assimilation, immigration is the policy area where the views of the governed and their government are farthest apart.[24] And as the fight over the Senate's 2007 amnesty bill showed, only an extraordinary—indeed, unprecedented—public uprising is able to derail the push for increased immigration by a united elite, including Big Business, Big Labor, Big Media, Big Religion, Big Academia, Big Philanthropy, and Big Government.

In a constitutional sense, it is surely true that immigration laws are legitimate, because Congress and the president are duly elected by the voters. But the question here is a political one—whether America's governing elites are acting in the interests of the people. It's especially relevant to the question of social engineering that no politician could get away with justifying continued high immigration by clearly stating its undisputed effects on the nation's population: "I'm voting to send another 100 million people to live in your communities," or "America's cities are insufficiently congested," or "My constituents are making the wrong decisions about childbearing, and those mistakes must be corrected through continued mass immigration."

A small caveat is in order. It's possible that with less immigration, the birthrates of Americans would actually increase. For instance, noted economist Richard Easterlin has long argued that one of the causes of the postwar Baby Boom was the higher wages young people were able to earn at the time because of the tight labor market caused by restricted immigration.[25] More recently, journalist Steve Sailer has tied birthrates to "affordable family formation."[26] His contention is that immigration increases population, and thus population density (since immigrants aren't settling in North Dakota, after all, but in the already-dense big cities). Especially in coastal cities (like Los Angeles, New York, Chicago, and Miami—which is where most immigrants settle), this drives up real estate prices, because there's less room to spread due to the presence of the ocean or lake. And higher real estate prices make it more difficult to afford a suburban home, and thus cause many people to delay marriage and delay or limit childbearing.

A suggestion of how immigration might be suppressing the

birthrates of Americans comes from California, where the fertility of overwhelmingly native-born groups (whites and blacks) went from being above the national average in 1990 to below it in 2002, after the massive surge in immigration during the 1990s.[27]

By the same token, Phillip Longman, in his book *The Empty Cradle,* suggests that one of the things holding down birthrates is what amounts to "double taxation" of those who bear children.[28] His argument is that, by raising children, parents are already ensuring the future viability of the Social Security system, making nonparents "free-riders." Longman's proposal is to reduce Social Security tax payments for parents of minor children, completely suspending such taxes for those with three or more children, until the youngest turns eighteen, but ensure that such parents will be credited toward future benefits as if they'd paid the taxes.

There's been a similar proposal in Congress, called the Parents' Tax Relief Act, which would make changes in Social Security and other taxes for parents of young children.

Such proposals are explicitly intended to be pronatalist—that is, specifically designed to get people to have more children, and thus are little different in intent from other forms of social engineering. But they might more accurately be seen as removing artificial obstacles to potential parents' childbearing decisions, and thus desirable purely as a matter of equity, regardless of the effects—if any—on birthrates.

In any case, if it were to turn out that reducing immigration or making the tax system more equitable resulted in an increase in birthrates among the native born, then that would mean that some of the population growth that would have been engineered by the government through immigration would take place naturally and democratically, as it were. But any effect would likely be small in any case; an analysis of the impact of France's elaborate efforts to boost its birthrates, for instance, has found that they were responsible for an increase of no more than 0.1 child per woman.[29] This means that birthrates here would almost certainly still be near replacement level, and population growth would still be lower than it would be with continued mass immigration.

QUALITY OF LIFE

This brings us to the second issue—that the artificial population growth caused by this government social-engineering program is undermining a variety of modern goals related to quality of life, including cleaner air and water, reduced congestion, and preservation of our nation's natural beauty and historic inheritance.

You don't have to subscribe to the apocalyptic fears of population-control doomsayers to be concerned about this subject. There's no doubt that much discussion of the population issue has been comically mistaken. Most notable, perhaps, was Paul Ehrlich's 1968 book *The Population Bomb,* in which he wrote, "The battle to feed all of humanity is over. In the 1970s and 1980s hundreds of millions of people will starve to death in spite of any crash programs embarked upon now. At this late date nothing can prevent a substantial increase in the world death rate."[30] Needless to say, this did not happen.

Even with 100 million extra people fifty years from now because of immigration, Americans can rest assured there will be enough food. But this engineered population growth *will* subvert many of the quality-of-life goals that modern societies cherish. Thus the real population question for Americans is not whether a Malthusian catastrophe awaits us but rather what kind of life we will bequeath to our grandchildren.

Let's start with conventional environmental matters. In the past, people just weren't all that concerned with how clean the air was or how pure the water. The fundamental reason these issues are now politically important is not because of the hyperventilating of environmental militants, but because the public in modern societies has come to see environmental stewardship as an important quality-of-life issue. Samuel Hays, a historian of the politics of environmentalism, has written that "environmental objectives arose out of deep-seated changes in preferences and values associated with the massive social and economic transformation in the decades after 1945."[31] In other words, as Americans became more prosperous, "Environmental quality was an integral part of this new search for a higher standard of living,"[32] making clean air and water and pristine nature into "environmental amenities." But immigration-driven population growth conflicts with the widely shared and deeply felt desire for such amenities.

The problem is not that the government's program of artificial population growth will choke us with pollutants; on the contrary, several indicators of environmental quality are actually improving.[33] Instead, the environmental progress that can stem from modern technology ends up being eroded, or even wiped out, by the artificially increased number of people.

For instance, the amount of carbon dioxide and other greenhouse gases released into the atmosphere *per person* actually decreased slightly from 1990 to 2005 in the United States. But the *total amount* of such gases went up 16 percent, with carbon dioxide from burning gasoline increasing 22 percent, because there were so many more people.[34]

It's the same with increases in fuel economy. In 1975, cars and light trucks got an average of 13.1 miles per gallon, and in 2006 that had increased to 21 miles per gallon.[35] But any possible reduction in emissions was wiped out by the addition of millions more cars on the road because of population growth, as well as longer commutes (also caused by population growth, which is discussed more fully later).

The pattern is repeated in total energy use. The average amount of energy used by each American in 2006 was about 7 percent lower than in 1979, the peak year, and the amount of energy it took to generate each dollar of national income was fully 44 percent lower.[36] But since there are so many more people, the total amount of energy used—generated mainly by burning coal in power plants—went up almost 25 percent.

Likewise with solid waste—trash. Even though the amount of solid waste generated per person was the same in 2005 as it had been in 1990, the overall amount of trash increased by 20 percent—because there were more people to generate the trash.[37] And the number of landfills to store this waste has been steadily declining for at least twenty years, partly because of increased size and efficiency of modern landfills, and partly because modern Americans don't want new landfills established near their homes. But continual immigration-driven population growth will inevitably keep generating increasing levels of trash, and it will have to go somewhere, creating political conflicts that would otherwise not exist or would be much milder—conflicts among legitimate political forces all seeking legitimate goals but set against one another by the imperatives of artificial population growth.

In the case of water use, the good news would have been much better had it not been for artificial, government-engineered population growth. Per-person water use has actually declined significantly; nationwide, we used slightly less water in 2000 than in 1975, even though the population was almost 70 million larger.[38] But how much larger would the drop in water use have been—and how much additional breathing room could we have afforded stressed municipal water systems, depleting aquifers, and polluted streams—if the drop in per-capita use of water had not been accompanied by such rapid growth in numbers?

Aside from cleaner air and water, another "amenity" whose enjoyment is undermined by mass immigration is protecting open space from development and sprawl. At first blush, the idea that immigration contributes to sprawl can seem more than a little ridiculous. Few of the developers, farmers, preservationists, or others involved in the various land-use fights that go on constantly all across the country are immigrants.

But rigorous examination of what actually causes undeveloped land to be paved over—based on data from the Census Bureau and from the Department of Agriculture's Natural Resources Conservation Service—has found that about 50 percent of the nation's sprawl is caused by land-use factors (zoning, bigger lots, and the like) and 50 percent by population growth (driven mainly by federal immigration policy).[39] In other words, half of sprawl is caused by each person occupying more space and the other half by the presence of ever more people, each one taking up that larger amount of space.

It's important to note that this means even areas with no population growth experience some sprawl. North Dakota, for instance, saw
its population decline 4 percent from 1982 to 1997, and yet the same
time period saw an increase of 6 percent in the state's developed
(paved-over, as it were) land area. But the states with the most rapid
population growth had far and away the most sprawl. For instance,
the ten states with the least sprawl (the smallest percentage increase in
developed land) grew in population only 4 percent during the time
period, while the ten states with most sprawl grew in population by
19 percent.

Likewise, of the nation's one hundred largest metropolitan areas,
eleven lost population between 1970 and 1990, but those eleven together nonetheless saw their urbanized area increase by 26 percent.
However, the eighty-nine other cities that increased in population col-
lectively sprawled 75 percent.

The first component of sprawl—increasing space for each person—
is generally a good thing, the result of modern affluence and technology. For instance, homes have gotten bigger and households smaller, so
that while in 1910 there were 1.13 people per room on average in
American homes, by 1997 that had fallen to only 0.42 people per
room.[40] The average American had nearly 700 square feet of living
space in 1995, more than double the average Japanese. All this is because the size of the average new home has grown, from 1,740 square
feet in 1980 to 2,469 square feet in 2006.[41]

But 100 million more people because of immigration means that
about 40 million more of these increasingly large housing units will
have to be built—and they will have to go somewhere. Either they
will be built on what little open land is left in built-up areas—called
in-fill development—or they will have to stretch ever farther into exur-
bia. Either way, trees are cut down, open land and protected places are
paved over, and people have progressively less access to nature and
green spaces.

Now, there's nothing necessarily bad about preferring bigger
homes. Modern Americans like them because they want the extra

space—a bedroom for each child, a rec room, a home office, maybe an enclosed deck. A 1999 survey found that "Americans overwhelmingly prefer a single-family detached home on a large lot in the suburbs to any other type of home," with 83 percent of respondents preferring single-family detached homes, 6 percent townhouses, and just 2 percent apartments.[42]

Facilitating this modern preference for more space is mass automobile ownership. In 1960, there were 417 cars per 1,000 Americans; by 2004, this had nearly doubled, to 806 cars per 1,000 Americans. As with bigger homes, mass ownership of cars is a good thing, affording drivers more freedom and a greater range of choices. But, assuming the same rate of car ownership, 100 million more people will mean 80 million more cars than today. And however fuel efficient and clean running these cars may become over the next several decades, this would still mean the burning of billions of additional gallons of gasoline and the release of huge additional amounts of noxious gases into our air, not to mention the need for more lane-miles of highway and more parking capacity.

But Americans have made demographic choices that can accommodate these modern preferences for more elbow room and mass mobility. With a stable or slow-growing population, people can spread out without having to pave over too much of the countryside, and still get to work and school and shopping in a reasonable amount of time. But when you combine the modern preference for less-dense living with the rapid population growth that is driven by government immigration policy, the result is increasingly intense competition between conflicting values, forcing us to make trade-offs we would otherwise not have to face, at least not as frequently or as starkly.

One such trade-off is between more living space and proximity to work. As people choose more space, commutes get longer and longer, with a 14 percent increase in the average commute time that people reported just from 1990 to 2000.[43] The Census Bureau has even had to develop the concept of "extreme commutes," lasting ninety minutes or more one way. It is no coincidence that the cities and states with the longest commutes are the very ones that have the largest immigrant populations.

A university report that took a more detailed look than the Census Bureau's broad averages found an even dimmer picture.[44] From 1982 to 2003, the amount of travel that took place during the worst congestion grew from 12 percent of all travel to 40 percent, with the amount of travel time on uncongested roads falling by more than half. The time spent stuck in traffic nearly tripled over that time period, and the number of cities nationwide with severe traffic congestion problems grew from five to fifty-one. What's more, the more populous the city, the more hours each driver ended up spending stuck in traffic.

Of course, it's not that any individual immigrant is responsible for lengthening your commute. Rather, population growth as a whole, driven mainly by the government's immigration policies, is forcing people to undertake longer and longer commutes if they want to enjoy the increased elbow room that modern conditions make possible. In effect, immigration forces us to choose between living like the Japanese, shoehorned into rabbit hutches, or enduring increasingly absurd commutes. More and more of us are picking absurd commutes, but this is a choice forced on us, in part, by federal policy.

Artificial population growth also forces us to choose between preserving important parts of our heritage and providing homes for our fellow citizens. An especially compelling example of this is the "Journey Through Hallowed Ground" corridor, from Gettysburg, Pennsylvania, to Monticello, Virginia, identified in 2005 by the National Trust for Historic Preservation as one of America's "11 Most Endangered Places."[45]

The region has "soaked up more of the blood, sweat, and tears of American history than any other part of the country," according to the late historian C. Vann Woodward,[46] including the Civil War battlefields of Gettysburg, Antietam, and Chancellorsville; the homes of presidents Jefferson, Madison, and Monroe; parts of the old National Road and the Underground Railroad; and much more. The reason for the endangered designation is that this area is in the path of residential development from the rapidly expanding Washington, D.C., area. In the words of the National Trust, "this once-tranquil landscape is being radically transformed by suburban sprawl from the fast-growing D.C. metropolitan area where new subdivisions sprout in the midst of corn-fields, meandering country roads are straightened and widened to accommodate traffic, traditional 'Main Street' towns find their character threatened by incompatible new development, and venerable landmarks are engulfed by sprawl."

Historian James McPherson aptly summarized the threat to this historic area posed by sprawl: "Although the region recovered from the Civil War, it could never recover from the blacktop and concrete revolution that threatens it today. To pave over the northern Piedmont would pave over much of America's past—permanently."[47]

At the same time, property-rights activists have complained of the many restrictions that would result from preservation efforts, such as proposed federal legislation to protect the region's character. Most colorful, perhaps, was Robert J. Smith, a senior fellow at the National Center for Public Policy Research: "This is a transparent effort by 'not in my back yard' elitists to milk millions of dollars from the nation's taxpayers to mandate gentrification of their rural landscape. These bluebloods want their pretty views and bucolic fields preserved in perpetuity at the expense of property rights, small landowners and farmers, and taxpayers."[48]

There are no bad guys here. Home buyers are naturally seeking more elbow room and relief from the rising prices and congestion closer to the city; developers are meeting a legitimate demand for housing; preservationists are trying to prevent the "creative destruction" of capitalism from destroying an irreplaceable inheritance; and property-rights activists are vigilantly trying to maximize the scope of individual freedom. But political conflicts like this are inevitable so long as the federal government artificially promotes population growth through immigration policy.

A similar choice forced on us is between more homes for a growing population and preserving the ability to live among or near trees and other greenery, making for more pleasant and healthier urban and sub-urban living. The historian Hays has written that as America grew after World War II, "Rivers, forests, wetlands, and deserts were seen as valu-able in their natural state as part of a modern standard of living."[49]

And it's true that nationwide we have significantly more forested land than during the nineteenth century; the end of the horse-and-buggy era freed millions of acres that had been devoted to growing hay for feed, causing much of that acreage to revert to forest. In fact, na-tionwide, forested land has been increasing slightly since the late 1980s, reaching 749 million acres in 2002.[50]

But more important for our purposes is the loss of forest cover where people actually live, in metropolitan areas. The group Ameri-can Forests has found that tree cover in urban areas east of the Missis-sippi has declined by about 30 percent over the last twenty years, while the area covered by these urban areas has increased by 20 percent.[51] This spreading development has led to a "tree deficit" of more than 600 million trees—in other words, our country's populated areas are more than 600 million trees short of conservative standards for the amount needed to provide shade, filter runoff, and otherwise maintain livable communities.

And the tree deficit caused by development isn't just a matter of how much rainwater soaks into the ground. As the Society of American Foresters writes, "As more forest land is permanently converted to non-forest land uses, fewer of our citizens will be able to enjoy the physical and spiritual renewal that their ancestors gained by spending leisure time within natural, forested landscapes."[52]

Lest this sound a little too touchy-feely, the human need for nature has been extensively documented.[53] Studies have shown that urban trees cause commercial properties to command higher rents, increase the price home buyers are willing to pay, increase the price shoppers are willing to pay in stores, help to reduce crime, help people heal faster after surgery, and improve job satisfaction and performance for office workers. This is not because of any magical qualities trees possess, but rather because human beings are designed to respond favorably to nature, at least in its benign forms. Thus, in this way too does immigration-driven population growth force us to degrade our quality of life in order to meet the undeniable need for more housing.

The final modern quality-of-life issue that conflicts with mass immigration is personal liberty. This is not about constitutional rights—for example, the right to own property, worship, bear arms, speak, vote, assemble, or petition. Rather, the issue is the more mundane one of increased governmental regulation of our day-to-day behavior. Regardless of population size or density, expanded government is an unavoidable part of modern life—in every country that underwent modernization, as the economy became more complex and people more mobile and cities more anonymous, government grew larger.

But in a mature, modern society, further growth of government, and of government intrusion in everyday life, is partly a function of how many people are packed into a place—more people means more laws. Thus the government's program to increase the population through immigration brings us closer to what Tocqueville called soft despotism, in which the government "covers the surface of society with a network of small complicated rules, minute and uniform, through which the most original minds and the most energetic characters cannot penetrate, to rise above the crowd."[54]

Take parking, as an example. Densely populated cities always, by necessity, have a complex system of parking regulations—rush-hour no-parking zones, loading zones, meters, and fire hydrants, all enforced by an army of (government) meter maids. Less-dense areas have less need for such regulation. But as people flee the congestion and regimentation of the city, the inner suburbs become denser (and more congested and more regimented), causing people to flee yet again.

Population growth doesn't just translate into more meter maids—perhaps worse, it also means a busier legislature. Wyoming, the least-populous state, with about half a million people, has a part-time legislature of sixty House members and thirty senators who meet no more than forty days each year, have no personal staff, and in 2005 were paid $125 per legislative day. In contrast, California, the most populous state, with more than 36 million people, has a full-time, professional legislature of eighty Assembly members and forty senators, receiving the highest pay of any state lawmakers, at $99,000 in 2005, and having permanent staffs, both in the capital of Sacramento and in their districts.

And more-populous states don't just have busier legislatures, but also more distant ones. In Wyoming, each House member represents an average of about 8,300 people, but each California Assembly member represents an average of 450,000 people. Likewise, a Wyoming senator has about 17,000 constituents, while one in California has about 900,000. In which state is a citizen more likely to run into his elected representative at the store or at church or on the street?

The underlying problem here is limited resources, though not in the way people usually mean that. No mineral dug out of the ground is truly limited; as oil or iron, say, become more scarce, their prices will rise, creating the incentive for the development of new sources and substitutes. This means that the last barrel of oil will never be pumped out of the ground, because it will have been rendered worthless long before that by changes in technology and the economy.

But Will Rogers's comment on land applies here: "They ain't making more of it." The natural beauty entrusted to us by the Creator, and the historical treasures bequeathed to us by our ancestors, really *are* limited resources—limited amenities, if you will—for which there are no substitutes or new supplies. A modern lifestyle can be compatible with enjoying these amenities, but not if the government keeps subverting Americans' revealed preference for slower population growth by importing more and more people from abroad.

With continued mass immigration, Americans would have to choose between two goods—either enjoy the modern, spacious, suburban, automobile-based lifestyle that most people aspire to, and kiss those environmental amenities good-bye; or, on the other hand, preserve these amenities by living increasingly cramped, uncomfortable, primitive lives, with more and more draconian government regulation of behavior. Having to make such a choice would not be the end of the world, but it's an unattractive future and not one that Americans have chosen.

CHAPTER 7

What Is to Be Done?

In determining what modern America's immigration policy should look like, there are four questions to answer: How do we control and reduce illegal immigration? How many, and which, legal immigrants do we admit? How do we handle temporary visitors? And how do we treat those immigrants we have admitted to live among us?

PRO-IMMIGRANT MEASURES

The first three of these questions relate to *immigration* policy, but perhaps we should start with the final question, which determines the shape of our *immigrant* policy. Think of immigrant and immigration policies as the X and Y axes on a graph, with high and low immigration on one axis, and pro- and anti-immigrant policies on the other axis. You can see that there are four general approaches to the immigration question:

1. **A PRO-IMMIGRANT POLICY OF HIGH IMMIGRATION.** In other words, admit large numbers of people from abroad, treat them generously, with easy access to welfare and other taxpayer-funded services, and shrink the distinctions between citizens and

noncitizens. This combination is what many people think we have now, though one could argue that mass immigration is itself not particularly pro-immigrant, given the harmful effects it has on the wages and government services of previous immigrants. People in this camp would include most of the Democratic leadership and their Republican echoes, such as President Bush and Senator John McCain.

2. **AN ANTI-IMMIGRANT POLICY OF HIGH IMMIGRATION.** This is what we really have now—take in lots of foreigners, but make sure they don't get too comfortable. This approach has been shaped by the libertarian faction among Republicans. Its anti-immigrant elements include the growing use of guest worker programs, welfare-eligibility bans even for lawful noncitizens whose sponsors are incapable of fulfilling their responsibilities, and lack of sustained investment to maintain an efficient immigration-services bureaucracy. Perhaps the purest expression of this approach came from then-senator Spencer Abraham, who led the fight in 1996 to kill the legal immigration cuts recommended by Barbara Jordan's Commission on Immigration Reform, but replaced them with draconian deportation and welfare rules that were opposed by supporters of the immigration cuts.

3. **AN ANTI-IMMIGRANT POLICY OF LOW IMMIGRATION.** That is to say, admit few immigrants and tighten the screws on those who do get in. This is the caricature of restrictionists, though usually a false one. This approach is often equated with the anti-Catholic Know-Nothing movement of the nineteenth century although, in fact, the Know Nothings were an example of approach number two. The 1856 platform of what was formally known as the American Party did *not* call for limits on immigration, except for paupers and criminals.[1] Instead, the party's goal was only to limit foreigners' access to citizenship by requiring twenty-one years' residence (instead of five years) for naturalization, and barring even naturalized immigrants from holding any government office.

4. **A PRO-IMMIGRANT POLICY OF LOW IMMIGRATION.** The
    final option is this book's recommendation and the approach im-
    plicitly supported by most Americans, whose support for less im-
    migration and tighter enforcement is clear from survey data, but
    who also make up the least xenophobic society in all human his-
    tory. The low immigration part of this approach is clear enough
    conceptually, and the policy specifics will be spelled out below. But
    what would the pro-immigrant part look like?

It should begin at the immigration office. Whatever number of immigrants we admit, they ought to be treated by our government with
professionalism and efficiency. The agency within the Department of
Homeland Security that deals with immigration-processing issues is
U.S. Citizenship and Immigration Services, and it is notorious for its
rudeness, inefficiency, and incompetence. Part of the problem is an unmanageable workload; a 2006 report from the Homeland Security Inspector General's office found that USCIS was incapable of handling its
current workload, let alone dealing with any kind of legalization or
guestworker program that might be passed by Congress.[2] But reducing
USCIS's workload (through immigration cuts) is only the first step
toward improving service. Because Congress has placated noisy business and ethnic interests by increasing immigration, but at the same
time sought to appear frugal with the people's money, it has based the
entire immigration services bureaucracy on user fees, making it extraordinarily difficult for the agency to make up-front investments that
would speed and improve service. For this reason, fees should be set so
they cover only the direct processing costs, with congressional appropriations covering needed technological upgrades as well as investiga-
tion and prosecutions of the endemic fraud.

Expanded English-language instruction is also vital to a pro-
immigrant approach. Most of the debate on language has been over the
noxious policy of bilingual education for school children, but adult
education is the biggest unfilled need. Whatever future changes are
made in immigration policy, helping those already here master English

is imperative, both to promote their attachment to America and to help them better provide for their families.

The 2000 census found that there were 21 million people who didn't speak English "very well," and this is a serious handicap, both to immigrants' economic success and to their Americanization. A large number of people are already enrolled in classes for English as a second language—there are more than 1 million people in Department of Education–funded ESL classes alone, not to mention classes run by various churches, businesses, ethnic associations, and the like. But because of the unprecedented scale of today's immigration, there remains a huge unmet demand; a 1997 Department of Education report found that the number of non-English speakers not in ESL classes but who were "very interested" in enrolling was half again as large as the number of people actually enrolled. By this measure, less than half the demand for English-language training is being met, something confirmed by anecdotal reports of thousands of immigrants on long waiting lists for classes. A more recent report concluded that 5.8 million legal immigrants require 277 million hours of English-language instruction per year for five years, at a cost of $200 million per year.[3]

Along these lines, Stanley Renshon has recommended the establishment of public-private welcome centers for legal immigrants, "whose sole purpose would be to help immigrants and their families adjust to the culture of this country and its institutional practices."[4]

A final pro-immigrant measure is the reduction in future immigration. Though this may seem improbable, a lower level of future immigration will benefit earlier immigrants first, by improving their prospects for jobs and raises and by lessening the burdens on the schools and hospitals they use.

Almost as important as jobs and schools is the fact that a lower level of immigration would make it less necessary to enact some of the tough measures that have been taken or proposed to deal with the ever-growing immigrant population—things like restrictions on access to welfare even for those whose sponsors are unable to meet their obligations, and stringent deportation rules for legal immigrants who commit relatively minor offenses. With less new immigration and a gradually shrinking immigrant population, mass immigration will again be allowed to recede into our history, permitting much more flexibility in the oversight of immigrants. We saw precisely this with the phasing-out in the early 1980s of the requirement for every green-card holder to mail in a postcard at the beginning of each year notifying the immigration authorities of his whereabouts. Also, the public-charge provisions of immigration law—providing for the deportation of immigrants who go on the dole—ceased to be enforced as immigration faded from memory. Whether these are good ideas in principle isn't the point; the fact that such concerns will become less and less salient as immigration pressures ease means their resolution one way or the other will be a matter of much less consequence for the future. Getting them right won't be as important and getting them wrong won't be as dangerous.

ATTRITION THROUGH ENFORCEMENT

On to immigration policy. Most immediate is deciding how to deal with 12 million illegal aliens. In considering this question, we are usually presented with two alternatives: quickly deport all the illegals by force, or legalize them—i.e., amnesty.

But this is a false choice, because there is a third way, and it is the only approach that can actually work: Shrink the illegal population through consistent, across-the-board enforcement of the immigration law.[5] By deterring the settlement of new illegals, by increasing deportations to the extent possible, and, most important, by increasing the number of illegals already here who give up and leave on their own, the United States can bring about an annual decrease in the illegal-alien population rather than allowing it to continually increase. The point, in other words, is not merely to block new illegal immigration through border enforcement (important as that is), but rather to bring about a steady reduction in the total number of illegal immigrants who are living in the United States. The result would be a shrinking of the illegal population over time to the status of a manageable nuisance rather than a crisis.

This is analogous to the approach a corporation might take to downsizing a bloated workforce: a hiring freeze (i.e., stop new illegal settlement), some layoffs (conventional deportations), plus new incentives to encourage excess workers to leave on their own (encouraging self-deportation through stringent controls on what illegals already here are able to do).

This strategy of attrition through enforcement is not a pipe dream. The central insight is that there is already significant churning in the illegal population, which can be used to speed the decline in overall numbers. According to a 2003 report from the Immigration and Naturalization Service, thousands of people are subtracted from the illegal population each year.[6] From 1995 to 1999, an average of 165,000 a year went back home on their own after residing here for at least a year; the same number received some kind of legal status, about 50,000 were deported, and 25,000 died, for a total of more than 400,000 people each year subtracted from the resident illegal population. The problem is that the average annual inflow of *new* illegal aliens over that same period was nearly 800,000, swamping the outflow and creating an average annual increase of close to 400,000. The annual increase is probably larger today, but the principle remains: There is a good deal of turnover in the illegal population, which we can use to our advantage.

Research shows that most illegal aliens are relatively recent arrivals and thus are more likely than people long settled to respond to increased enforcement of the immigration laws. The Pew Hispanic Center has estimated that two thirds of the illegal population (7.3 million people, at the time of the study) had been here ten years or less, and only 16 percent of the population had been here more than fifteen years.[7] And Princeton University's Mexican Migration Project has documented a significant churning in the flow of Mexican illegals specifically, with about 25 percent of them leaving within twelve months of arrival.[8] Unfortunately, that's down from 45 percent twenty years ago, because we have made it so much easier to stay by virtually abandoning interior immigration enforcement and accommodating the presence of the illegal aliens in a variety of ways. As bad as that is, it clearly suggests that illegal aliens do, in fact, respond to changes in government policies.

Another study confirms the responsiveness of illegal immigrants to U.S. enforcement decisions. A researcher at the University of Pennsylvania created a model of the behavior of Mexican illegal immigrants in response to two kinds of policies: more intense border enforcement on the one hand, and increased penalties for employers of illegal workers on the other. He found that tighter controls on employment could cause a 40 percent drop in the existing illegal population over a period of five years, while stricter border enforcement alone caused no noticeable reduction in the existing illegal population.[9]

The goal of an attrition strategy would be to harness these trends to ensure that the outbound flow of illegals is much larger than the inbound flow. This would be a measured approach to the problem, and its proponents need not aspire to an immediate, magical solution to a long-brewing crisis, as the advocates of both mass deportations and amnesty do.

And we've actually seen this work on a small scale already. In the wake of 9/11, there was a "Special Registration" program for visitors from Islamic countries. The affected nation with the largest illegal-alien population was Pakistan, with an estimated 26,000 illegals here in 2000. Once it became clear that our government was actually serious about enforcing the immigration law—at least with regard to Middle Easterners—Pakistani illegals (mostly visa overstayers) started leaving in droves, on their own. They essentially deported themselves to Pakistan, to Canada, and to Europe. The Pakistani embassy estimated that more than 15,000 of its illegal aliens have left the United States,[10] and the *Washington Post* reported the "disquieting" fact that in Brooklyn's Little Pakistan, the mosque was one-third empty, business was down, there were fewer want ads in the local Urdu paper, and FOR RENT signs were sprouting everywhere.[11]

Even enforcement at the state level has resulted in attrition. In New York City, there was a noticeable decline in the size of the illegal Irish population, attributed in part to a state effort to do a better job of denying driver's licenses to illegal aliens. The Irish government estimated that about 14,000 Irish, out of an estimated population of at least 20,000, returned home from the United States in the five years after 2001, a large percentage of whom were likely illegal aliens; compare that with the fact that immigration authorities deported only 43 Irish in 2005.[12] While the strong Irish economy also helped persuade people to go back, the inability to obtain a license, which limits job opportunities and other aspects of a normal daily life, clearly contributed to the attrition of the Irish illegal population.

The same was true for Argentine illegal aliens in Florida, who cited their inability to get a driver's license and travel, in addition to the rebounding economy in Argentina, as factors in their decision to return home.[13] Records from the international airport in Buenos Aires showed that from 2002 to 2005, 35,000 more Argentines arrived from Miami than departed, and the Argentine consulate noted that the number of citizens seeking a certificate of residence to return home had nearly quadrupled over the same time period. In comparison, the immigration authorities apprehend no more than a few hundred Argentine illegal aliens a year.

Legalizing the illegal population, as some suggest—whether it's called amnesty or regularization or normalization or some other euphemism—is clearly no solution at all, since it's an act of surrender that will merely lead to new amnesties in the future. But if our goal is to reduce the size of the illegal population, why not stage a reprise of the ill-named Operation Wetback? This was the 1954 federal government initiative that used neighborhood sweeps to arrest and deport a large portion of the illegal Mexican population, about 1 million people, in an (unsuccessful) attempt to prevent the huge Bracero temporary worker program from resulting in permanent settlement.

It's true that raids at workplaces and elsewhere will always be needed as an enforcement tool (like speed traps or random tax audits in other contexts), because every illegal alien must understand that he or she may be deported at any time. But mass roundups aren't going to happen, for three reasons: First, we simply don't have the capacity to find, detain, and deport 12 million people in a short period of time. And this isn't simply a matter of needing more officers, buses, and detention beds; the invention of new rights for illegal aliens over the past thirty years and the growth of a cadre of activist attorneys and legal clinics whose mission is to obstruct enforcement of the immigration law by any and all means make it much more difficult to remove illegals than in the past. Congress can do much to improve our capacity to deport illegal aliens, by increasing resources and radically streamlining the entire process—from the moment they're apprehended to the time they step onto an outbound plane or bus—but Washington has permitted the illegal population to grow so large that simply arresting them all really is not feasible.

Second, even if we had the capacity to magically relocate the millions of illegals, the economic disruption from such an abrupt change would make the transition more painful than it needs to be for those businesses that have become addicted to illegal labor. There are perhaps 7 million illegal aliens in the American workforce, concentrated in farm work, construction, hotels, and restaurants; their presence was not and is not economically necessary. Our remarkably flexible and responsive market economy can easily adjust to the absence of these illegal workers, but it will take some time. But since new enforcement initiatives will have to be phased in, simply as a practical matter, businesses will have time to adjust.

And finally, political support for a new commitment to enforcement might well be undermined if an exodus of biblical proportions were to be televised in every American living room. As it is, the media and antienforcement political figures would pounce on every misstep by the government, every heart-wrenching story, every inconvenienced employer. Mass roundups would provide such a superabundance of these anecdotes (while media coverage of those benefiting from the new enforcement environment would be almost completely lacking), that it would almost certainly undermine whatever political consensus had developed in favor of immigration law enforcement.

None of this means that a new strategy of attrition wouldn't include a significant increase in deportations. But the numbers of deportations are quite low to begin with, so even a big increase couldn't address the whole problem. In fiscal year 2005, only about 41,000 aliens were actually deported from the interior of the United States, a decrease of 18 percent from the previous year (and most of these were criminals completing their prison sentences, not ordinary illegals).[14] The number of "removals" often reported in the media is much larger (about 204,000 in fiscal year 2005), but that is only because the immigration statistics aggregate actual deportations with findings of "inadmissibility," which is to say, aliens who are not let through immigration checkpoints at airports or land crossings, and so were never living in the United States to begin with. Thus, if there are 12 million illegal aliens and we actually deport only about 40,000 a year, deportations would have to be increased by a factor of 300 in order to solve the illegal-alien problem in this way alone. A more realistic goal of doubling or tripling the number of deportations, as important and as beneficial as that would be, would by itself have only a small numerical effect on the total illegal population. This means that promoting self-deportation is essential.

SEVEN ELEMENTS

While there is a very long list of reforms that would help reduce the illegal population and limit future illegal immigration, seven specific policies are key:

1. End illegal aliens' access to jobs.
2. Secure identification.
3. Ensure that the IRS cooperates with immigration enforcement.
4. Increase cooperation between federal immigration authorities and state and local law enforcement.
5. Reduce visa overstays.
6. Double deportations of ordinary, noncriminal illegal aliens.
7. Pass state and local laws to discourage illegal settlement.

1. The key to preventing illegal aliens from getting jobs is an electronic system to verify immigration status, one that would detect basic identity fraud and determine whether the new hire had the legal right to work in the United States. The Department of Homeland Security has been operating a pilot system for more than a decade now (started by the now-defunct INS) and is working to add more and more participants. Employers have found this Web-based system easy to use, but two changes are needed for it to realize its potential as a deterrent to illegal immigration. The first, smaller change is to enable scanning for identity theft. The system, now called E-Verify, matches the name, date of birth, and Social Security number of a newly hired employee against government databases. Unfortunately, it was not designed to flag multiple uses of the same legitimate name and number; as a result, many illegals successfully secured jobs even with employers who participate in the system, as was made clear during the 2006 raids at the Swift & Co. meatpacking plants. The second, larger change is that participation in the system has to eventually become universal and mandatory, so that there is an even playing field that does not put legitimate employers at a competitive disadvantage. The first step in that direction would be to require all federal contractors to enroll in the system.

2. A modern society needs a reasonably secure means of identifying people—for a wide variety of purposes, of course, but especially for immigration control.[15] Denying legitimate identification to illegal aliens is essential to preventing them from embedding themselves in our society by getting jobs, and so on. Unlike many nations, the United States doesn't have a single national ID card but rather a hybrid federal-state system, based mainly on Social Security numbers on the federal side, and on birth certificates and driver's licenses on the state side. In 2005, Congress passed the REAL ID Act, which established minimum standards for state driver's licenses and nondriver IDs to be accepted for federal purposes (such as boarding an airplane or presenting to a new employer). The act

includes a requirement that states check the legal status of nonciti-zen applicants. Unfortunately, the law left open the possibility of issuing special driving certificates to illegal aliens, documents that could not be used for federal purposes but would nonetheless help illegals embed themselves; Utah and Tennessee are the only two states that have gone this route so far, but the loophole needs to be closed. Even more pressing is the need for a standardized, secure system of vital records (birth and death certificates), which are maintained by the states (and in some states by local officials) and can be used to invent a whole new identity, with which one can obtain a Social Security card, driver's license, and passport.

3. In 1996, the Internal Revenue Service started issuing Individual Tax Identification Numbers (ITINs) to foreigners not eligible for a Social Security number but who had investments here that require them to pay taxes.[16] It also issued these numbers to millions of illegal aliens, who have used them in place of a Social Security number (which they can't legally get) to acquire driver's licenses, bank ac-counts, and mortgages, and generally to embed themselves in Amer-ican society. In 2001, illegal aliens filed more than half a million tax returns using ITINs, claiming more than $500 million in refunds. The IRS refuses to end this practice or to share information with immigration enforcement agents, citing the supposed privacy rights of illegal aliens and its desire for them to file tax returns. Congress must amend the tax code to explicitly permit the IRS to disclose tax information on illegal aliens to the Department of Homeland Secu-rity, just as it already shares information from tax returns with the Department of Education (on student loan defaulters) and the Social Security Administration and the Centers for Medicare and Medic-aid Services (to confirm eligibility for benefits).

4. The seven hundred thousand state and local law enforcement offi-cers around the country encounter illegal immigrants every day in the normal course of their duties, and they have always had the authority to make arrests for violations of immigration law. Facili-tating cooperation between them and the federal immigration

authorities is a vital force-multiplier that can significantly increase apprehension and detention of illegal aliens.[17] A particularly powerful example of the importance of such cooperation is the experience of the Duka brothers, the Albanian Muslim illegal aliens arrested for plotting an attack on Fort Dix; over a period of more than nine years, they had been stopped seventy-five times for various traffic violations, including driving without a license, and never once did police check into their immigration status.[18] Unfortunately, the Bureau of Immigration and Customs Enforcement (ICE), the agency within Homeland Security responsible for immigration enforcement in the interior of the country, has been cool to working with state and local police, partly because such cooperation would dramatically increase the number of illegals it would have to deal with. One important way to expand this cooperation is for ICE to enter into training agreements with more state and local police agencies, so that trained officers are deputized to enforce immigration law beyond the initial arrest authority. Florida and Alabama were the first states to do this, in what is called the 287(g) program, with several other states and localities following their lead. In addition, the federal government must crack down on states and cities that have in place sanctuary laws prohibiting their officers from asking about immigration status or cooperating with ICE.

5. The United States has no good way of knowing whether foreign visitors ever leave, rendering irrelevant the time limits imposed by immigration inspectors. The US-VISIT program is supposed to be an electronic check-in/check-out system for foreigners, and even its very limited rollout so far has shown its worth. But most Mexicans and Canadians (the overwhelming majority of foreign visitors) are exempt from being checked in when they arrive, and only a relative handful of people are checked out, because the exit-tracking is in place only in some airports and seaports.[19] The result is that we still have little idea who is entering the country and almost no idea whether they have left. But reducing illegal immigration requires a

means of determining which foreign visitors have overstayed their permission to stay, because such overstayers account for at least one third of all illegal immigrants—people who did not sneak across the border but were legally admitted and never left. US-VISIT is already providing a level of deterrence as prospective overstayers realize the immigration agency is paying some attention to their movements in and out, and it has been cited by Irish illegals as a factor contributing to their decision to give up and return home. A fully functioning US-VISIT program would generate leads for enforcement agents and would alert immigration inspectors to past lawbreaking if the overstayer eventually leaves and then seeks to return. In addition, it would provide reliable information for consular officers abroad making decisions about who should be issued visas.

6. Immigration authorities have responded to the ambivalence about enforcement in Congress and successive administrations by adopting a triage approach to their overwhelming workload. The focus of enforcement has been on arresting and deporting criminal aliens and illegals working at airports and other sensitive locations. That means ordinary illegal aliens have almost no reason to expect they will ever be apprehended. Changing this expectation requires a "broken windows" approach to immigration law enforcement.[20] Ignoring minor immigration violations has created the same atmosphere of disorder as leaving broken windows unrepaired does in a run-down neighborhood; and, as Mayor Giuliani demonstrated in New York, the reassertion of control by the government over seemingly minor matters reestablishes a sense of order, leading to decreased lawbreaking in general. Immigration enforcement, therefore, must combine its current focus on major crimes with an effort to significantly increase the number of noncriminal deportations—the goal being not only to bring down the number of illegals directly but also to create a new climate of enforcement, encouraging more self-deportation as the likelihood of actually being caught increases. This would include, for instance,

a new commitment to arresting, prosecuting, and deporting those who are apprehended in workplace raids and other compliance efforts, as well as those who commit fraud in immigration applications.

7. An additional way to discourage illegals from embedding themselves here, and encouraging those already here to leave, is through state and local legislation. As the illegal population has ballooned, states and localities have considered an avalanche of measures, including barring illegals from receiving welfare benefits and in-state tuition discounts, requiring proof of legal residence to get a driver's license, denying bail to illegal aliens, barring illegals from winning punitive damages, denying the tax deductibility of wages paid to illegals, requiring state agencies and contractors to check new employees with the federal Employment Eligibility Verification Program, barring landlords from renting to illegals, and even suing the federal government over nonenforcement of the immigration laws. Rather than swat away this flurry of enthusiasm from below, which is the natural inclination of an administration uninterested in immigration enforcement, the federal government should try to harness it. This might take the form of establishing an office within ICE devoted to helping coordinate state and local efforts by spelling out what kinds of measures are appropriate, serving as a clearing house for the various local efforts, and actively marketing the verification programs for both employment and for people seeking government benefits (called the SAVE Program) to local and state governments.

Note that none of these seven recommendations involves border control. This is not because the work of the Border Patrol is unimportant—after all, as much as 70 percent of the illegal population got here by sneaking across our frontier with Mexico. Nor is this because we are already devoting adequate attention to border control; our effort remains laughably inadequate, with an average of probably no more than two agents per mile stationed on the Mexican border during any one shift, and only a fraction of the border having any modern security fencing.

It's just that, however inadequate, at least we *have* a border enforcement effort. Even the Bush administration, headed by a president who is emotionally repelled by the very idea of enforcing our southern border, has launched the Secure Border Initiative, which is supposed to increase the number of Border Patrol agents and detention beds and expand the use of technology, like unmanned aerial vehicles and remote video surveillance. This is still not enough, but at least politicians and the public don't need any persuading about the importance of enforcement efforts at the border.

But too many people, usually supporters of high levels of immigration, think border enforcement ends at the border and that measures in the interior of the country are unnecessary or even undesirable. But without the kind of broad enforcement strategy outlined above, border enforcement will end up serving mainly as political cover, a means of persuading the public that something is being done about immigration without actually doing anything effective.

An effective strategy of immigration law enforcement requires no land mines, no tanks, no tattooed arms—none of the cartoonish images routinely invoked by supporters of loose borders. The consistent application of ordinary law-enforcement tools is all that's needed. "Consistent," though, is the key word. Enforcement personnel need to know that their work is valued, that their superiors actually want them to do the jobs they've been assigned, and that they will be backed up when the inevitable complaints roll in. Only with an unambiguous commitment to enforcement of the law, from the top down, will it be possible to establish control over immigration.

CUT THE NUMBERS

Once the law is properly enforced, levels of legal immigration could theoretically still be very high.[21] But the object of this book has been to demonstrate that high levels of immigration—legal or not—are in conflict with the needs of a modern society. So not only illegal immigration must be reduced, but legal immigration also. After all, the majority of immigrants are legal.

So what should the level be? Some just pick a number. Borjas, for instance, suggests 500,000 immigrants a year, half today's level, though he readily acknowledges that there's no reason this should be a magic number.[22] The U.S. Commission on Immigration Reform, headed by the late Barbara Jordan, recommended in 1995 a similar cut to about 550,000 per year.[23] Some environmentalists have argued for zero net immigration, so immigration would match emigration; no one really knows what the level of emigration is, but it's estimated to be 250,000 to 300,000 per year.[24] Yet others suggest a level of immigration of 250,000 per year, near the average over the first two centuries of our national history.[25]

These and other proposals approach the issue of numbers as a matter of adjusting the existing level of immigration; in other words, how to shave off some numbers here and there to get the total down to some desired level.

A better approach would be to learn from the principle of zero-based budgeting, defined in one dictionary as "a process in government and corporate finance of justifying an overall budget or individual budgeted items each fiscal year or each review period rather than dealing only with proposed changes from a previous budget."

So in considering the amount and nature of legal immigration, we shouldn't start from the existing level and work down; instead, we should start from zero immigration and work up. Zero is not where we'll end, but it must be where we start. From zero we must then consider what categories of immigrant are so important to the national interest that their admission warrants risking the kinds of problems that the rest of this book has outlined.

Most immigration flows, regardless of the source or destination, have three components: family, employment, and humanitarian. **Family-based immigration**—admitting immigrants because they have relatives in the United States—is different from other categories because it involves a delegation of authority. The American people grant the right to their fellow citizens to decide, in their individual capacity and without any affirmative determination by the government, who will move to the United States. Some categories are, of course, numerically limited and the community retains the right to veto relatives considered undesirable, but the fact remains that these private decisions by individual citizens will determine the future makeup of the American people.

This is a profound responsibility that we devolve onto each other individually, as profound in its way as the decision to bear children. And because the consequences of such individual decisions are of such import, their scope must be as narrow as possible, limited only to marriage to a foreign spouse or adoption of a foreign child. In other words, family-based immigration should not be subject to any numerical cap but should include only the legitimate spouses and minor children of U.S. citizens.

This means eliminating altogether today's immigration categories for the adult siblings of citizens, the married and unmarried adult sons and daughters of citizens, the parents of adult citizens, and the adult sons and daughters of legal residents. These are grown people with their own lives, for whom "family reunification" is a misnomer.

The remaining question regarding family immigration is what to do about the spouses and minor children of permanent residents (green-card holders who aren't citizens yet). When people receive green cards under some non-family-based category, then their spouses and minor children also receive green cards. But *unmarried* people who immigrate for one reason or another should only be permitted to import spouses or children *after* they become citizens. Unfortunately, we have admitted such immigrants with the expectation that, before becoming citizens, they can marry foreigners and bring those spouses here. While there is no right to immigrate—none whatsoever—prudence suggests that we not contribute to the separation of spouses and young children. Therefore, unmarried permanent residents who subsequently married and have filed an immigration petition for their new spouses by the date of the new law's enactment should be grandfathered in.

Restricting family immigration to spouses and minor children of American citizens would still result in a substantial amount of immigration. The average number of such immigrants admitted annually from 2001 through 2005 was about 340,000. By comparison, the total average family immigration during those years was 623,000. It is likely that, once other categories of immigration were eliminated, this category would decline, since a large portion of U.S. citizens marrying foreigners are themselves earlier immigrants.

The next major component is **skills-based immigration**, which selects people based on education, skill, or experience, often with specific offers of employment. The five employment-based categories in current law, with their numerous subcategories, are commonly imagined to provide for the immigration of the world's best and brightest—Einstein immigration, if you will. In fact, in addition to a handful of actual geniuses, the employment-based categories admit a wide array of ordinary people who should not receive special immigration rights. There's no reason any employer should be permitted to make an end run around our vast, mobile, continent-spanning labor force of more than 150 million people unless the prospective immigrant in question has unique, remarkable abilities and would make an enormous contribution to the productive capacity of the nation.

Perhaps the simplest way to approach this would be to admit anyone who scores above 140 on an IQ test. A more bureaucratic approach would be to admit "aliens of extraordinary ability" and outstanding professors and researchers, as defined by the top employment-based category in current law. The 2001–2005 average number of people admitted annually under this targeted definition of skilled workers was about 15,000, though we could do without a cap so long as standards for admission are set sufficiently high. Such a refinement would eliminate the largest of the employment-based divisions, the third employment-based preference category, which admits people with few special skills; in addition, the catch-all "special immigrants" category and the investor-visa category would be eliminated.

The third major component is **humanitarian immigration**. Under this broad heading are three main parts: refugee resettlement (bringing into the country refugees from overseas), grants of asylum (reclassifying as a refugee someone who is already here illegally or on a temporary visa), and cancellation of removal (a grant of amnesty to an illegal alien whose deportation would cause "exceptional and extremely unusual hardship" to the alien's legally resident parent, spouse, or child).

The Refugee Act of 1980, which incorporated the international definition of a refugee into U.S. law, foresaw an annual intake of 50,000 refugees and asylum seekers per year. As you might expect, the number has almost always exceeded this target, except in the two years after 9/11. The average annual number of refugees resettled 2001–2005 was about 46,000 and the average number of people awarded the cancellation-of-removal amnesty was about 25,000. In 2005 about 20,000 people were granted asylum.

The number of refugees to be admitted in the coming year is set by the president in consultation with Congress; but the number of grants of asylum and of cancellation of removal are out of the executive's control, since they are for illegal aliens trying to avoid deportation and are usually granted by judges of one sort or another.

To introduce some predictability and control over the numbers, it would be advisable to set an overall ceiling for humanitarian immigration of fifty thousand per year, with the element over which we have the most control—refugee resettlement—dependent on the numbers of asylum grants and cancellations of removal. In other words, an increase in asylum and/or cancellation of removal would trigger a reduction in available slots for refugee resettlement; conversely, fewer grants of asylum or cancellations of removal would free up more slots for refugee resettlement.

A further problem is that refugee resettlement is no longer viewed by the State Department as the option of last resort, but rather the first resort, as though America's streets were a safety valve for the diplomatic flashpoint du jour.[26] Whole populations are selected for resettlement, without any assessment of individual cases or search for alternatives. Instead, only the most desperate people on the planet should be offered resettlement in the United States—genuine refugees in immediate danger who have no hope of ever finding another solution. Considering that there are more than 8 million refugees in the world, the only morally defensible approach is to resettle some share of those who are the most desperate (often specifically identified as such by the UN High Commissioner for Refugees), not those who are the most appealing or politically well connected.

Finally, asylum law is developing in troubling ways, moving away from granting protection to people who have been persecuted due to race, religion, nationality, or political opinion, and increasingly concocting rationales for asylum based on the final criterion in the law, "membership in a particular social group." This is a catch-all category aggressively exploited by lawyers and activist judges trying to obstruct deportations. Asylum has been granted for reasons that have nothing whatever to do with government persecution, including to women abused by their husbands, homosexuals taunted by neighbors, even a disabled boy whose relatives considered him a stain on the family. The backwardness of the third world is not a matter to be addressed through American immigration policy, and Congress must act by eliminating the "particular social group" category from the refugee law.

TEMPORARY MEANS TEMPORARY

A reconsideration of immigration policy must also include nonimmigrant, or temporary, visas, since they are the source of much permanent immigration—in 2006, nearly two thirds of new green-card recipients were already living in the United States, some illegally but most on some sort of temporary visa. In 2006, 33.7 million foreigners entered on such visas or the equivalent, and most returned home after a vacation (24.9 million admissions) or business trip (5 million). But hundreds of thousands used these temporary visas as shortcuts to permanent immigration, even though they formally affirmed to our visa officers abroad and to our immigration inspectors at the border that they had no such intent.

The main types of temporary visas that lead to permanent immigration are F visas for students and H visas for temporary workers and trainees. There are various ways of counting the de facto immigrants who use these means of gaining access to the United States, and all the numbers are large. For instance, the State Department reports that it issued more than nearly 300,000 new student visas in fiscal year 2006, while the Bureau of Customs and Border Protection reports more than 730,000 entries in the same period using such visas (some had been issued in earlier years and some represent multiple entries by the same person).[27] Meanwhile, the Institute for International Education, using data from colleges, calculates that there were 565,000 foreign students actually here during the 2005–2006 school year.[28]

The number of people using H visas is also very large—372,000 new visas issued in fiscal year 2006, with 745,000 admissions on those visas. Other temporary visa categories that are routinely used for permanent immigration are J (exchange visitors: 340,000 visas issued, 427,000 admissions), L (intracompany transferees: 134,000 visas issued, 466,000 admissions), and E (treaty traders and investors: 37,000 visas issued, 217,000 admissions).

To end the practice of using temporary visas for permanent immigration, all long-term nonimmigrant visas (those good for more than six months) should be made available only to those countries whose nationals do not often adjust from temporary visitor to permanent immigrant. This would be modeled on the Visa Waiver Program, which allows short-term entry to people from countries whose nationals generally do not end up overstaying their visas and becoming illegal immigrants.

The categories themselves must be streamlined and reined in. The H visas for workers should be eliminated entirely—any foreign worker actually worth letting in is worth admitting as a permanent immigrant rather than what amounts to an indentured servant. The L visa for intracompany transferees should be limited to three years and available only to large companies with multiple millions in annual sales, so as to prevent its use as a legal form of alien smuggling, with people ostensibly being transferred to the American "branch office" of a tiny business abroad.

Student visas are for foreigners admitted specifically to attend college, as opposed to legal immigrants already here, who may pursue whatever kind of higher education they choose without any kind of special visa. People admitted on student visas should be limited to no more than 1 percent of total national enrollment in higher education, which would translate, generously, to 150,000. Also, no more than a small share, say 5 percent, of any particular school's total enrollment should consist of foreign students; currently, more than 20 percent of the enrollment at Stanford, Columbia, and the University of Southern California are student visa holders.

Student visas should be issued only for colleges granting bachelor's degrees or higher; more than 10 percent of foreign students are enrolled at community colleges, whose mission is supposed to be serving the local community and providing training, including remedial and vocational training, to local residents who would not otherwise go on to higher education. The admission of foreign students is directly contrary to the mission of community colleges and should never be permitted. Finally, because the education of every college student in the nation is hugely subsidized by the public (even at ostensibly private universities), foreign students should be required to pay double the normal full tuition rate and should not be permitted to receive any form of financial aid from the college.

Even if they somehow did not lead to permanent legal immigration, large-scale temporary programs should never be instituted. Whether the guestworkers are tomato pickers or computer programmers, such schemes distort the economy in the same way as permanent immigration; they inevitably promote illegal immigration, and they lead to the creation of a servile class.

Thus a new blueprint for a modern American immigration policy: a firm commitment to reducing the illegal population over time and keeping it low; a level of legal immigration, built up from zero, which is still quite high, perhaps four hundred thousand per year, though likely to decline as time passes; a temporary visa system that welcomes the legitimate visitor but is not a means to sidestep the immigration laws; and pro-immigrant measures to offer a warmer welcome to those we admit as our future countrymen.

ACKNOWLEDGMENTS

This book is a work of synthesis. A new and provocative and illuminating synthesis, I hope, but nonetheless one that uses as its raw material the work of others.

Much of that raw material comes from the published work of the Center for Immigration Studies, the organization I head, even though the views herein are not necessarily those of the center. The center's funders, board, and staff have helped make it the nation's premier institution examining immigration from the perspective of the broad national interest. In particular, I simply could not have written this book without the extensive research and invaluable guidance of Director of Research Steven Camarota and Senior Policy Analyst Jessica Vaughan.

The raw material also includes the work of anonymous legions at the Census Bureau, the Government Accountability Office, the Congressional Research Service, the Department of Homeland Security's Office of Immigration Statistics, and the various agencies' inspector general offices. Without them we would know even less than we do about the workings and consequences of our immigration system, or any other part of our government, and it is too seldom that they receive a word of thanks.

The other writers and researchers whose work informs this book can be gleaned from the endnotes, but special mention should go to George Borjas, Janice Kephart, Heather Mac Donald, Philip Martin, and Robert Rector. And even before them, it was Patrick Burns who got me into this business, and whose passion inspired me.

I'm especially grateful to the following, not only for their contributions to my understanding of immigration, but also for reading all or part of the manuscript and offering suggestions that inevitably improved it: Roy Beck, Vernon Briggs, Glynn Custred, John Fonte, Otis Graham, Stanley Renshon, Peter Skerry, and John Wahala.

Of course, all opinions and any errors are mine alone.

I'm indebted to Rich Lowry and Glenn Hartley; Rich ran my *National Review* cover story which caught the eye of my future agent, Glenn, who worked assiduously to find a home for a book that didn't fit nicely into existing categories.

My editor, Bernadette Malone Serton, has been a patient and insightful guide; I owe her a lot, though she owes me a doughnut.

I'd also like to thank Rupi, just because.

Most important, I'm deeply grateful to my long-suffering wife, Amelie, and sons, Alex, Ben, and Theo, for putting up with my procrastination, isolation, and irritation. Without their faith and encouragement, there could have been no book.

NOTES

Introduction

1. John D. Fonte, "Does America Have an Assimilation Problem? Yes, It's Not 1900 Any More," *The American Enterprise,* Dec. 2000.
2. *Statistical Abstract of the United States,* http://www.census.gov/compendia/ statab/hist_stats.html. Other data from *It's Getting Better All the Time: The Greatest Trends of the Last 100 Years,* by Stephen Moore and Julian L. Simon—ironically, boosters of mass immigration—(Washington, DC: Cato Institute, 2000) and from Federal Reserve Bank of Dallas, *1997 Annual Report,* http://www.dallasfed.org/fed/annual/1999p/ar97 .html.
3. Leon F. Bouvier, "The Impact of Immigration on United States' Population Size: 1950 to 2050," *NPG Forum,* Nov. 1998, http://www.npg .org/forum_series/imm_impact_usgrowth.htm.
4. John Higham, *Strangers in the Land: Patterns of American Nativism, 1860– 1925,* 2nd ed. (New York: Atheneum, 1978), p. 324.
5. "Three Decades of Mass Immigration: The Legacy of the 1965 Immigration Act," Center for Immigration Studies *Backgrounder,* Sept. 1995, http://www.cis.org/articles/1995/back395.html.

6. Betty Kay Koed, "The Politics of Reform: Policymakers and the Immigration Act of 1965," University of California at Santa Barbara, unpublished dissertation, 1999, ch. 6, p. 35.

7. "President Lyndon B. Johnson's Remarks at the Signing of the Immigration Bill, Liberty Island, New York," Oct. 3, 1965, *Public Papers of the Presidents of the United States: Lyndon B. Johnson, 1965* (Washington, DC: Government Printing Office, 1966), vol. 2, entry 546, pp. 1037–1040, http://www.lbjlib.utexas.edu/johnson/archives.hom/speeches.hom/651003.asp.

8. Starting in prehistoric times, a total of perhaps 73 million people have moved to what is now the United States, about 29 million of them since 1965.

Chapter 1. Assimilation: The Cracked Melting Pot

1. Letter to Mr. Hurd, Jan. 3, 1919, http://67.19.222.106/politics/graphics/troosevelt.pdf.

2. Speech at Chicago, Illinois, July 10, 1858, http://www.founding.com/library/lbody.cfm?id=323&parent=63.

3. Lawrence H. Fuchs, *The American Kaleidoscope: Race, Ethnicity, and the Civic Culture* (Middletown, CT: Wesleyan University Press, 1990), p. 225.

4. "True Americanism," address of Louis D. Brandeis at Faneuil Hall, Boston, July 5, 1915, http://library.louisville.edu/law/brandeis/whatis.html.

5. John Fonte, "We Need a Patriotic Assimilation Policy: It's Time the United States Got Serious Again About Americanizing Its Immigrants," *American Outlook,* Winter 2003, http://www.hudson.org/index.cfm?fuseaction=publication_details&id=2855.

6. Stanley A. Renshon, *The 50% American: Immigration and National Identity in an Age of Terror* (Washington, DC: Georgetown University Press, 2005), p. 2.

7. Ruth 1:16–17.

8. Stephen Castles, "Migration and Community Formation Under Conditions

of Globalization," *International Migration Review,* vol. 36, no. 4, Winter 2002, p. 1157.

9. Office of Immigration Statistics, U.S. Department of Homeland Security, *Yearbook of Immigration Statistics: 2005,* http://www.uscis.gov/graphics/shared/statistics/yearbook/LPR05.htm, table 2.

10. Steven A. Camarota, "Immigrants at Mid-Decade: A Snapshot of America's Foreign-Born Population in 2005," Center for Immigration Studies, Dec. 2005, http://www.cis.org/articles/2005/back1405.html, table 4.

11. David Hollinger employs a similar concept in asking, "How wide the circle of the 'we'?" in David A. Hollinger, ed., *Postethnic America: Beyond Multiculturalism* (New York: Basic Books, 2000), p. 68.

12. Benjamin Franklin, "Observations Concerning the Increase of Mankind, Peopling of Countries, etc.," 1751. Franklin went on to say "that the Number of purely white People in the World is proportionably very small. All Africa is black or tawny. Asia chiefly tawny. America (exclusive of the new Comers) wholly so. And in Europe, the Spaniards, Italians, French, Russians and Swedes, are generally of what we call a swarthy Complexion; as are the Germans also, the Saxons only excepted, who with the English, make the principal Body of White People on the Face of the Earth."

13. See the 1856 platform of the American (Know-Nothing) Party, which made no reference at all to restrictions on immigration but instead sought to postpone naturalization of immigrants with a twenty-one-year residency requirement and to limit officeholding to the native born. Online at http://www.yale.edu/glc/archive/974.htm.

14. Peter Brimelow, *Alien Nation* (New York: Random House, 1995), p. xv.

15. Gillian Stevens, Mary E. M. McKillip, and Hiromi Ishizawa, "Intermarriage in the Second Generation: Choosing Between Newcomers and Natives," Migration Information Source, Oct. 1, 2006, http://www.migration information.org/Feature/display.cfm?id=444.

16. And 43 percent picked "some other race." Thanks to Peter Skerry for supplying these numbers.

17. Paula D. McClain et al., "Racial Distancing in a Southern City: Latino Immigrants' Views of Black Americans," *Journal of Politics,* vol. 68, no. 3, Aug. 2006, http://journalofpolitics.org/art68_3.html#a7.

18. Peter Whoriskey, "States, Counties Begin to Enforce Immigration Law," *Washington Post,* Sept. 27, 2006.

19. Steven A. Camarota and Nora McArdle, "Where Immigrants Live: An Examination of State Residency of the Foreign Born by Country of Origin in 1990 and 2000," Center for Immigration Studies, Sept. 2003, http://www.cis.org/articles/2003/back1203.html.

20. Steven A. Camarota, "Immigrants in the United States—2002: A Snapshot of America's Foreign-Born Population," Center for Immigration Studies, Nov. 2002, http://www.cis.org/articles/2002/back1302.html, table 5.

21. Camarota and McArdle, "Where Immigrants Live."

22. Michael S. Teitelbaum, "Right Versus Right: Immigration and Refugee Policy in the United States," *Foreign Affairs,* vol. 59, no. 1, Fall 1980, pp. 26–7.

23. "Mother Tongue of the Foreign White Stock," *Thirteenth Census of the United States Taken in the Year 1910* (Washington, DC: Government Printing Office, 1913), vol. 1, Population, ch. 9, http://www2.census.gov/prod2/decennial/documents/36894832v1ch12.pdf.

24. Samuel Huntington, *Who Are We?* (New York: Simon & Schuster, 2004), pp. 247–51.

25. Ibid., p. 250.

26. Barry R. Chiswick and Paul W. Miller, "Do Enclaves Matter in Immigrant Adjustment?" IZA Discussion Paper no. 449 (Bonn: Institute for the Study of Labor, Mar. 2002), http://ftp.iza.org/dp449.pdf.

27. "The State of the News Media 2006," Project for Excellence in Journalism, Columbia University Graduate School of Journalism, http://www.stateofthemedia.com/2006/narrative_ethnicalternative_intro.asp?cat=1&media=10.

28. Frank Ahrens, "Accent on Higher TV Ratings: Spanish-Language Network Telemundo Coaches Actors to Use Mexican Dialect," *Washington Post,* Aug. 2, 2004, http://www.washingtonpost.com/wp-dyn/articles/A32693-2004Aug1.html.

29. Ruben G. Rumbaut, Douglas S. Massey, and Frank D. Bean, "Linguistic Life Expectancies: Immigrant Language Retention in Southern California," *Population and Development Review,* vol. 32, no. 3, Sept. 2006, pp. 447–60, http://www.popcouncil.org/PDR_LinguisticLifeExpectancy.pdf.

30. They are the diversity visa lottery and the per-country limits on certain immigration categories.

31. See, for instance, Mark Krikorian, "Taking Chances: The Folly of the Visa Lottery," Center for Immigration Studies, July 2004, http://www.cis.org/articles/2004/back804.html.

32. Vilhelm Moberg, *The Last Letter Home,* trans. Gustaf Lannestock (New York: Simon & Schuster, 1961).

33. Alejandro Portes, "Global Villagers: The Rise of Transnational Communities," *American Prospect,* Mar. 1996, http://www.prospect.org/print/V7/25/portes-a.html.

34. Deborah Sontag and Celia W. Dugger, "The New Immigrant Tide: A Shuttle Between Worlds," *New York Times,* July 19, 1998.

35. Peggy Levitt, *The Transnational Villagers* (Berkeley: University of California Press, 2001).

36. Ibid., p. 24.

37. Sontag and Dugger, "The New Immigrant Tide."

38. Deborah Sontag, "A Mexican Town That Transcends All Borders," *New York Times,* July 21, 1998.

39. Sontag and Dugger, "The New Immigrant Tide."

40. Renshon, *The 50% American,* ch. 1. See also: *Citizenship Laws of the World,* U.S. Office of Personnel Management, Mar. 2001, http://www.opm.gov/extra/investigate/IS-01.pdf.

41. Renshon, *The 50% American,* p. xix.

42. This rough estimate of the annual increase includes 80 percent of the roughly 1 million legal immigrants admitted per year (legal immigrants eventually are eligible for U.S. citizenship, unlike illegal aliens) plus 80 percent of the more than 1 million babies born each year with at least one immigrant parent, minus deaths and emigration.

43. John Fonte, "Dual Allegiance: A Challenge to Immigration Reform and

Patriotic Assimilation," Center for Immigration Studies, Nov. 2005, http://www.cis.org/articles/2005/back1205.html.

44. Pew Hispanic Center, "Survey of Mexican Migrants, Part Two: Attitudes about Voting in Mexican Elections and Ties to Mexico," Mar. 14, 2005, http://pewhispanic.org/reports/report.php?ReportID=42.

45. Fonte, "Dual Allegiance."

46. Arthur M. Schlesinger Jr., *The Disuniting of America: Reflections on a Multicultural Society,* rev. ed. (New York: Norton, 1998), p. 31.

47. Fonte, "Dual Allegiance."

48. John Higham, *Strangers in the Land: Patterns of American Nativism, 1860–1925* (New York: Atheneum, 1978), pp. 247–8.

49. John Miller, *The Unmaking of Americans: How Multiculturalism Has Undermined the Assimilation Ethic* (New York: Free Press, 1998), p. 49.

50. Miller, *The Unmaking of Americans,* pp. 55–6.

51. Huntington, *Who Are We?* pp. 269–70.

52. See Mark Krikorian, "Post-Americans: They've Just 'Grown' Beyond Their Country," *National Review Online,* June 22, 2004, http://www.nationalreview.com/comment/krikorian200406220944.asp.

53. "U.S. Corporations Pledge Allegiance to No-Pledge Plans; Not Time or Place, Officials Tell Nader," *Washington Times,* July 3, 1998.

54. The editorials are "In Praise of Huddled Masses," July 3, 1984; "The Rekindled Flame," July 3, 1986; "Simpson-Volstead-Mazzoli," July 3, 1987; "The Rekindled Flame," July 3, 1989; "The Rekindled Flame," July 3, 1990. In addition, editorial-page editor Robert Bartley reiterated the open-borders stance in two columns: "Liberty's Flame Beckons a Bit Brighter," July 3, 2000, and "Open Nafta Borders? Why Not? Immigration Is What Made This Country Great," July 2, 2001.

55. Huntington, *Who Are We?* p. 267.

56. *Worldviews 2002,* http://www.worldviews.org/detailreports/usreport/index.htm, summarized and analyzed by Roy Beck and Steven A. Camarota in "Elite vs. Public Opinion: An Examination of Divergent Views on Immigration," Center for Immigration Studies, Dec. 2002, http://www.cis.org/articles/2002/back1402.html.

57. Francis Fukuyama, "Identity, Immigration, and Liberal Democracy," *Journal of Democracy,* Apr. 2006, http://www.journalofdemocracy.org/articles/gratis/Fukuyama-17-2.pdf.

58. Miller, *The Unmaking of Americans,* p. 81.

59. Victor Davis Hanson, *Mexifornia: A State of Becoming* (San Francisco: Encounter Books, 2003), p. 79.

60. Ibid., p. 82.

61. Ibid., p. 84.

62. Ibid., p. 101.

63. Randall Hanson, "The Free Economy and the Jacobin State, or How Europe Can Cope with the Coming Immigration Wave," in *Debating Immigration,* Carol M. Swain, ed. (Cambridge: Cambridge University Press, 2007), p. 236.

64. Letter to Mr. Hurd, Jan. 3, 1919, http://67.19.222.106/politics/graphics/troosevelt.pdf.

65. *Miami Herald* editorial, Nov. 1, 1980; Jo Thomas, "Miami Area Divided Over Ballot Proposal to Drop Spanish as Second Official Language," *New York Times,* Nov. 2, 1980.

66. Peter Duignan, "Bilingual Education: A Critique," the Hoover Institution, 1998, http://www.hoover.org/publications/he/2896386.html.

67. See testimony of Roger Clegg, president and general counsel, Center for Equal Opportunity, before the House Judiciary Committee's Subcommittee on the Constitution regarding the reauthorization of the Voting Rights Act, May 4, 2006, http://judiciary.house.gov/media/pdfs/clegg050406.pdf.

68. Executive Order 13166, "Improving Access to Services for Persons with Limited English Proficiency," Aug. 11, 2000, http://www.usdoj.gov/crt/cor/Pubs/eolep.htm.

69. Poll conducted by Zogby International, Mar. 14–16, 2006, commissioned by ProEnglish. Detailed results available from ProEnglish; for general results, see http://www.proenglish.org/newsreleases/060321.html.

70. Friedrich A. Hayek, *The Constitution of Liberty* (Chicago: University of Chicago Press, 1960), p. 377.

71. John Fonte, "Is the Purpose of Civic Education to Transmit or Transform

the American Regime?" in *Civic Education and Culture,* Bradley C. S. Watson, ed. (Wilmington, DE: ISI Books, 2005), pp. 73–111.

72. See, for instance, John Fonte, "We the Peoples: The Multiculturalist Agenda Is Shattering the American Identity," *National Review,* Mar. 25, 1996.

73. Nathan Glazer and Reed Ueda, *Ethnic Groups in History Textbooks* (Washington, DC: Ethics and Public Policy Center, 1983); quoted by Heather Mac Donald in "The Sobol Report: Multiculturalism Triumphant," *The New Criterion,* Jan. 1992.

74. Intercollegiate Studies Institute, *The Coming Crisis in Citizenship: Higher Education's Failure to Teach America's History and Institutions,* Oct. 2006, http://www.americancivicliteracy.org/.

75. Alejandro Portes and Ruben Rumbaut, *Legacies: The Story of the Immigrant Second Generation* (Berkeley: University of California Press, 2001), ch. 7.

76. Ibid. p. 157.

77. Fonte, "Dual Allegiance."

78. Stanley A. Renshon, *Dual Citizenship and American National Identity,* Center for Immigration Studies, paper no. 20, Oct. 2001, http://www.cis.org/articles/2001/paper20/renshondual.pdf, p. 43.

79. 8 U.S.C. 1448(a).

80. *Afroyim v. Rusk,* 387 U.S. 253 (1967).

81. Alejandro Portes, "Global Villagers: The Rise of Transnational Communities," *American Prospect,* Mar. 1996, http://www.prospect.org/print/V7/25/portes-a.html.

82. Portes and Rumbaut, *Legacies,* p. 157.

83. Hugh Davis Graham, *Collision Course: The Strange Convergence of Affirmative Action and Immigration Policy in America* (New York: Oxford University Press, 2002), p. 134.

84. Ibid., p. 12.

85. Ibid., pp. 146–7.

86. Miller, *The Unmaking of Americans.* Curiously, despite the logic of his statement, Miller defended continued mass immigration.

87. Peter Skerry, "Immigration and Social Disorder," in *Uniting America: Restoring the Vital Center to American Democracy,* Norton Garfinkle and Daniel Yankelovich, eds. (New Haven, CT: Yale University Press, 2005), p. 128.

88. Noah Pickus and Peter Skerry, "Good Neighbors and Good Citizens: Beyond the Legal-Illegal Immigration Debate," in *Debating Immigration,* Carol M. Swain, ed. (Cambridge: Cambridge University Press, 2007), p. 97.

89. Steven Greenhouse, "Crossing the Border Into the Middle Class," *New York Times,* June 3, 2004; quoted in Skerry, *Uniting America,* p. 129.

90. Robert D. Putnam, *Bowling Alone: The Collapse and Revival of American Community* (New York: Simon & Schuster, 2000), p. 19.

91. Ibid., pp. 283–4.

92. Peter Skerry, *Mexican Americans: The Ambivalent Minority* (New York: Free Press, 1993), p. 374.

93. Ibid., p. 346.

94. For Mexican hometown associations, see Robert S. Leiken, "The Melting Border: Mexico and Mexican Communities in the United States" (Falls Church, VA: Center for Equal Opportunity, 2000), http://www.ceousa.org/pdfs/MELTBORDER.pdf.

95. Skerry, *Mexican Americans,* p. 325.

96. Gregory Rodriguez, "Mexican Americans Are Building No Walls," *Los Angeles Times,* Feb. 29, 2004.

97. John Lloyd, "Study Paints Bleak Picture of Ethnic Diversity," *Financial Times,* Oct. 8, 2006, http://www.ft.com/cms/s/c4ac4a74-570f-11db-9110-0000779e2340.html.

98. Robert D. Putnam, *"E Pluribus Unum:* Diversity and Community in the Twenty-first Century; The 2006 Johan Skytte Prize Lecture," *Scandinavian Political Studies,* vol. 30, no. 2, June 2007, pp. 150–1.

99. Ibid., p. 149.

100. Dora L. Costa and Matthew E. Kahn, "Civic Engagement and Community Heterogeneity: An Economist's Perspective," *Perspectives on Politics,* vol. 1, no. 1, Mar. 2003, p. 104.

101. René Böheim and Karin Mayr, "Immigration and Public Spending," IZA Discussion Paper no. 1834, Nov. 2005, ftp://ftp.iza.org/dps/dp1834.pdf.

102. Putnam, *"E Pluribus Unum,"* p. 137.

103. Arjun Appadurai, *Modernity at Large: Cultural Dimension of Globalization* (Minneapolis: University of Minnesota Press, 1996), p. 171.

Chapter 2. Mass Immigration Versus American Sovereignty

1. Manuel Roig-Franzia, "Mexican Presidential Hopefuls Vow to Seek Immigration Pact: Front-Runners Also Stress Human Rights, Economic Issues in Debate," *Washington Post,* June 7, 2006.
2. For other explorations of this issue, see: Maria Hsia Chang, "Multiculturalism, Immigration and Aztlan," paper presented at the second action conference of the Alliance for Stabilizing America's Population, at Breckenridge, CO, Aug. 6, 1999, http://www.diversityalliance.org/docs/Chang-aztlan.html; Yeh Ling-Ling, "Mexican Immigration and Its Potential Impact on the Political Future of the United States," *Journal of Social, Political and Economic Studies,* vol. 29, no. 4, Winter 2004, http://www.diversityalliance.org/docs/article_2004winter.html; Allan Wall, "Undue Influence—the Government of Mexico and U.S. Immigration Policies," *Social Contract,* Winter 2002, http://www.thesocialcontract.com/cgi-bin/showarticle.pl?articleID=1122; Scott McConnell, "Americans No More," *National Review,* Dec. 31, 1997, http://www.nationalreview.com/31dec97/mcconnell123197.html; and Lawrence Auster, "The Second Mexican War," *Front Page,* Feb. 17, 2006, http://www.frontpagemag.com/Articles/ReadArticle.asp?ID=21309.
3. Ron Maxwell, "What Bush Fails to See at the Border," *Washington Times,* Apr. 6, 2006.
4. Michelle Malkin, "Reconquista Is Real," TownHall.com, May 3, 2006.
5. See, for instance, James R. Edwards Jr., "The Security and Prosperity Partnership: Its Immigration Implications," Center for Immigration Studies, June 2007, http://www.cis.org/articles/2007/back607.html and Eagle Forum's "North American Union" page at http://www.eagleforum.org/topics/NAU/.
6. See Mark Krikorian, "Post-Americans: They've Just 'Grown' Beyond Their Country," *National Review Online,* June 22, 2004, http://www.nationalreview.com/comment/krikorian200406220944.asp.
7. Steven A. Camarota, "Immigrants at Mid-Decade: A Snapshot of America's Foreign-Born Population in 2005," Center for Immigration Studies, Dec. 2005.

8. Steven A. Camarota, *Immigration From Mexico: Assessing the Impact on the United States,* Center for Immigration Studies, paper no. 19, July 2001.

9. Kevin G. Hall, "Fox Claim of Begging for Mexican Workers: U.S. Will Clamor for Mexican Workers in Coming Years, Fox Says," Knight/Ridder Tribune News Service, Mar. 1, 2006; Mariusa Reyes, "Fox: 'En 10 años EE.UU. suplicara,'" BBC Mundo, Mexico, in Spanish, Mar. 2, 2006, http://news.bbc.co.uk/hi/spanish/latin_america/newsid_4765000/4765242.stm; translated by Allan Wall, "Memo from Mexico," Vdare.com, Mar. 30, 2006, http://www.vdare.com/awall/060330_fox.htm.

10. David Simcox, "Another 50 Years of Mass Mexican Immigration: Mexican Government Report Projects Continued Flow Regardless of Economics or Birth Rates," Center for Immigration Studies, Mar. 2002, http://www.cis.org/articles/2002/back202.html.

11. See Population Division of the UN Department of Economic and Social Affairs, *World Population Prospects: 2006 Revision,* http://www.un.org/esa/population/publications/wpp2006/wpp2006.htm.

12. Steven A. Camarota, "Birth Rates Among Immigrants in America: Comparing Fertility in the U.S. and Home Countries," Center for Immigration Studies, Oct. 2005, http://www.cis.org/articles/2005/back1105.html.

13. California Department of Finance Demographic Research Unit, "Population Projections by Race/Ethnicity, Gender and Age for California and Its Counties, 2000–2050," May 2004, http://www.dof.ca.gov/HTML/DEMOGRAP/DRU_Publications/Projections/P3/P3.htm.

14. Office of the State Demographer, "Projections of the Population of Texas and Counties in Texas by Age, Sex and Race/Ethnicity for 2000–2040," Institute for Demographic and Socioeconomic Research, University of Texas at San Antonio, June 2004, http://txsdc.utsa.edu/tpepp/2004projections/2004_txpoprj_txtotnum.php.

15. See translation at http://www.americanpatrol.com/RECONQUISTA/GreatMexInvasDeMola820720.html.

16. Quoted by Allan Wall, in "Memo From Mexico: Spanish and the New Conquistadors," Vdare.com, Feb. 21, 2002, http://www.vdare.com/awall/conquistadors.htm.

17. Ibid.

18. John Rice, "An Old War Haunts a New Debate Between Mexico, United States," Associated Press, Apr. 30, 2006.

19. Sam Howe Verhovek, "Torn Between Nations, Mexican-Americans Can Have Both," *New York Times,* Apr. 14, 1998; audio file at http://www .americanpatrol.com/AUDIO/osunarecon020798.ra.

20. See poll results at http://www.immigrationcontrol.com/AIC_Zogby _Mexican_Poll.htm.

21. Federation for American Immigration Reform, "Chicano Nationalism, Revanchism and the Aztlan Myth," Jan. 2005, http://www.fairus.org/ site/PageServer?pagename=iic_immigrationissuecenters861a.

22. Frank Zoretich, "N.M. Will Secede to New Nation, Prof Says," *Albuquerque Tribune,* Jan. 31, 2000.

23. Allan Wall, "Who Is Jose Angel Gutierrez—And What Does He Want?" Vdare.com, June 2, 2004, http://www.vdare.com/awall/ gutierrez.htm.

24. *Congressional Record,* Apr. 3, 1969, p. 8590.

25. Lewis W. Diuguid, "Hispanics Will Help Build Future of U.S.," *Kansas City Star,* Apr. 28, 2004.

26. Diana Hull, "La Raza—Chicano Activism in California," *Social Contract,* Summer 1999.

27. Audio clips of statements by Obledo, Torres, and Alatorre at http://ccir .net/AUDIO/TakeoverOfAmericaCD/Menu.html.

28. CBS News, *48 Hours,* July 28, 1993.

29. Allan Wall, " 'Somos Mas Americanos'—We Are More American!" Vdare .com, Oct. 16, 2002, http://www.vdare.com/awall/americanos.htm.

30. Skerry, *Mexican Americans,* p. 4.

31. https://travelregistration.state.gov/ibrs/home.asp.

32. George J. Sanchez, *Becoming Mexican American* (New York: Oxford University Press, 1993), p. 113.

33. María Rosa García-Acevedo, "Politics Across Borders: Mexico's Policies Toward Mexicans in the United States," *Journal of the Southwest,* vol. 45, no. 4, Winter 2003.

34. Robert Smith, "Transnational Public Spheres and Changing Practices of Citizenship, Membership and Nation: Comparative Insights from the Mexican and Italian Cases," draft paper to be presented at International Center for Cooperation and Conflict Resolution Conference on Transnationalism, May 18, 1998, http://les.man.ac.uk/sa/Transnationalism/rsmith.htm.

35. Audio clip of Zedillo's comments at http://americanpatrol.com/WMV/zedilloaffirmedincontext01.wmv.

36. "Plan Nacional de Desarrollo, 1995–2000," http://www.cddhcu.gob.mx/bibliot/publica/otras/pnd/pndind.htm.

37. Fonte, "Dual Allegiance."

38. Allan Wall, "Hernandez Out—But His Soul Goes Marching On," Vdare.com, Aug. 20, 2002, http://www.vdare.com/awall/rise_and_fall.htm.

39. ABC News, *Nightline,* June 7, 2001.

40. Stephen Dinan and Jerry Seper, "Mexican Envoy Hits Own Policies," *Washington Times,* July 20, 2007.

41. Traci Carl, "Mexican President Blasts U.S. for Deportations; Promises to Fight for Immigrant Rights," Associated Press, Sept. 2, 2007.

42. Peter Prengaman, "Majority of Mexican Expats Voting Absentee Support Conservative," Associated Press, July 4, 2006.

43. "Let Us Not Repeat the Amnesty Mistake of 1986," testimony before the House Judiciary Committee by John Fonte, Sept. 1, 2006, http://acc.hudson.org/index.cfm?fuseaction=publication_details&id=4182.

44. Antonio Olivo and Oscar Avila, "Influence on Both Sides of the Border," *Chicago Tribune,* Apr. 6, 2007; Antonio Olivo, "Few Decide to Register for Mexican Election," *Chicago Tribune,* July 4, 2007.

45. J. Michael Waller, "Mexico's Glass House: How the Mexican Constitution Treats Foreign Residents, Workers and Naturalized Citizens," Center for Security Policy, Apr. 1, 2006.

46. Nancy Cleeland, "Mexican Ambassador Rips Immigration Law Changes, Politics: 'Racism and Xenophobia' Have Infected U.S. Policies, He Tells LULAC Members Meeting in Anaheim," *Los Angeles Times,* June 26, 1997.

47. José Luis Ruiz, "Acusa Presidente al PRI de liderar trabas," *El Universal,*
     Apr. 10, 2002.

48. Allan Wall, "Mexico's Terrified Tancredo-Bashing," Vdare.com, May
     26, 2003, http://www.vdare.com/awall/tancredo.htm.

49. Mark Stevenson, "Mexico, Central America Demand U.S. Allow More
     Legal Immigration," Associated Press, Jan. 9, 2006. See also: Sergio de
     Leon, "Latin American Diplomats to Protest U.S. Immigration Bill,
     Border Fence," Associated Press, Feb. 14, 2006, and Craig Gilbert, "Latin
     America Joins Immigration Debate: 8 Countries Gently Press U.S. for
     Reform," *Milwaukee Journal Sentinel,* May 3, 2006.

50. For foreign diplomatic missions in the United States, see http://www
     .state.gov/s/cpr/rls/; for Mexican missions abroad, see http://www.sre
     .gob.mx/english/.

51. Allan Wall, "Immigration Policy in Mexico and the U.S.," *FrontPage,*
     Sept. 19, 2002, http://www.frontpagemag.com/Articles/ReadArticle
     .asp?ID=3224.

52. Margot Louria, "The Boldness of Charles Evans Hughes," *National
     Interest,* Summer 2003, p. 116.

53. Peter R. D'Agostino, "The Scalabrini Fathers, the Italian Emigrant
     Church, and Ethnic Nationalism in America," *Religion and American
     Culture,* vol. 7, no. 1, Winter 1997, pp. 141–2.

54. Gilbert G. Gonzalez, *Mexican Consuls and Labor Organizing: Imperial Poli-
     tics in the American Southwest* (Austin: University of Texas Press, 1999), pp.
     47–8.

55. Alfredo Corchado, "Mexico Tries to Move Immigration Debate from
     Washington to U.S. Communities," *Dallas Morning News,* Feb. 9, 2003.

56. The text of the convention can be found at http://untreaty.un.org/ilc/
     texts/instruments/english/conventions/9_2_1963.pdf.

57. Scholars are developing a theoretical justification for this expansion of
     Mexican sovereignty at the expense of the United States, making the
     case for immigration as an "intermestic" matter (both international and
     domestic). See Marc R. Rosenblum, *The Transnational Politics of U.S.
     Immigration Policy* (La Jolla, CA: Center for Comparative Immigration
     Studies, University of California at San Diego, 2004).

58. Matthew Brayman, "Immigration Law Controversy: Defiant Zedillo Breaks Silence," *The News* (Mexico City), Apr. 4, 1997.

59. Translated and quoted by Howard Sutherland, in "Mexico's Northern Strategy: Vicente Fox Takes Active Measures to Keep Mexico's Emigrants from Assimilating," *American Conservative,* Mar. 10, 2003.

60. Dave Montgomery, "Summit to Take up Immigrant Initiative," *Fort Worth Star-Telegram,* Nov. 24, 2002.

61. Natalia Gómez Quintero, "'Hay que devolverle a la embajada en EU poder de cabildeo': Sarukhan," *El Universal,* Dec. 5, 2006, translated by Allan Wall, in "Arturo Sarukhan on Beachheads," Vdare.com, Dec. 11, 2006, http://blog.vdare.com/archives/2006/12/11/arturo-sarukhan-on -beachheads/.

62. Chris Hawley, "Mexico Publishes Guide to Assist Border Crossers," *Arizona Republic,* Jan. 1, 2005. The Mexican foreign ministry removed the Web version from its site, but a scanned image is at http://www.steinreport .com/GuiaDelMigranteMexicano.pdf, and a translation with the color images is at http://www.dallas.org/node/108.

63. "Diez reglas de oro para el inmigrante en EEUU," *El Mensajero,* May 22, 2005, http://www.elmensajero.com/index.php?option=com_content& task=view&id=46&Itemid=84.

64. Edward Hegstrom, "Mexico Official: U.S. Policy Leading to Deaths on Border," *Houston Chronicle,* June 27, 2002.

65. Alfredo Corchado and Ricardo Sandoval, "Fox to Intensify Bid for Immigration Changes: He'll Tell Lawmakers in U.S., Unions of Job Force Need for Migrants," *Dallas Morning News,* Oct. 25, 2002.

66. See Jennifer K. Elsea and Michael John Garcia, *Implications of the Vienna Convention on Consular Relations Upon the Regulation of Consular Identification Cards,* Congressional Research Service, May 23, 2005, http://www.fas .org/sgp/crs/misc/RS21627.pdf.

67. Randal C. Archibold, "Mexico Adds to Consulates Amid Debate," *New York Times,* May 23, 2007.

68. See Heather Mac Donald, "Mexico's Undiplomatic Diplomats," *City Journal,* Autumn 2005, http://www.city-journal.org/html/15_4_mexico .html; and Marti Dinerstein, "IDs for Illegals: The 'Matricula Consular'

Advances Mexico's Immigration Agenda," Center for Immigration Studies, Jan. 2003, http://www.cis.org/articles/2003/back303.html.

69. Jennifer Mena, "Mexican ID Card Gains Status, and Long Lines of Applicants," *Los Angeles Times,* Jan. 20, 2002.

70. "Consular ID Cards in a Post-9/11 World," testimony of Steve McCraw, assistant director of the Office of Intelligence, FBI, before the House Judiciary Subcommittee on Immigration, Border Security, and Claims on Consular ID Cards, June 26, 2003, http://www.fbi.gov/congress/congress03/mccraw062603.htm.

71. Andorra Bruno and K. Larry Storrs, *Consular Identification Cards: Domestic and Foreign Policy Implications, the Mexican Case, and Related Legislation,* Congressional Research Service, order code RL32094, May 26, 2005, http://www.ilw.com/immigdaily/news/2005,1128-crs.pdf.

72. "Fox Thanks L.A. Mayor for Accepting Mexican ID Cards," Agencia EFE, May 24, 2002.

73. Chris Hawley, "Calderon Talks Foreign Policy," *Arizona Republic,* July 8, 2006.

74. Cecilia M. Vega, "Napa Council OKs Mexican ID Card," *Santa Rosa Press-Democrat* (California), June 4, 2003.

75. Fred Alvarez, "Mexico ID Cards Backed; The Oxnard Council Is Expected to Allow Immigrants to Use Documents from Their Native Country as Valid Identification in the City," *Los Angeles Times,* Jan. 14, 2003.

76. Jerry Kammer and Leonel Sanchez, "Debate Intensifies over the Matricula ID Card from Mexico," Copley News Service, Feb. 3, 2003.

77. Rachel L. Swarns, "Old ID Card Gives New Status to Mexicans in U.S.," *New York Times,* Aug. 25, 2003.

78. Daniel Gonzalez, "Mexican Envoy Rips Immigration Bills," *Arizona Republic,* Feb. 12, 2003.

79. Allan Wall, "Undue Influence—the Government of Mexico and U.S. Immigration Policies," *Social Contract,* Winter 2002.

80. Paul Foy, "Mexican Consul, Mormon Church Denounce Anti-Immigration Group," Associated Press, Feb. 26, 2004.

81. Marla Sowards, "BYU-Area Mexican Consulate Issues IDs to Illegal Immigrants," *Daily Universe* (Brigham Young University), Mar. 3, 2003.

82. Leslie Casimir, "Want Immigrant IDs OKd," *New York Daily News,* Dec. 20, 2004.

83. Mark Bixler, "Walking a Tightrope: Mexican Consul Balances Roles as Latino Advocate," *Atlanta Journal and Constitution,* Jan. 24, 2000.

84. John J. Sanko and Hector Gutierrez, "Owens Questions Mexican Consulate: Colorado's Chief Exec Wants Official to Clarify Status of Spokesman," *Rocky Mountain News,* Jan. 16, 2003; "An Undiplomatic Consul" (editorial), *Denver Post,* Mar. 25, 2004.

85. "California Legislators Ask Mexican Senate to Intervene," Mexidata.info, Sept. 7, 2004.

86. Elizabeth Pierson, "Mexican Government Honors Wise," *Brownsville Herald,* Sept. 26, 2004.

87. Seth Rowe, "Mexican Consulate Representative Joins in Ordinance Debate," Sun Newspapers (Minnesota), Nov. 10, 2005.

88. Valerie Richardson, "Anti-Sanctuary Law Sets Off Consular Tiff," *Washington Times,* May 7, 2006; and Elizabeth Aguilera, "New Law Raises Profiling Fears," *Denver Post,* May 5, 2006.

89. Mark Fineman, "Mexico Fights Prop. 187—Delicately," *Los Angeles Times,* Oct. 29, 1994.

90. Patrick J. McDonnell, "Mexican Official Denounces Ballot Measure," *Los Angeles Times,* Aug. 15, 1994.

91. Fineman, "Mexico Fights Prop. 187."

92. K. L. Billingsley, "Mexico Rallies Against Initiative: Meddling Alarms Many in California," *Washington Times,* Nov. 2, 1994.

93. Tracey Eaton, "California Measure's Passage Angers Mexicans; Attack on 'Human Rights' Draws Fire," *Dallas Morning News,* Nov. 10, 1994.

94. Georgie Anne Geyer, "Mexico's 'Friendly' Intrusions on U.S. Sovereignty," *Chicago Tribune,* Oct. 21, 1994.

95. Tim Golden, "The 1994 Campaign: Mexico; Government Joins Attack on Ballot Idea," *New York Times,* Nov. 3, 1994.

96. Esther Schrader, "In Mexico, Prop. 187 Protests," *San Jose Mercury News,* Oct. 29, 1994.

97. Mark Fineman, "Mexico Condemns California Measure," *Houston Chronicle,* Oct. 30, 1994.

98. Bernardo Mendez, "Mexican Government Regrets Passage of Prop 200 in Arizona," *Hispanic Vista* (www.hispanicvista.com), Nov. 8, 2004.

99. "Pathways to Greatness: Espinoza, Gutierrez Earn Ohtli Awards," Arizona State University press release, June 6, 2005.

100. "Mexican Government Opposes Ban of Public Benefits for Undocumented in Arizona," *El Universal,* Dec. 24, 2004.

101. "Mexico May Appeal to International Tribunals," *El Universal,* Jan. 26, 2005.

102. Will Weissert, "Mexico Warns of Lawsuits Against U.S. If National Guard Detains Migrants," Associated Press, May 16, 2006.

103. "Mexico Weighs Lawsuit Against U.S. Army Reservist Who Detained Migrants," Associated Press, May 6, 2005.

104. Steven G. Vegh, "Mexico Sues DeCoster for Discrimination: Lawyers Say the Class-Action Suit Against the Egg Firm Is the First Filed in Maine by a Foreign Government," *Portland Press Herald* (Maine), May 19, 1998.

105. Alfredo Corchado, "Mexico, U.S. Farm Settle Suit: Landmark Case Alleged That Migrants Toiled in Horrid Conditions," *Dallas Morning News,* July 2, 2002.

106. Jerry Seper, "Mexico Urges Immigrants to Join Class-Action Suit: U.S. Grocers That Employed Them Accused of Discrimination," *Washington Times,* Mar. 22, 2004.

107. Michael Kiefer, "Thomas Irate at Mexico Official's Challenge of Law: Envoy Discusses Ariz. Measure with Attorney," *Arizona Republic,* May 10, 2006.

108. Dan McLean, "Illegal Immigrant's Lawyer Says Law Misused," *Union Leader* (Manchester, NH), May 12, 2005.

109. Pam Belluck, "Novel Tack on Illegal Immigrants: Trespass Charges," *New York Times,* July 13, 2005.

110. Consular Fact Sheet for Mexico, Feb. 23, 2007, http://travel.state.gov/travel/cis_pa_tw/cis/cis_970.html.

111. Stuart Eskenazi, "Mexico Expels Evergreen Students: Group Accused of Violating Political-Activities Ban in May Day Parade," *Seattle Times,* May

4, 2002; and Allan Wall, "Gringo Meddlers Expelled From Mexico! (Now What About Mexican Meddlers Here?)," Vdare.com, May 7, 2002.

112. See "Manifestaciones Hispanas" at http://www.ime.gob.mx/agenda _migratoria/debate.htm.

113. Chris Hawley and Susan Carroll, "Mexico Praises Immigrant Support, Decries Burning of Flag in Tucson," *Arizona Republic,* Apr. 11, 2006.

114. Ruben G. Rumbaut, Roberto G. Gonzales, Golnaz Komaie, and Charlie V. Morgan, "Debunking the Myth of Immigrant Criminality: Imprisonment Among First- and Second-Generation Young Men," *Migration Information Source,* June 2006, http://www.migrationinformation.org/Feature/ display.cfm?id=403. See also: Ruben G. Rumbaut and Walter A. Ewing, "The Myth of Immigrant Criminality and the Paradox of Assimilation: Incarceration Rates among Native and Foreign-Born Men," Immigration Policy Center, Spring 2007, http://www.ailf.org/ipc/special_report/sr _022107.pdf.

115. Sara A. Carter, "Officials Disclaim Bulletin 'Tipping' Report," *Inland Valley Daily Bulletin* (Ontario, CA), May 10, 2006.

116. Louie Gilot, "Mexican Consulate Criticizes Sheriff's Role in Arrests," *El Paso Times,* Apr. 20, 2006.

117. Jerome R. Corsi, "Sheriff: Deputy Prosecuted by Mexico's Demand; Claims There Were No Plans to Charge Gilmer Hernandez Until Intervention," *WorldNet Daily,* Feb. 22, 2007, http://www.worldnetdaily .com/news/article.asp?ARTICLE_ID=54379; John MacCormack, "An Immigration Ruckus in Rocksprings: City Cries, 'Free Gilmer!'" *San Antonio Express-News,* Dec. 16, 2006.

118. Greg Sowinski, "Beck Responds to Letter from Mexican Consulate," *Lima News* (Ohio), Oct. 4, 2005.

119. "International Law Influences Government Legal Work, Taft Says," remarks of William Howard Taft IV to National Association of Attorneys General, Mar. 21, 2003, http://usinfo.org/wf-archive/2003/ 030321/epf516.htm.

120. Warren Richey, "Treaty Doesn't Force US to Exclude Incriminating Testimony, Court Rules," *Christian Science Monitor,* June 29, 2006.

121. Patrick Timmons, "La Abogada de Mexico: Sandra Babcock's Battle Against the Death Penalty," *Texas Observer,* Oct. 25, 2002.

122. Rebecca Romani, "High Court to Hear Case on Foreign Suspects' Rights," Inter Press Service, May 24, 2006.

123. Sandra Hernandez, "José Luis Bernal: Growing Pains, Healing Wounds at Mexico's Outpost in L.A.," *Los Angeles Times,* Mar. 26, 2000.

124. K. L. Billingsley, "L.A. Police Tongues Tied to Mexican Teaching," *Washington Times,* Jan. 1, 1995.

125. "Gov't Teaching Spanish to U.S. Cops," *El Universal,* Mar. 16, 2005.

126. Don Thompson, "Mexican Inmates Offered Classes," Associated Press, Oct. 18, 2000.

127. Jorge Amselle, "Reverse Imperialism, North of the Border: America Gets Some Help in Formulating Its Education Policy—from the Mexican Government," *National Review,* Oct. 12, 1998.

128. Ibid.

129. Sarah Tully and Raksha Varma, "Bilingual-Class Request Granted: Teaching in Spanish and English Achieves Parents' Goal at Placentia School," *Orange County Register,* Jan. 22, 2004.

130. Mac Donald, "Mexico's Undiplomatic Diplomats."

131. Ibid.

132. Elia Gonzalez, "School Marks Mexican Flag Day: Consul General Presents Pupils with Banner," *Californian* (Salinas), Feb. 26, 2002.

133. Hector Gutierrez, "New Classes Target Teen Immigrants: Mexican Government Has Hand in Classes for Spanish-Speaking Kids," *Rocky Mountain News,* Sept. 25, 1998.

134. "U.S. Labor Secretary Elaine L. Chao and Mexican Foreign Secretary Luis Ernesto Derbez Sign Joint Declaration to Improve Working Conditions for Mexican Workers," OSHA news release, July 21, 2004, http://www.dol.gov/opa/media/press/osha/OSHA20041371.htm.

135. "Mexican Consulate Partners with OSHA, Georgia Tech, Opens Hotline to Assist Callers with Work-Related Concerns," OSHA Region 4 news release, Mar. 28, 2005, http://www.osha.gov/pls/oshaweb/owadisp.show_document?p_table=NEWS_RELEASES&p_id=11297.

136. Bart Jones, "Mexico Backing Day Laborers: The Nation's Consul General Blasts Levy for Farmingville Evictions, Saying They Have Increased Tensions," *Newsday,* July 6, 2005.

137. "Somos un país bisagra: Jorge Castañeda," *El Universal,* Nov. 6, 2002.

138. "Dermot Ahern Will Fight for Undocumented Irish in US," UTV (Northern Ireland), June 8, 2007, http://www.utvlive.com/newsroom/indepth.asp?id=82805&pt=n.

139. Fonte, "Dual Allegiance."

Chapter 3. National Security: Safety in Lower Numbers

1. http://www.whitehouse.gov/news/releases/2003/02/20030226-11.html.

2. See *9/11 and Terrorist Travel: Staff Report of the National Commission on Terrorist Attacks Upon the United States,* Aug. 2004, http://www.9-11commission.gov/staff_statements/911_TerrTrav_Monograph.pdf.

3. John M. Broder, "Shredder Ended Work Backlog, U.S. Says," *New York Times,* Jan. 31, 2003.

4. Remarks as prepared for delivery by Deputy Secretary of Defense Paul Wolfowitz, Petersen AFB, Colorado Springs, CO, Oct. 1, 2002, http://www.defenselink.mil/speeches/2002/s20021001-depsecdef1.html.

5. Mark Krikorian, "Keeping Terror Out: Immigration Policy and Asymmetric Warfare," *National Interest,* Spring 2004.

6. "'Why We Fight America': Al-Qa'ida Spokesman Explains September 11 and Declares Intentions to Kill 4 Million Americans with Weapons of Mass Destruction," Middle East Media Research Institute (MEMRI) Special Dispatch, no. 388, June 12, 2002, http://memri.org/bin/articles.cgi?Page=subjects&Area=jihad&ID=SP38802.

7. Naval Historical Center, "German Espionage and Sabotage Against the U.S. in World War II: George John Dasch and the Nazi Saboteurs," Department of the Navy, http://www.history.navy.mil/faqs/faq114-2.htm.

8. See James R. Edwards Jr., "Keeping Extremists Out: The History of Ideological Exclusion and the Need for Its Revival," Center for

Immigration Studies, Sept. 2005, http://www.cis.org/articles/2005/back1005.html.

9. Office of the Under Secretary of Defense (Policy), *Quadrennial Defense Review Report,* Feb. 6, 2006, http://www.defenselink.mil/qdr/report/Report20060203.pdf.

10. George Borjas, "An Evaluation of the Foreign Student Program," Center for Immigration Studies, June 2002, http://www.cis.org/articles/2002/back602.html; and Richard Haitch, "Follow Up on the News: Counting Iranians," *New York Times,* Aug. 16, 1981.

11. Chicago Council on Foreign Relations and German Marshall Fund of the United States, "Worldviews 2002," Oct. 2, 2002. See "American Public Opinion and Foreign Policy," and specifically "Gaps Between Leaders and the Public" in chapter 8, http://www.worldviews.org/detailreports/usreport/html/ch8s3.html.

12. See Steven A. Camarota, "Immigrants from the Middle East: A Profile of the Foreign-Born Population from Pakistan to Morocco," Center for Immigration Studies, Aug. 2002, http://www.cis.org/articles/2002/back902.html.

13. "FBI Warns of Chechen-Led al Qaeda Plot," *Los Angeles Times,* Sept. 19, 2002.

14. Robert S. Leiken, "Europe's Mujahideen: Where Mass Immigration Meets Global Terrorism," Center for Immigration Studies, Apr. 2005, http://www.cis.org/articles/2005/back405.html.

15. "Report to Congress on Chinese Espionage Activities Against the United States," Dec. 12, 1999, http://www.fas.org/irp/threat/fis/prc_1999.html.

16. Peter Grier, "Spy Case Patterns the Chinese Style of Espionage," *Christian Science Monitor,* Nov. 30, 2005.

17. Fund for Peace, "Failed States Index 2006," http://www.fundforpeace.org/programs/fsi/fsindex2006.php.

18. Office of Homeland Security, *National Strategy for Homeland Security,* July 2002, http://www.whitehouse.gov/homeland/book/.

19. See http://www.northcom.mil/about_us/about_us.htm.

20. Steven A. Camarota, *The Open Door: How Militant Islamic Terrorists Entered*

and Remained in the United States, 1993–2001, Center for Immigration Studies, paper no. 21, May 2002, http://www.cis.org/articles/2002/Paper21/terrorism.html.

21.   Janice L. Kephart, *Immigration and Terrorism: Moving Beyond the 9/11 Staff Report on Terrorist Travel*, Center for Immigration Studies, paper no. 24, Sept. 2005, http://www.cis.org/articles/2005/kephart.html.

22.   U.S. Department of State, Office of Inspector General, "Review of Nonimmigrant Visa Issuance Policy and Procedures," Memorandum Report ISP-I-03-26, Dec. 2002, http://oig.state.gov/documents/organization/16215.pdf.

23.   Ibid.

24.   Testimony of Asa Hutchinson before the Senate Judiciary Committee, Subcommittee on Immigration, Border Security, and Citizenship, Sept. 30, 2003, http://judiciary.senate.gov/testimony.cfm?id=944&wit_id=2705.

25.   Nikolai Wenzel, "America's Other Border Patrol: The State Department's Consular Corps and Its Role in U.S. Immigration," Center for Immigration Studies, Aug. 2000, http://www.cis.org/articles/2000/back800.html.

26.   Statement of Mary A. Ryan to the National Commission on Terrorist Attacks Upon the United States, Jan. 26, 2004, http://www.9-11commission.gov/hearings/hearing7/witness_ryan.htm.

27.   Joel Mowbray, "Visas for Terrorists: They Were Ill-Prepared. They Were Laughable. They Were Approved," *National Review,* Oct. 28, 2002.

28.   John Crewdson, "Tracking a 9/11 Linchpin: Suspect's Capture in Pakistan Hailed as a Major Break," *Chicago Tribune,* Sept. 15, 2002.

29.   Testimony of John E. Lange, deputy inspector general, U.S. Department of State and Broadcasting Board of Governors, before the House Committee on Government Reform, Subcommittee on National Security, Emerging Threats, and International Relations, Sept. 13, 2005, http://oig.state.gov/documents/organization/53248.pdf.

30.   Immigration and Naturalization Act Section 212(a)(6)(C)(i).

31.   *Foreign Affairs Manual,* 9 FAM 40.63, notes, http://foia.state.gov/masterdocs/09fam/0940063N.pdf.

32. Wenzel, "America's Other Border Patrol."

33. Joel Mowbray, "Catching the Visa Express: The Awful Program That Allows Saudis to Skip Into the U.S.," *National Review,* July 1, 2002.

34. Charlie Savage, "Probe Finds Churches' Visa Program Riddled with Fraud," *Boston Globe,* July 11, 2006.

35. Statement of Jill M. Esposito, Directorate for Visa Services, Department of State, before the Subcommittee on Immigration and Claims, Committee on the Judiciary, U.S. House of Representatives, May 5, 1999, http://judiciary.house.gov/legacy/jill0505.htm.

36. "Review of Nonimmigrant Visa Issuance Policy," (see note 22, p. 261).

37. Testimony of John E. Lange (see note 29). See also: other statements at the same hearing, online at http://reform.house.gov/NSETIR/Hearings/EventSingle.aspx?EventID=34259.

38. See *9/11 and Terrorist Travel* (see note 2, p. 259).

39. Ibid.

40. Elizabeth M. Grieco, "Temporary Admissions of Nonimmigrants to the United States: 2005," Department of Homeland Security, Office of Immigration Statistics, July 2006, http://www.uscis.gov/graphics/shared/statistics/publications/2005_NI_rpt.pdf. See also, "National Workload Statistics," U.S. Customs and Border Protection, May 26, 2006, http://www.cbp.gov/xp/cgov/toolbox/about/accomplish/national_workload_stats.xml; and "FY04 Crossing Volume," provided to the author by the US-VISIT program office, received Aug. 17, 2006. The totals in these three reports do not match exactly, probably because the number of Mexicans and Canadians legally entering the United States is just an estimate.

41. See *9/11 and Terrorist Travel.*

42. Rosemary Jenks, "The Enhanced Border Security and Visa Reform Act of 2002; H.R. 3525," Center for Immigration Studies, June 2002, http://www.cis.org/articles/2002/back502.html.

43. Deborah Meyers, "'One Face at the Border'—Is It Working?" Migration Policy Institute, July 1, 2005, http://www.migrationinformation.org/Feature/display.cfm?id=320.

44. Tamara Audi, "Inspectors: Security Lags When Traffic Jams," *Detroit Free Press,* Mar. 29, 2006.

45. Office of Inspector General, *Implementation of the United States Visitor and Immigrant Status Indicator Technology Program at Land Border Ports of Entry,* Department of Homeland Security, OIG-05-11, Feb. 2005, http://www.dhs.gov/interweb/assetlibrary/OIG_05-11_Feb05.pdf.

46. "Border Security: Continued Weaknesses in Screening Entrants into the United States," statement of Gregory D. Kutz, managing director, Forensic Audits and Special Investigations, Government Accountability Office, before the Senate Finance Committee, Aug. 2, 2006, GAO-06-976T, http://www.gao.gov/new.items/d06976t.pdf.

47. See *9/11 and Terrorist Travel*, p. 52.

48. Ibid., p. 17.

49. Camarota, *The Open Door*.

50. Pauline Arrillaga and Olga R. Rodriguez, "Terror-Linked Migrants Crossing into U.S.," Associated Press, July 2, 2005.

51. See *9/11 and Terrorist Travel*, p. 30.

52. Jessica M. Vaughan, "Modernizing America's Welcome Mat: The Implementation of US-VISIT," Center for Immigration Studies, Aug. 2005, http://www.cis.org/articles/2005/back905.html.

53. National Commission on Terrorist Attacks Upon the United States, *The 9/11 Commission Report,* http://www.9-11commission.gov/report/911Report_Ch12.pdf, p. 389.

54. Department of Homeland Security, "Fact Sheet: Improving Border Security and Immigration Within Existing Law," Aug. 10, 2007, http://www.dhs.gov/xnews/releases/pr_1186757867585.shtm.

55. Vaughan, "Modernizing America's Welcome Mat."

56. David Lorey, *The U.S.-Mexican Border in the Twentieth Century* (Wilmington, DE: SR Books, 1999), p. 126.

57. Kephart, *Immigration and Terrorism*.

58. See *9/11 and Terrorist Travel,* p. 132.

59. See Mark Krikorian, "Eternal Vigilance; Handing Out Green Cards Is a Security Matter," *National Review Online,* July 3, 2002, http://www.nationalreview.com/comment/comment-krikorian072302.asp.

60. Kephart, *Immigration and Terrorism*.

61. Ibid.

62. Lance Williams, "Bin Laden's Bay Area Recruiter; Khalid Abu-al-Dahab Signed Up American Muslims to Be Terrorists," *San Francisco Chronicle*, Nov. 21, 2001.

63. Government Accountability Office, *Immigration Benefits: Additional Controls and a Sanctions Strategy Could Enhance DHS's Ability to Control Benefit Fraud*, GAO-06-259, Mar. 2006, http://www.gao.gov/new.items/d06259.pdf.

64. "A Day in the Life of USCIS," Department of Homeland Security Fact Sheet, June 29, 2005, http://www.uscis.gov/files/nativedocuments/dayinlife_050629.pdf.

65. Statement of Michael Chertoff before the Senate Judiciary Committee, Oct. 18, 2005, http://judiciary.senate.gov/testimony.cfm?id=1634&wit_id=66.

66. Marcus Stern, "Mishandled Address-Change Cards a Major Failure for INS," *San Diego Union-Tribune*, July 27, 2002.

67. Government Accountability Office, *Immigration Benefits*.

68. General Accounting Office, *Immigration Benefit Fraud: Focused Approach Is Needed to Address Problems*, Jan. 31, 2002, http://www.gao.gov/new.items/d0266.pdf.

69. "Checking Terrorism at the Border," testimony of Michael J. Maxwell before the House Subcommittee on International Terrorism and Nonproliferation, Committee on International Relations, Apr. 6, 2006, http://wwwc.house.gov/international_relations/109/max040606.pdf, pp. 16–17.

70. Ibid., pp. 19–20.

71. Michael A. Fletcher, "Bush Promises Latinos He'll Speed Up Immigration Process," *Washington Post*, July 6, 2000.

72. *Lou Dobbs Tonight*, Ap. 6, 2006, http://transcripts.cnn.com/TRANSCRIPTS/0604/06/ldt.01.html.

73. General Accounting Office, *Immigration Benefit Fraud*.

74. Government Accountability Office, *Immigration Benefits*, p. 14.

75. Department of Labor, Office of Inspector General, *Restoring Section 245(i) of the Immigration and Nationality Act Created a Flood of Poor Quality Foreign*

Labor Certification Applications Predominantly for Aliens Without Legal Work Status, report number 06-04-004-03-321, Sept. 30, 2004, http://www.oig.dol.gov/public/reports/oa/2004/06-04-004-03-321.pdf.

76. Government Accountability Office, *Immigration Benefits,* pp. 17–18.

77. U.S. Citizenship and Immigration Services, "The USCIS/ICE Anti-Fraud Initiative Progress Report," prepared for the House Committee on Appropriations, Aug. 2005, p. 1.

78. Congressional Research Service, "Immigration Enforcement in the United States," presentation for the House Committee on the Judiciary, Apr. 27, 2006, http://www.ilw.com/immigdaily/news/2006,0817-crs.pdf, p. 25.

79. Department of Homeland Security, Office of Inspector General, *A Review of U.S. Citizenship and Immigration Services' Alien Security Checks,* OIG-06-06, Nov. 2005, http://www.dhs.gov/interweb/assetlibrary/OIG_06-06_Nov05.pdf, p.3.

80. Ibid., p. 18.

81. Sara A. Carter, "Terrorist Screening Missed 75% of Time: Green Card and Visa Applications Not Checked Against Terror Watch List," *Daily Bulletin,* Aug. 23, 2006; and Sara A. Carter, "Reports of Flawed Screening Process Prompt Call for Probe," *Daily Bulletin,* Sept. 1, 2006.

82. "Checking Terrorism at the Border," testimony of Michael J. Maxwell, p. 13.

83. USCIS operating instructions for adjudicators, quoted in "Checking Terrorism at the Border," testimony of Michael J. Maxwell, p. 16.

84. "Address to a Joint Session of Congress and the American People," President George W. Bush, Sept. 20, 2001, http://www.whitehouse.gov/news/releases/2001/09/20010920-8.html.

85. Francis A. J. Ianni, "Formal and Social Organization in an Organized Crime Family: A Case Study," *University of Florida Law Review,* vol. 24, 1971.

86. Steven Erlanger, "In Germany, Terrorists Made Use of a Passion: An Open Democracy," *New York Times,* Oct. 5, 2001.

87. "A Hub for Hijackers Found in New Jersey," *New York Times,* Sept. 27, 2001.

88. Statement of Charles E. Allen, chief intelligence officer and assistant

secretary for intelligence and analysis, Department of Homeland Security, before the Select Committee on Intelligence, U.S. House of Representatives, Jan. 18, 2007.

89. "Hijackers Found Welcome Mat on West Coast: San Diego Islamic Community Unwittingly Aided 2 Who Crashed into Pentagon," *Washington Post,* Dec. 29, 2001.

90. Susan Schulman, Lou Michel, Charity Vogel, and Jay Rey, "A Separate World," *Buffalo News,* Sept. 23, 2002.

91. Jerry Zremski, "On Call to Aid al-Qaida from Unlikely Places," *Buffalo News,* Sept. 18, 2002.

92. "From Pakistan to Lodi: A Special Report," *Lodi News-Sentinel* (CA), Nov. 24, 2001, http://www.lodinews.com/pakistan/.

93. Julia Priest, "Lodi's Pakistani Women Struggle with Clash of Cultures," *Lodi News-Sentinel* (CA), Nov. 24, 2001, http://www.lodinews.com/pakistan/html/women.shtml.

94. Ko-lin Chin, *Chinatown Gangs* (New York: Oxford University Press, 1996), p. 18.

95. William Kleinknecht, *The New Ethnic Mobs: The Changing Face of Organized Crime in America* (New York: Free Press, 1996), p. 292.

96. U.S. Department of Justice press conference, Oct. 31, 2002.

97. Statement of James W. Ziglar Before the House Subcommittee on Immigration and Claims Regarding Using Information Technology to Secure America's Borders, Oct. 11, 2001, http://judiciary.house.gov/legacy/ziglar_101101.htm.

98. Dena Bunis, "Amnesty May Lose Support: Backers Fear Concerns About Border Security Will Hurt Their Cause," *Orange County Register,* Sept. 13, 2001.

99. Gary Martin, "Lawmakers Want Tighter Border," *San Antonio Express-News,* Sept. 19, 2001.

Chapter 4. Economy: Cheap Labor Versus Modern America

1. "Union Members in 2005," Bureau of Labor Statistics press release USDL 06-99, Jan. 20, 2006, http://www.bls.gov/news.release/pdf/union2.pdf.

2. Vernon M. Briggs Jr., *Immigration and American Unionism* (Ithaca, NY: Cornell University Press, 2001), p. 113.

3. George J. Borjas, *Heaven's Door: Immigration Policy and the American Economy* (Princeton, NJ: Princeton University Press, 1999), p. 35.

4. George J. Borjas, Jeffrey Grogger, and Gordon H. Hanson, "Immigration and African-American Employment Opportunities: The Response of Wages, Employment, and Incarceration Rates to Labor Supply Shocks," National Bureau of Economic Research, Working Paper no. 12518, Sept. 2006, p. 49.

5. See Steven A. Camarota, "Immigrants at Mid-Decade: A Snapshot of America's Foreign-Born Population in 2005," Center for Immigration Studies, Dec. 2005, http://www.cis.org/articles/2005/back1405.html.

6. Borjas, *Heaven's Door,* p. 21.

7. Steven A. Camarota, "Dropping Out: Immigrant Entry and Native Exit from the Labor Market, 2000–2005," Center for Immigration Studies, Mar. 2006, http://www.cis.org/articles/2006/back206.html.

8. William Julius Wilson, *When Work Disappears: The World of the New Urban Poor* (New York: Knopf, 1996), p. 145.

9. Quoted by George J. Borjas, in "Increasing the Supply of Labor Through Immigration: Measuring the Impact on Native-born Workers," Center for Immigration Studies, May 2004, http://www.cis.org/articles/2004/back504.html, p. 2.

10. James P. Smith and Barry Edmonston, eds., *The New Americans: Economic, Demographic, and Fiscal Effects of Immigration* (Washington, DC: National Academies Press, 1997), p. 140.

11. Borjas, "Increasing the Supply of Labor," p. 5.

12. Ibid., p. 6.

13. Camarota, "Dropping Out."

14. Katherine D. Newman and Chauncy Lennon, "The Job Ghetto," *American Prospect,* June 23, 1995, http://www.prospect.org/print/V6/22/newman-k.html.

15. Wilson, *When Work Disappears,* p. 144.

16. Borjas, Grogger, and Hanson, "Immigration and African-American Employment Opportunities," p. 49.

17. Ibid., p. 4.

18. Wilson, *When Work Disappears,* p. 132.

19. Borjas, Grogger, and Hanson, "Immigration and African-American Employment Opportunities," p. 5.

20. Andrew Sum, Paul Harrington, and Ishwar Khatiwada, "The Impact of New Immigrants on Young Native-Born Workers, 2000–2005," Center for Immigration Studies, Sept. 2006, http://www.cis.org/articles/2006/back806.html, p. 1.

21. Ibid., p. 2.

22. Peter Drucker and Brent Schlender, "Peter Drucker Sets Us Straight: The 94-Year-Old Guru Says That Most People Are Thinking All Wrong About Jobs, Debt, Globalization, and Recession," *Fortune,* Jan. 12, 2004.

23. Borjas, *Heaven's Door,* p. 21.

24. See Steven A. Camarota, "The Slowing Progress of Immigrants: An Examination of Income, Home Ownership, and Citizenship, 1970–2000," Center for Immigration Studies, Mar. 2001, http://www.cis.org/articles/2001/back401.html, figure 1; and Camarota, "Immigrants at Mid-Decade," table 7.

25. Camarota, "The Slowing Progress of Immigrants."

26. Borjas, *Heaven's Door,* p. 30.

27. Ibid., p. 31. Emphasis in the original.

28. George J. Borjas, "Making It in America: Social Mobility in the Immigrant Population," National Bureau of Economic Research, Working Paper 12088, Mar. 2006.

29. Ibid., p. 22.

30. Ibid., p. 23.

31. "The Rich, the Poor and the Growing Gap Between Them," *Economist,* June 15, 2006.

32. See Robert Rector and Rea Hederman Jr., "Two Americas: One Rich, One Poor? Understanding Income Inequality in the United States," Heritage Foundation, Backgrounder no. 1791, Aug. 24, 2004, http://www.heritage.org/Research/Taxes/bg1791.cfm.

33. White House Office of the Press Secretary, "President Bush Delivers

State of the Economy Report," Jan. 31, 2007, http://www.whitehouse.gov/news/releases/2007/01/20070131-1.html.

34. See, for instance, Kathryn Neckerman, ed., *Social Inequality* (New York: Russell Sage Foundation, 2004); Eric M. Uslaner and Mitchell Brown, "Inequality, Trust, and Civic Engagement," *American Politics Research,* vol. 33, no. 6, pp. 868–94 (2005); and Putnam, *Bowling Alone,* pp. 358–363.

35. U.S. Census Bureau, Historical Income Tables—Income Equality, Table IE-6. Measures of Household Income Inequality: 1967 to 2001, http://www.census.gov/hhes/income/histinc/ie6.html.

36. U.S. Census Bureau, Historical Income Tables—Households, Table H-2. Share of Aggregate Income Received by Each Fifth and Top 5 Perc of Households (All Races): 1967 to 2001, http://www.census.gov/hhes/income/histinc/h02.html.

37. Isabel Sawhill and John E. Morton, *Economic Mobility: Is the American Dream Alive and Well?* Economic Mobility Project, May 24, 2007, http://www.economicmobility.org/assets/pdfs/EMP%20American%20Dream%20Report.pdf%20, p. 3.

38. Ron Haskins, *Economic Mobility of Immigrants in the United States,* Economic Mobility Project, July 24, 2007, http://www.economicmobility.org/reports_and_research/?id=0003.

39. Stephanie Bell-Rose and Frank D. Bean, eds., *Immigration and Opportunity: Race, Ethnicity, and Employment in the United States* (New York: Russell Sage Foundation, 1999), p. 13.

40. Steven A. Camarota, *Importing Poverty: Immigration's Impact on the Size and Growth of the Poor Population in the United States,* Center for Immigration Studies, paper no. 15, Sept. 1999, http://www.cis.org/articles/poverty_study/index.html.

41. Deborah Reed, *California's Rising Income Inequality: Causes and Concerns,* Public Policy Institute of California, Feb. 1999, http://www.ppic.org/content/pubs/report/R_299DRR.pdf.

42. Jack Martin, *Immigration and Income Inequality,* Federation for American Immigration Reform, Apr. 2004, http://www.fairus.org/site/DocServer/inequality2.pdf?docID=401.

43. Michael Lind, *The Next American Nation: The New Nationalism and the Fourth American Revolution* (New York: Free Press, 1996), p. 209.

44. Jane Sneddon Little and Robert K. Triest, "The Impact of Demographic Change on U.S. Labor Markets," in *Seismic Shifts: The Economic Impact of Demographic Change,* proceedings from the Federal Reserve Bank of Boston Conference Series no. 46, 2001, www.bos.frb.org/economic/conf/conf46/conf46e1.pdf.

45. Philip L. Martin and Michael S. Teitelbaum, "The Mirage of Mexican Guest Workers," *Foreign Affairs,* Nov.–Dec. 2001.

46. Julian L. Simon, *The Ultimate Resource 2,* rev. ed. (Princeton, NJ: Princeton University Press, 1996), p. 59.

47. Yoav Sarig, James F. Thompson, and Galen K. Brown, "Alternatives to Immigrant Labor? The Status of Fruit and Vegetable Harvest Mechanization in the United States," Center for Immigration Studies, Dec. 2000, www.cis.org/articles/2000/back1200.html.

48. Orachos Napasintuwong and Robert D. Emerson, "Induced Innovations and Foreign Workers in U.S. Agriculture," paper presented at the American Agricultural Economics Association annual meeting, Long Beach, CA, July 28–31, 2002, http://agecon.lib.umn.edu/cgi-bin/pdf_view.pl?paperid=4576&ftype=.pdf.

49. Sarig, Thompson, and Brown, "Alternatives to Immigrant Labor?"

50. Philip Martin, Wallace Huffman, Robert Emerson, J. Edward Taylor, and Refugio I. Rochin, eds., *Immigration Reform and U.S. Agriculture,* University of California Division of Agricultural and Natural Resources, publication 3358, 1995.

51. See Bert Mason, R. Keith Striegler, and Gregory T. Berg, "Alternatives to Immigrant Labor? Raisin Industry Tests New Harvesting Technology," Center for Immigration Studies, June 1997, www.cis.org/articles/1997/back297.html.

52. Eduardo Porter, "In Florida Groves, Cheap Labor Means Machines," *New York Times,* Mar. 22, 2004.

53. Julia Malone, "Farmers, Inventors Explore Automation as Answer to Labor Shortage," Cox News Service, June 1, 2006.

54. See Marie Brenner, "In the Kingdom of Big Sugar," *Vanity Fair,* Feb. 2001;

and "Southeast, Florida Sugar, FLOC," *Rural Migration News,* vol. 8 no. 1, Jan. 2001, http://migration.ucdavis.edu/rmn/more.php?id=488_0_3_0.

55. Sarig, Thompson, and Brown, "Alternatives to Immigrant Labor?"

56. Southern California Edison Co. with the assistance of DRI/McGraw-Hill, "Southern California's Apparel Industry: Building a Path to Prosperity," Feb. 1995, p. 22. Emphasis in original.

57. Ethan Lewis, "Immigration, Skill Mix, and the Choice of Technique," Federal Reserve Bank of Philadelphia, working paper no. 05-8, May 2005, http://www.phil.frb.org/files/wps/2005/wp05-8.pdf.

58. Maryann Haggerty, "Shrinking Labor Pool Strains Home Builders," *Washington Post,* Aug. 8, 1998, p. G1.

59. MIT Open Source Building Alliance White Paper, for discussion at the Oct. 15 OSBA Workshop, rev. Sept. 1, 2002, http://architecture.mit.edu/~kll/OSBA_proposal.htm.

60. Bill Lurz, "Mod Moves Up: Modular Manufacturers Are Courting Home Builders with Products—and Quality—Light Years Beyond the Double-Wide," *Professional Builder,* Oct. 1, 2006, p. 64, http://www.housingzone.com/probuilder/article/CA6377012.html.

61. John Caulfield, "Hard Labor: Immigrants Help Balance Housing's Fragile Labor Supply, but Contractors Keep Scrambling to Keep Up with Big Builders' Demands, and They Worry . . . Where Will All the Workers Come From?" *Big Builder,* Nov. 1, 2004.

62. Susan Okie, "Robots Make the Rounds to Ease Hospitals' Costs: VA Experience May Herald New Uses for 'Droids,'" *Washington Post,* Apr. 3, 2002, p. A3.

63. "With Japan Aging, Toyota to Staff Factories with Robots," Agence France Presse, Jan. 6, 2005.

64. "By 2010, Toyota Will Fetch Tea and Tidy Your Home," *Asahi Shimbun,* June 1, 2005.

65. Otis L. Graham Jr., *Rethinking Purposes of Immigration Policy,* Center for Immigration Studies, paper no. 6, May 1991, http://www.cis.org/articles/1991/paper6.html.

66. Guillermina Jasso, Douglas S. Massey, Mark R. Rosenzweig, and James P. Smith, "The New Immigrant Survey Pilot (NIS-P): Overview and

New Findings About U.S. Legal Immigrants at Admission," *Demography,* vol. 37, no. 1, Feb. 2000.

67. Deborah Cole, "Germany Issues Fresh Call for Indian High-Tech Experts," Agence France Presse, July 21, 2004.

68. Smith and Edmonston, eds., *The New Americans,* p. 141.

69. Gordon C. Winston, "Toward a Theory of Tuition: Prices, Peer Wages, and Competition in Higher Education," Williams College Project on the Economics of Higher Education, discussion paper DP-65, Jan. 2003, http://www.williams.edu/wpehe/DPs/DP-65.pdf.

70. Institute of International Education, *Open Doors 2006,* Nov. 13, 2006, http://www.opendoors.iienetwork.org.

71. George Borjas, "An Evaluation of the Foreign Student Program," Center for Immigration Studies, June 2002, http://www.cis.org/articles/2002/back602.html.

72. Borjas, *Heaven's Door,* p. 201.

73. Ibid.

74. For instance, immigrants with a bachelor's degree or more have about the same median annual income as similarly educated natives ($42,000 vs. $45,000) but are more than twice as likely to be uninsured (17.1 percent vs. 7.1 percent) or use at least one major welfare program (12.8 percent vs. 6 percent). Camarota, "Immigrants at Mid-Decade."

75. Smith and Edmonston, eds., *The New Americans,* p. 334.

76. Quoted by Stephen J. Blank, in *Rethinking Asymmetric Threats,* Strategic Studies Institute, U.S. Army War College, Sept. 2003, http://www.strategicstudiesinstitute.army.mil/pubs/display.cfm?PubID=103, p. 26.

77. See, for instance, "The Invasion of the Chinese Cyberspies," *Time,* Sept. 5, 2005; see also the witness statements from "Sources and Methods of Foreign Nationals Engaged in Economic and Military Espionage," a hearing of the Subcommittee on Immigration, Citizenship, Refugees, Border Security, and International Law, U.S. House of Representatives Judiciary Committee, Sept. 15, 2005, http://judiciary.house.gov/Oversight.aspx?ID=187 and http://judiciary.house.gov/Oversight.aspx?ID=189.

78. Douglas S. Massey and Ilana Redstone Akresh, "Immigrant Intentions and Mobility in a Global Economy: The Attitudes and Behavior of

Recently Arrived U.S. Immigrants," *Social Science Quarterly,* vol. 87, no. s1, Dec. 2006, p. 954.

79. Alejandro Portes, Cristina Escobar, and Alexandria Walton Radford, "Immigrant Transnational Organizations and Development: A Comparative Study," *International Migration Review,* vol. 41, no. 1, Spring 2007, p. 242.

80. Massey and Redstone Akresh, "Immigrant Intentions and Mobility."

81. Ernest Gellner, *Nations and Nationalism* (Ithaca, NY: Cornell University Press, 1983).

82. Stephan Thernstrom, ed., *Harvard Encyclopedia of American Ethnic Groups* (Cambridge, MA: Belknap Press, 1980), p. 555.

83. Ibid., p. 182.

84. Ibid., pp. 920–1.

Chapter 5. Government Spending

1. Peter Brimelow, "Milton Friedman at 85," *Forbes,* Dec. 29, 1997.

2. Robert E. Rector, "Setting the Record—and the Research—Straight: Heritage Responds (Again) to the *Wall Street Journal,*" June 12, 2007, http://www.heritage.org/Press/Commentary/ed061207b.cfm.

3. Using the *Columbia Journalism Review* inflation calculator (http://www.cjr .org/tools/inflation/) results in $525 million of 1901 dollars becoming $11.9 billion in 2002 dollars. Then the Bureau of Labor Statistics inflation calculator (http://data.bls.gov/cgi-bin/cpicalc.pl) converted that amount into $13.524 billion in 2006 dollars.

4. The historical data is from *Historical Tables, Budget of the United States Government, Fiscal Year 2007* (Washington, DC: U.S. Government Printing Office, 2006), http://www.gpoaccess.gov/usbudget/fy07/pdf/ hist.pdf.

5. Chris Edwards, "Downsizing the Federal Government," Cato Institute, Nov. 2005.

6. Richard Estrada, "Immigration Magnets' Power," *Dallas Morning News,* July 22, 1994.

7. Steven A. Camarota, "Immigrants at Mid-Decade: A Snapshot of America's Foreign-Born Population in 2005," Center for Immigration

Studies, Dec. 2005, http://www.cis.org/articles/2005/back1405.pdf, table 6.

8. Ibid., table 14.

9. Ibid., table 10.

10. Ibid., table 13.

11. Cash assistance includes state-run general-assistance programs, TANF, and SSI.

12. Steven A. Camarota, "Back Where We Started: An Examination of Trends in Immigrant Welfare Use Since Welfare Reform," Center for Immigration Studies, Mar. 2003, http://www.cis.org/articles/2003/back503release.html.

13. Robert E. Rector and Christine Kim, "The Fiscal Cost of Low-Skill Immigrants to the U.S. Taxpayer," Heritage Foundation, special report no. 14, May 22, 2007, http://www.heritage.org/Research/Immigration/sr14.cfm.

14. Office of the Actuary, "National Health Care Expenditures Projections: 2005–2015," Centers for Medicare and Medicaid Services, 2006, http://www.cms.hhs.gov/NationalHealthExpendData/downloads/proj2005.pdf.

15. Camarota, "Immigrants at Mid-Decade," table 11.

16. Ibid., p. 15.

17. Paul Fronstin, "The Impact of Immigration on Health Insurance Coverage in the United States," *Employee Benefit Research Institute Notes,* June 2005, http://www.ebri.org/pdf/notespdf/EBRI_Notes_06–2005.pdf.

18. Dana P. Goldman, James P. Smith, and Neeraj Sood, "Legal Status and Health Insurance Among Immigrants," *Health Affairs,* vol. 24, no. 6, Nov.–Dec. 2005, pp. 1640–53.

19. Committee on the Future of Emergency Care in the United States Health System, *Hospital-Based Emergency Care: At the Breaking Point* (Washington, DC: National Academies Press, 2006), prepublication copy, http://newton.nap.edu/catalog/11621.html, p. 2.

20. U.S. General Accounting Office, *Undocumented Aliens: Questions Persist About Their Impact on Hospitals' Uncompensated Care Costs,* GAO-04-472, May 2004, http://www.gao.gov/new.items/d04472.pdf, pp. 3–4.

21. Committee on the Future of Emergency Care, *Hospital-Based Emergency Care,* p. 41.

22. Camarota, "Immigrants at Mid–Decade," table 18.

23. Committee on the Future of Emergency Care, *Hospital-Based Emergency Care,* p. 44.

24. Ibid., p. 43.

25. Jack Martin, *The Costs of Illegal Immigration to New Yorkers,* Federation for American Immigration Reform, Sept. 2006, http://www.fairus.org/site/DocServer/NYCosts.pdf?docID=1161.

26. Jack Martin and Ira Mehlman, *The Costs of Illegal Immigration to Floridians,* Federation for American Immigration Reform, Oct. 2005, http://www.fairus.org/site/DocServer/fla_study.pdf?docID=601.

27. Jack Martin and Ira Mehlman, *The Costs of Illegal Immigration to Texans,* Federation for American Immigration Reform, Apr. 2005, http://www.fairus.org/site/DocServer/texas_costs.pdf?docID=301.

28. Jack Martin and Ira Mehlman, *The Costs of Illegal Immigration to Californians,* Federation for American Immigration Reform, Nov. 2004, http://www.fairus.org/site/DocServer/ca_costs.pdf?docID=141.

29. Jack Martin and Ira Mehlman, *The Costs of Illegal Immigration to Arizonans,* Federation for American Immigration Reform, 2004, http://www.fairus.org/site/DocServer/azcosts2.pdf?docID=101.

30. Steven A. Camarota, *The High Cost of Cheap Labor: Illegal Immigration and the Federal Budget,* Center for Immigration Studies, paper no. 23, Aug. 2004, http://www.cis.org/articles/2004/fiscal.pdf, p. 5.

31. Families USA, *Paying a Premium: The Added Cost of Care for the Uninsured,* publication no. 05–101, June 2005, http://www.familiesusa.org/assets/pdfs/Paying_a_Premium_rev_July_13731e.pdf.

32. Committee on the Future of Emergency Care, *Hospital-Based Emergency Care,* p. 29.

33. Ibid., p. 44.

34. Fronstin, "The Impact of Immigration on Health Insurance Coverage."

35. National Center for Education Statistics, *Digest of Education Statistics 2004,* U.S. Department of Education, http://nces.ed.gov/programs/digest/d04/index.asp, ch. 1, table 29.

36. Camarota, "Immigrants at Mid-Decade," table 16.

37. National Center for Education Statistics, *Digest of Education Statistics 2004,* ch. 2, table 3.

38. National Center for Education Statistics, *Condition of America's Public School Facilities: 1999,* U.S. Department of Education, June 2000, http://nces.ed.gov/pubs2000/2000032.pdf.

39. Jack Martin, *Breaking the Piggy Bank: How Illegal Immigration Is Sending Schools into the Red,* Federation for American Immigration Reform, June 2005, http://www.fairus.org/site/PageServer?pagename=research_researchf6ad.

40. Patricia Gandara, *Review of Research on the Instruction of Limited English Proficient Students: A Report to the California Legislature,* University of California Linguistic Minority Research Institute, Feb. 1999, http://lmri.ucsb.edu/publications/97_gandara.pdf, p. 14.

41. David Denslow and Carol Weissert, "Tough Choices: Shaping Florida's Future," LeRoy Collins Institute, University of Florida, Oct. 2005, http://www.bebr.ufl.edu/system/files/Tough_Choices.pdf, p. 216.

42. Rafael Lara-Alecio, et al., *Texas Dual Language Program Cost Analysis,* Jan. 2005, http://ldn.tamu.edu/Archives/CBAReport.pdf, p. 4.

43. Kristen A. Hughes, *Justice Expenditure and Employment in the United States, 2003,* Bureau of Justice Statistics, NCJ 212260, rev., May 10, 2006, http://www.ojp.usdoj.gov/bjs/abstract/jeeus03.htm.

44. U.S. Government Accountability Office, *Information on Criminal Aliens Incarcerated in Federal and State Prisons and Local Jails,* GAO-05–337R, Apr. 7, 2005, http://www.gao.gov/new.items/d05337r.pdf, p. 2.

45. Carl F. Horowitz, *An Examination of U.S. Immigration Policy and Serious Crime,* Center for Immigration Studies, Apr. 2001, http://www.cis.org/articles/2001/crime/toc.html.

46. Ruben G. Rumbaut, Roberto G. Gonzales, Golnaz Komaie, and Charlie V. Morgan, "Debunking the Myth of Immigrant Criminality: Imprisonment Among First- and Second-Generation Young Men," *Migration Information Source,* June 2006, http://www.migrationinformation.org/Feature/display.cfm?id=403.

47. Ruben G. Rumbaut and Walter A. Ewing, "The Myth of Immigrant

Criminality and the Paradox of Assimilation: Incarceration Rates Among Native and Foreign-Born Men," Immigration Policy Center, Spring 2007, http://www.ailf.org/ipc/special_report/sr_022107.pdf.

48. U.S. Government Accountability Office, *Information on Criminal Aliens,* p. 3.

49. Martin, *The Costs of Illegal Immigration to New Yorkers.*

50. Martin and Mehlman, *The Costs of Illegal Immigration to Floridians.*

51. Martin and Mehlman, *The Costs of Illegal Immigration to Texans.*

52. Martin and Mehlman, *The Costs of Illegal Immigration to Californians.*

53. Martin and Mehlman, *The Costs of Illegal Immigration to Arizonans.*

54. Rector and Kim, "The Fiscal Cost of Low-Skill Immigrants."

55. Rector, "Setting the Record—and the Research—Straight."

56. James P. Smith and Barry Edmonston, eds., *The New Americans: Economic, Demographic, and Fiscal Effects of Immigration,* (Washington, DC: National Academies Press, 1997), http://newton.nap.edu/catalog/5779.html, ch. 6–7.

57. Robert Rector, "Amnesty and Continued Low Skill Immigration Will Substantially Raise Welfare Costs and Poverty," Heritage Foundation, backgrounder no. 1936, May 12, 2006, http://www.heritage.org/Research/Immigration/bg1936.cfm.

58. Denslow and Weissert, "Tough Choices: Shaping Florida's Future," p. 385.

59. Camarota, *The High Cost of Cheap Labor.*

60. Martin and Mehlman, *The Costs of Illegal Immigration to New Yorkers,* and comparable reports for other states.

61. Tom Bethell, "Immigration, Si; Welfare, No," *American Spectator,* Nov. 1993.

62. Rector and Kim, "The Fiscal Cost of Low-Skill Immigrants."

63. Karlyn H. Bowman, "Attitudes About Welfare Reform," *AEI Studies in Public Opinion,* American Enterprise Institute, Mar. 6, 2003, http://www.aei.org/publications/pubID.14885/pub_detail.asp.

64. Grover G. Norquist, "Reducing the Government by Half: How and Why We Can Cut the Size and Cost of Government in Half in One Generation—the Next Twenty-five Years," *Heritage Insider,* May 2000, http://www.atr.org/content/html/2000/may/000501op-govt_in_half.htm.

65. James R. Edwards Jr., "Public Charge Doctrine: A Fundamental Principle of American Immigration Policy," Center for Immigration Studies, May 2001, http://www.cis.org/articles/2001/back701.html, p. 2.

66. Ibid., p. 4.

67. George J. Borjas, *The Impact of Welfare Reform on Immigrant Welfare Use,* Center for Immigration Studies, Mar. 2002, http://www.cis.org/articles/2002/borjas.htm.

68. Camarota, "Back Where We Started."

69. *Time*/SRBI poll, Mar. 31, 2006, http://www.srbi.com/TimePoll_Final_Report-2006–03–31.pdf.

70. Camarota, *The High Cost of Cheap Labor.*

71. Robert Rector, "Amnesty and Continued Low Skill Immigration Will Substantially Raise Welfare Costs and Poverty," Heritage Foundation, backgrounder no. 1936, May 12, 2006, http://www.heritage.org/Research/Immigration/bg1936.cfm.

72. Camarota, "Immigrants at Mid-Decade," table 15.

Chapter 6. Population

1. Charles Krauthammer, "Saved by Immigrants: The U.S. Fertility Rate Is Barely at Replacement Level," *Washington Post,* July 17, 1998, p. A21.

2. Ben J. Wattenberg, *Fewer: How the New Demography of Depopulation Will Shape Our Future* (Chicago: Ivan R. Dee, 2004), p. 5.

3. Central Intelligence Agency, *The World Factbook,* 2007 estimates, https://www.cia.gov/library/publications/the-world-factbook/rankorder/2127rank.html.

4. Kevin Kinsella and Victoria A. Velkoff, *An Aging World: 2001,* U.S. Census Bureau, Series P95/01–1, http://www.census.gov/prod/2001pubs/p95–01–1.pdf.

5. U.S. Census Bureau, *Global Population Profile: 2002,* International Population Reports WP/02, Mar. 2004, http://www.census.gov/ipc/prod/wp02/wp-02.pdf.

6. Steven A. Camarota, "Immigration in an Aging Society: Workers, Birth

Rates, and Social Security," Center for Immigration Studies, Apr. 2005, http://www.cis.org/articles/2005/back505.html.

7. Steven A. Camarota, "Birth Rates Among Immigrants in America: Comparing Fertility in the U.S. and Home Countries," Center for Immigration Studies, Oct. 2005, http://www.cis.org/articles/2005/back1105.html.

8. Camarota, "Immigration in an Aging Society," pp. 2–3.

9. Ibid., pp. 4–5.

10. U.S. Census Bureau, "Methodology and Assumptions for the Population Projections of the United States: 1999 to 2100," Population Division, working paper no. 38, Jan. 13, 2000, http://www.census.gov/population/www/documentation/twps0038.pdf, p. 21.

11. Camarota, "Immigration in an Aging Society," pp. 11–15.

12. U.S. Census Bureau, "Methodology and Assumptions."

13. Steven A. Camarota, "100 Million More: Projecting the Impact of Immigration on the U.S. Population, 2007 to 2060," Center for Immigration Studies, Aug. 2007, http://www.cis.org/articles/2007/back707.html.

14. Steven A. Camarota, "Births to Immigrants in America, 1970 to 2002," Center for Immigration Studies, July 2005, http://www.cis.org/articles/2005/back805.html.

15. Steven A. Camarota, "Immigrants in the United States—2002: A Snapshot of America's Foreign-Born Population," Center for Immigration Studies, Nov. 2002, http://www.cis.org/articles/2002/back1302.html.

16. United Nations Population Division, "World Population Prospects: The 2006 Revision," http://esa.un.org/unpp/.

17. U.S. Census Bureau, "Ranking Tables for Counties: Population in 2000 and Population Change from 1990 to 2000," PHC-T-4, http://www.census.gov/population/www/cen2000/phc-t4.html.

18. The comments about the 1965 immigration bill are from "Three Decades of Mass Immigration: The Legacy of the 1965 Immigration Act," Center for Immigration Studies, Sept. 1995, http://www.cis.org/articles/1995/back395.html.

19. See note 8 to the Introduction.

20. Center for Immigration Studies, "New Poll: Americans Prefer House Approach on Immigration; Poll Is First to Offer the Public a Choice Between House and Senate Plan," press release, May 3, 2006, http://www.cis.org/articles/2006/2006poll.html.

21. Polling Company, Sept. 2007, http://www.numbersusa.com/hottopic/100306comm.html.

22. Wattenberg, *Fewer,* p. 216.

23. Fredo Arias-King, "Immigration and Usurpation: Elites, Power, and the People's Will," Center for Immigration Studies, July 2006, http://www.cis.org/articles/2006/back706.html.

24. Roy Beck and Steven A. Camarota, "Elite vs. Public Opinion: An Examination of Divergent Views on Immigration," Center for Immigration Studies, Dec. 2002, http://www.cis.org/articles/2002/back1402.html.

25. See Richard A. Easterlin, "The American Baby Boom in Historical Perspective," *American Economic Review,* vol. 51, no. 5, Dec. 1961, pp. 869–911; and Richard A. Easterlin, *Birth and Fortune: The Impact of Numbers on Personal Welfare* (London: Grant McIntyre, 1980).

26. Steve Sailer, "Affordable Family Formation—the Neglected Key to GOP's Future," Vdare.com, May 8, 2005, http://www.vdare.com/sailer/050508_family.htm. See also: Steve Sailer, "Baby Gap: How Birthrates Color the Electoral Map," *American Conservative,* Dec. 20, 2004, http://www.amconmag.com/2004_12_06/cover.html.

27. "Trends in Characteristics of Births by State: United States, 1990, 1995, and 2000–2002," *National Vital Statistics Reports,* vol. 52, no. 19, May 10, 2004; see table 4, "Total Fertility Rates and Birth Rates by Age, Race, and Hispanic Origin of Mother: United States and Each State, 1990, 1995, 2000, 2001, and 2002," http://www.cdc.gov/nchs/data/nvsr/nvsr52/nvsr52_19acc.pdf.

28. Phillip Longman, *The Empty Cradle: How Falling Birthrates Threaten World Prosperity and What to Do About It* (New York: Basic Books, 2004).

29. Gary S. Becker, "Missing Children," *Wall Street Journal,* Sept. 1, 2006.

30. Paul R. Ehrlich, *The Population Bomb* (New York: Ballantine Books, 1971), p. xi.

31. Samuel P. Hays, *Beauty, Health and Permanence: Environmental Politics in the United States, 1955–1985* (Cambridge: Cambridge University Press, 1989), p. 13.

32. Ibid., p. 4.

33. See, for instance, Steven F. Hayward and Amy Kaleita, "Index of Leading Economic Indicators, 2007," Pacific Research Institute, April 2007, http://liberty.pacificresearch.org/docLib/20070418_07EnvIndex .pdf.

34. U.S. Environmental Protection Agency, "Inventory of U.S. Greenhouse Gas Emissions and Sinks: 1990–2005," Apr. 15, 2007, http://www.epa .gov/climatechange/emissions/downloads06/07CR.pdf.

35. U.S. Environmental Protection Agency, "Light-Duty Automotive Technology and Fuel Economy Trends: 1975 through 2006," July 2006, http://www.epa.gov/otaq/cert/mpg/fetrends/420r06011.pdf.

36. Energy Information Administration, "Annual Energy Review 2006," U.S. Department of Energy, June 27, 2007, http://www.eia.doe.gov/ emeu/aer/overview.html.

37. U.S. Environmental Protection Agency, "Municipal Solid Waste in the United States: 2005 Facts and Figures," Oct. 2006, http://www.epa.gov/ msw/pubs/mswchar05.pdf.

38. U.S. Geological Survey, "Estimated Use of Water in the United States in 2000," Mar. 2004, http://pubs.usgs.gov/circ/2004/circ1268/index.html.

39. Roy Beck, Leon Kolankiewicz, and Steven A. Camarota, *Outsmarting Smart Growth: Population Growth, Immigration, and the Problem of Sprawl,* Center for Immigration Studies, paper no. 22, Aug. 2003, http://www .cis.org/articles/2003/sprawl.html.

40. Stephen Moore and Julian L. Simon, *It's Getting Better All the Time: The Greatest Trends of the Last 100 Years* (Washington, DC: Cato Institute, 2000), pp. 120–1.

41. U.S. Census Bureau, "Characteristics of New Housing," http://www .census.gov/const/www/charindex.html.

42. Cited by Beck, Kolankiewicz, and Camarota in *Outsmarting Smart Growth*.

43. U.S. Census Bureau News, "Americans Spend More Than 100 Hours Commuting to Work Each Year, Census Bureau Reports," CB05-AC.02, Mar. 30, 2005, http://www.census.gov/Press-Release/www/releases/archives/american_community_survey_acs/004489.html.

44. David Schrank and Tim Lomax, *The 2005 Urban Mobility Report,* Texas Transportation Institute, May 2005, http://tti.tamu.edu/documents/mobility_report_2005.pdf.

45. See http://www.nationaltrust.org/11Most/list.asp?i=171.

46. C. Vann Woodward, "A Mickey Mouse Idea," *New Republic,* June 20, 1994.

47. Rudy Abramson, *Hallowed Ground: Preserving America's Heritage* (Charlottes-ville, VA: Thomasson-Grant & Lickle, 1996), p. 19.

48. "Anti–Property Rights Initiative Gets Boost from Unlikely Source: Senator George Allen," U.S. Newswire, Aug. 18, 2006.

49. Hays, *Beauty, Health and Permanence,* p. 3.

50. W. Brad Smith, Patrick D. Miles, John S. Vissage, and Scott A. Pugh, *Forest Resources of the United States, 2002,* gen. tech. report NC-241 (St. Paul, MN: USDA Forest Service, North Central Forest Experiment Station), http://ncrs.fs.fed.us/pubs/gtr/gtr_nc241.pdf.

51. See "Setting Urban Tree Canopy Goals," http://www.americanforests.org/resources/urbanforests/treedeficit.php.

52. "Loss of Forest Land: A Position Statement of the Society of American Foresters," Dec. 5, 2004, http://www.safnet.org/policyandpress/psst/loss_of_forest_land.cfm.

53. See "Human Dimensions of Urban Forestry and Urban Greening," Center for Urban Horticulture, College of Forest Resources, University of Washington, http://www.cfr.washington.edu/research.envmind/; and the Human-Environment Research Laboratory, University of Illinois, Urbana-Champaign, http://www.herl.uiuc.edu/.

54. Alexis de Tocqueville, *Democracy in America* (New York: Mentor Books, 1956), p. 303.

Chapter 7. What Is to Be Done?

1. See "American Platform of Principles," http://www.yale.edu/glc/archive/974.htm.

2. Spencer S. Hsu, "Immigrant Processors Fall Behind: System Overwhelmed Even Without 'Amnesty,' Guest Workers," *Washington Post,* Jan. 4, 2007, p. A3.

3. Margie McHugh, Julia Gelatt, and Michael Fix, "Adult English Language Instruction in the United States: Determining Need and Investing Wisely," Migration Policy Institute, July 2007, http://www.migrationpolicy.org/pubs/NCIIP_English_Instruction073107.pdf.

4. Stanley A. Renshon, "Becoming American: The Hidden Core of the Immigration Debate," Center for Immigration Studies, Jan. 2007, http://www.cis.org/articles/2007/back107.html.

5. The recommendations in this chapter are drawn from a variety of earlier analyses: Mark Krikorian, "Downsizing Illegal Immigration: A Strategy of Attrition Through Enforcement," Center for Immigration Studies, May 2005, http://www.cis.org/articles/2005/back605.html; Jessica M. Vaughan, "Attrition Through Enforcement: A Cost-Effective Strategy to Shrink the Illegal Population," Center for Immigration Studies, Apr. 2006, http://www.cis.org/articles/2006/back406.html; Mark Krikorian, "Fewer Immigrants, a Warmer Welcome: Fixing a Broken Immigration Policy," Center for Immigration Studies, Nov. 2003, http://www.cis.org/articles/2003/back1503.html; Mark Krikorian, "Legal Immigration: What Is to Be Done," in *Blueprints for an Ideal Legal Immigration Policy,* Richard D. Lamm and Alan Simpson, eds., Center for Immigration Studies, paper no. 17, Mar. 2001, http://cis.org/articles/2001/blueprints/toc.html; and Jessica M. Vaughan, "Shortcuts to Immigration: The 'Temporary' Visa Program Is Broken," Center for Immigration Studies, Jan. 2003, http://www.cis.org/articles/2003/back103.html.

6. Office of Policy and Planning, "Estimates of the Unauthorized Immigrant Population Residing in the United States: 1990 to 2000," U.S. Immigration and Naturalization Service, Jan. 31, 2003; executive summary at http://www.dhs.gov/xlibrary/assets/statistics/publications/2000ExecSumm.pdf.

A more recent report does not break out emigration rates by year: Michael Hoefer, et al., "Estimates of the Unauthorized Immigrant Population Residing in the United States: January 2005," Office of Immigration Statistics, Department of Homeland Security, Aug. 2006.

7.   Jeffrey S. Passel, *The Size and Characteristics of the Unauthorized Migrant Population in the U.S.: Estimates Based on the March 2005 Current Population Survey,* Pew Hispanic Center, Mar. 2006, http://pewhispanic.org/reports/report.php?ReportID=61.

8.   Douglas S. Massey, "Beyond the Border Buildup: Towards a New Approach to Mexico–US Migration," *Immigration Policy in Focus,* vol. 4, issue 7, Sept. 2005, http://www.ailf.org/ipc/policy_reports_2005_beyond border.shtml.

9.   Aldo Colussi, "Migrants' Networks: An Estimable Model of Illegal Mexican Immigration," Department of Economics, University of Pennsylvania, Nov. 2003, http://www.econ.upenn.edu/~acolussi/JMP.pdf.

10. Rachel L. Swarns, "Thousands of Arabs and Muslims Could Be Deported, Officials Say," *New York Times,* June 7, 2003, p. A1.

11. Michael Powell, "An Exodus Grows in Brooklyn: 9/11 Still Rippling Through Pakistani Neighborhood, *Washington Post,* May 29, 2003, p. A1.

12. Michelle Garcia, "Irish Immigration Slips Into Reverse," *Washington Post,* Feb. 20, 2006.

13. Casey Woods, "Argentines Leaving Miami for Home as Economy Rises," *Miami Herald,* Mar. 22, 2006.

14. This figure does not include the large number of Mexicans apprehended at the border and simply turned back; the total number of Southwest border apprehensions in fiscal year 2005 was 1.17 million.

15. See Marti Dinerstein, "America's Identity Crisis: Document Fraud Is Pervasive and Pernicious," Center for Immigration Studies, Apr. 2002, http://www.cis.org/articles/2002/back302.html.

16. See Marti Dinerstein, "Giving Cover to Illegal Aliens: IRS Tax ID Numbers Subvert Immigration Law," Center for Immigration Studies, Oct. 2002, http://www.cis.org/articles/2002/back1202.html.

17. See Kris W. Kobach, "State and Local Authority to Enforce Immigration Law: A Unified Approach for Stopping Terrorists," Center for Immigra-

tion Studies, June 2004, http://www.cis.org/articles/2004/back604.html; and James R. Edwards Jr., "Officers Need Backup: The Role of State and Local Police in Immigration Law Enforcement," Center for Immigration Studies, Apr. 2003, http://www.cis.org/articles/2003/back703.html.

18. For a list of the violations, see Newt Gingrich, "75 Reasons to Be Angry with Government; 75 Reasons to Oppose the Senate Immigration Bill," Newt.org, May 21, 2007, http://www.newt.org/backpage.asp?art=4451.

19. See Jessica M. Vaughan, "Modernizing America's Welcome Mat: The Implementation of US-VISIT," Center for Immigration Studies, Aug. 2005, http://www.cis.org/articles/2005/back905.html.

20. George L. Kelling and James Q. Wilson, "Broken Windows: The Police and Neighborhood Safety," *Atlantic Monthly,* Mar. 1982.

21. In the real world, though, high legal immigration necessarily leads to high illegal immigration, since the two phenomena are inextricably connected. See James R. Edwards Jr., "Two Sides of the Same Coin: The Connection Between Legal and Illegal Immigration," Center for Immigration Studies, Feb. 2006, http://www.cis.org/articles/2006/back106.html.

22. George J. Borjas, *Heaven's Door: Immigration Policy and the American Economy* (Princeton, NJ: Princeton University Press, 1999), pp. 200–03.

23. U.S. Commission on Immigration Reform, *Legal Immigration: Setting Priorities,* 1995.

24. *2000 Statistical Yearbook of the Immigration and Naturalization Service,* chapter 7, "Estimates," http://www.dhs.gov/xlibrary/assets/statistics/yearbook/2000/Est2000.pdf.

25. Numbers USA, "Honoring Our Immigration and Other Traditions," http://www.numbersusa.com/about/goals_honoring.html. See also: Numbers USA Education and Research Foundation, "History of Traditional Levels of U.S. Immigration," http://www.numbersusa.com/PDFs/TraditionalLevelsofUSImmigration.pdf.

26. See Don Barnett, "A New Era of Refugee Resettlement," Center for Immigration Studies, Dec. 2006, http://www.cis.org/articles/2006/back1006.html; and Don Barnett, "Out of Africa: Somali Bantu and the Paradigm Shift in Refugee Resettlement," Center for Immigration Studies, Oct. 2003, http://www.cis.org/articles/2003/back1303.html.

27. See *Report of the Visa Office 2006,* http://travel.state.gov/visa/frvi/statistics/statistics_3163.html; and Office of Immigration Statistics, "Temporary Admissions of Nonimmigrants to the United States: 2006," U.S. Department of Homeland Security, July 2007, http://www.dhs.gov/xlibrary/assets/statistics/publications/NI_FR_2006_508_final.pdf.

28. Institute for International Education, *Open Doors 2006,* http://opendoors.iienetwork.org/?p=89251.

INDEX